Feminism and Women's Writing

.890

Feminism and Women's Writing

An Introduction

Catherine Riley with Lynne Pearce

EDINBURGH
University Press

Edinburgh University Press is one of the leading university presses in the UK. We publish academic books and journals in our selected subject areas across the humanities and social sciences, combining cutting-edge scholarship with high editorial and production values to produce academic works of lasting importance. For more information visit our website: edinburghuniversitypress.com

Edinburgh University Press Ltd
The Tun – Holyrood Road, 12(2f) Jackson's Entry, Edinburgh EH8 8PJ

Typeset in sabon and Gill Sans Nova
by R. J. Footring Ltd, Derby, UK, and
printed and bound in Great Britain.

A CIP record for this book is available from the British Library

ISBN 978 1 4744 1559 0 (hardback)
ISBN 978 1 4744 1561 3 (webready PDF)
ISBN 978 1 4744 1560 6 (paperback)
ISBN 978 1 4744 1562 0 (epub)

Contents

Case studies

Note on the authors

With the exception of this Introduction which was co-authored, all the chapters which comprise *Feminism and Women's Writing* have been first-authored by Catherine Riley with editorial support from Lynne Pearce. Lynne Pearce has taught feminist theory and women's writing courses at Lancaster University – where Catherine was also a student in the 1990s – for over twenty years, and has published widely in the field. Catherine Riley wrote her doctoral thesis on the second-wave British publisher Virago, the research for which included a series of interviews with key people in the industry, some of which are quoted within the present text. The material from her thesis forms the basis for Catherine's monograph *The Virago Story – Assessing the Impact of a Feminist Publishing Phenomenon*, published by Berghahn Books (in April 2018). Catherine has taught on literature and gender courses at Birkbeck College and elsewhere, spent two years working to establish the Women's Equality Party, and now works in communications in the third sector.

Acknowledgements

Our first acknowledgement must be to the many writers, critics and publishers cited and extolled in the pages of this book without whose passion and commitment the feminist literary revolution would never have happened. Both of us have been privileged to know several of them in person, and a historical overview of this kind is a great reminder of the way in which our *collective* effort has brought about such a transformation in the way literature is thought about and taught. So, thanks to you all – too numerous to name individually – who have given so much!

As explained in the Introduction, the immediate genesis of this volume was Catherine's PhD thesis entitled 'Do We Still Need Virago?' and Catherine would like to extend special thanks to Virago's key women, past and present, in particular Lennie Goodings.

Catherine also wishes to thank her PhD supervisors, Hilary Fraser and Jo Winning, and the students and faculty of Birkbeck's English department. Further, she would like to thank wholeheartedly her former team at the Women's Equality Party who showed her the need for, and value of, feminism as praxis, and helped support her intellectually and with their friendship through the process of writing this book.

Lynne, meanwhile, would like to pay tribute to all the students who have participated in Lancaster University's 'Women Writers' course – past and present – and who were the 'model readers' for this volume. The enthusiasm for women's writing that you have shown over the years has told us, repeatedly, that this is far from being a specialism that has had its day. Thanks, too, to Lancaster colleagues Tess Cosslett and Alison Easton, who first put the course on the books way back in 1984 and who were both truly inspirational teachers; and, more recently, to Alison Findlay, Rose Jack, Lindsey Moore and Hilary Hinds, who have all contributed eagerly to the course and taken it in new directions.

Lynne would also like pay a special acknowledgement to Paul Poplawski, whose amazing guide *English Literature in Context* (Cambridge University Press, second edition 2017) she drew upon in preparing the timeline for this volume. Many thanks Paul – your historical research into the key historical-social events of the twentieth century was very useful and much appreciated!

Finally, both authors would like say a huge thank you to the editors and production team at Edinburgh University Press for their support in putting the volume together: in particular, Jackie Jones – who has been the publisher behind so many fantastic volumes of feminist literary criticism in the UK over the years – and Adela Rauchova.

Timeline

Year	Landmark social/ historical events in Britain and America (including the history of publishing)	Landmark British and American literary texts	Landmark works of feminist theory and criticism
1792			Mary Wollstonecraft publishes *A Vindication of the Rights of Woman* – the first 'manifesto' for feminism
1818		Mary Shelley publishes *Frankenstein*	
1847		Charlotte Brontë publishes *Jane Eyre*	
1869	Girton College, Cambridge, is founded for female students (but women cannot receive a degree until 1948)		Matthew Arnold institutes the concept of the English canon with his text *Culture and Anarchy*
1870	The Married Women's Property Act (with a further Act in 1882) ends the system of 'coverture', the legal doctrine that meant that women's identities – and thus rights – were subsumed under that of their husband upon marriage		
1878	University of London admits women to all its degree programmes (and allows them to graduate)		
1899		Kate Chopin publishes *The Awakening*	
1905	Suffragette movement underway and the imprisonment of some activists		

1907	The Women's Social and Political Union (WSPU) begins publishing its newspaper *Votes for Women*	
1914	The First World War begins (ends 1918)	
1915		Charlotte Perkins Gilman publishes the feminist utopia *Herland*
1917	Virginia Woolf co-founds the Hogarth Press, arguing that women's control of their words equates to control of their bodies, and their lives	
1918	The Representation of the People Act extends the vote to women over the age of 30 years if they are a member or are married to a person on the Local Government Register, a property owner, or a graduate	
1926	The General Strike in the UK lasts nine days	
1928	The universal franchise is established – the right to vote is extended to all socioeconomic groups, including women, from the age of 21	Virginia Woolf publishes *Orlando* Radclyffe Hall's lesbian love narrative *The Well of Loneliness* is published
1929		Virginia Woolf publishes *A Room of One's Own*
1932	'Hunger March' ends in London as unemployment tops 3 million	
1933		Vera Brittain publishes her First World War autobiography *Testament of Youth*
1934		Crime writer Agatha Christie publishes *Murder on the Orient Express*

Year	Historical events	Literature by women	Literature and criticism
1936		Rosamond Lehmann publishes her novel featuring a clandestine affair, *The Weather in the Streets* Margaret Mitchell publishes *Gone with the Wind*	
1937		Black American author Zora Neale Hurston publishes *Their Eyes Were Watching God*	
1938		Daphne du Maurier publishes *Rebecca*	
1939	The Second World War begins (ends 1945)		
1948	The National Health Service is established		F. R. Leavis publishes *The Great Tradition* which reinstitutes the canonical ideal and the marginalisation of women writers
1949			Simone de Beauvoir publishes *The Second Sex*
1951		Elizabeth Taylor publishes *A Game of Hide and Seek*	
1952		Patricia Highsmith publishes the lesbian thriller *The Price of Salt* (later *Carol*) under a pseudonym	
1954	End of post-war rationing in the UK		
1957	Wolfenden report recommends decriminalising homosexuality		
1958		Barbara Pym publishes *A Glass of Blessings*	
1962		Doris Lessing publishes the feminist consciousness-raising classic *The Golden Notebook*	
1963			Betty Friedan publishes *The Feminine Mystique*, problematising the role and status of the American 'housewife'

1964	The Labour Party under Harold Wilson is elected		
	Mass opposition to the Vietnam War (1955–75) begins		
1965		Margaret Drabble publishes *The Millstone*	
		Margaret Atwood publishes *The Edible Woman*	
1967	Homosexuality is decriminalised; abortion is legalised in Britain (not Northern Ireland)		
1968	Race Relations Act makes racial discrimination illegal in the UK		
1969	The Booker Prize for Fiction is founded	Ursula Le Guin publishes early feminist science fiction text *The Left Hand of Darkness*	Kate Millett publishes *Sexual Politics*
1970	The Equal Pay Act is passed in the UK		Germaine Greer publishes *The Female Eunuch*
1973	Virago is founded by Carmen Callil	Erica Jong publishes *Fear of Flying*	Sheila Rowbotham's *Hidden from History: 300 Years of Women's Oppression and the Fight Against It* directly challenges the orthodoxy of the male-centric English canon
1975			Hélène Cixous publishes *The Laugh of the Medusa*, which is followed by Julia Kristeva's *Revolution in Poetic Language* (1984) and Luce Irigaray's *This Sex Which Is Not One* (1985), which together launch the 'French feminist' movement

1976			Shulamith Firestone publishes *The Dialectic of Sex: The Case for Feminist Revolution*, in which she argues that reproduction itself is the basis of women's unequal status with men
			Michel Foucault publishes *The History of Sexuality*
1977	Virago establishes its reprint library – a selection of works of fiction by historical women writers – inspired by Sheila Rowbotham's book *Hidden from History* (1973)	Marilyn French publishes *The Women's Room* Angela Carter publishes *The Passion of New Eve*	Elaine Showalter coins the term 'gynocriticism' in her book *A Literature of Their Own*
1978	The Women's Press is established Virago publishes the first title in its Modern Classics series: *Frost in May*, by Antonia White, originally published in 1933		Susie Orbach's polemical text *Fat Is a Feminist Issue* is published in the US
1979	The Conservative Party under Margaret Thatcher comes to power and remains in office for 18 years Southall Black Sisters is founded in London – it presently remains the UK's longest-standing organisation supporting the human rights of black and minority ethnic (BME) women		Barbara Christian publishes *Black Women Novelists* Angela Carter publishes *The Sadeian Woman: An Exercise in Cultural History* Sandra Gilbert and Susan Gubar publish the now iconic *Madwoman in the Attic: The Woman Writer and the Nineteenth-Century Literary Imagination* Lilian Faderman publishes *Surpassing the Love of Men: Romantic Friendship and Love Between Women from the Renaissance to the Present* (UK paperback 1985)

1980	Sheba Press is established to publish writings by BME women		
1981			Adrienne Rich publishes *Compulsory Heterosexuality and Lesbian Existence* Elaine Showalter publishes her essay 'Feminist Criticism in the Wilderness' in the journal *Critical Inquiry*
1982	The Women's Press launches its crime fiction series	Audre Lorde publishes the black lesbian 'biomythography' *Zami: A New Spelling of My Name*	bell hooks publishes *Ain't I a Woman? Black Women and Feminism* Annette Kuhn publishes *Women's Pictures: Feminism and Cinema*
1983		Alice Walker publishes *The Color Purple*	
1984	Unemployment in Britain tops 3 million The Silver Moon bookshop (for women) is founded by Jane Cholmeley and Sue Butterworth, and from 1990 publishes titles under the Silver Moon Books imprint	Maya Angelou publishes *I Know Why The Caged Bird Sings*	
1985	Pandora Press is established to court the growing feminist academic market	Black British writer Joan Riley publishes *The Belonging* Jeanette Winterson publishes *Oranges Are Not The Only Fruit* Margaret Atwood publishes *The Handmaid's Tale*	Gayatri Spivak publishes her essay 'Can the Subaltern Speak?', which fosters new connections between feminist and postcolonial studies Donna Haraway first publishes her 'Cyborg Manifesto' (reproduced in her *Simians, Cyborgs and Women*, 1991) Toril Moi publishes her Marxist critique of French Feminism, *Sexual/Textual Politics* Deborah Cameron publishes *Feminist Theory and Linguistics*

1986		Ruth Rendell publishes *A Dark-Adapted Eye* under the pseudonym Barbara Vine, marking the introduction of the 'whydunit' thriller	Cora Kaplan publishes *Sea Changes: Essays on Culture and Feminism*, which was at the vanguard of a wave of British Marxist-feminist publications in the UK at this time
		Mary Eagleton publishes *Feminist Literary Theory: A Reader* (third edition 2010)
1987		Toni Morrison publishes *Beloved*	
1988	Clause 28 of the Local Government Act makes it illegal for local authority agencies (including schools) to promote homosexuality (repealed in Scotland in 2000 and in the rest of the UK in 2003)		
1989			Rita Felski publishes *Beyond Feminist Aesthetics: Feminist Literature and Social Change*
			Patricia Waugh publishes *Feminine Fictions: Revisiting the Postmodern*
1990	Margaret Thatcher resigns (but the Conservatives retain power in the 1992 general election)		Judith Butler publishes *Gender Trouble*, instituting the beginning of 'queer' theory and politics
			Naomi Wolf publishes *The Beauty Myth*

1991		Pat Barker publishes *Regeneration*	Rosi Braidotti publishes *Nomadic Subjects: Embodiment and Sexual Difference in Contemporary Feminist Theory*, which spearheads a decade of work on feminism and the body
			Susan Faludi's *Backlash: The Undeclared War Against Women* examines the anti-feminist agenda
1993		Jeanette Winterson publishes *Written on the Body*	Judith Butler publishes her follow-up to *Gender Trouble – Bodies That Matter*, which develops her ideas further
			Eve Kosofsky Sedgwick publishes *Tendencies* (a landmark collection of queer readings of literary texts)
			Jackie Stacey publishes *Stargazing: Hollywood Cinema and Female Spectatorship* during a decade which saw interest in feminist film studies soar
1994			Elizabeth Grosz publishes *Volatile Bodies: Towards a Corporeal Feminism*
			Kate Bornstein begins articulation of trans identities in *Gender Outlaw: On Men, Women and the Rest of Us*
1996	The Orange Prize, now known as the Women's Prize for Fiction, is founded	Helen Fielding publishes *Bridget Jones's Diary*	
1997	The Labour Party under Tony Blair comes to power		Lynne Pearce publishes *Feminism and the Politics of Reading*

1998		Jackie Kay publishes *Trumpet*	
		Sarah Waters publishes *Tipping the Velvet*	
2000		Zadie Smith's debut *White Teeth* is published	
2001	The Twin Towers in New York are destroyed by terrorists on 11 September ('9/11')		
2003	American and British forces invade Iraq		
2004		Andrea Levy publishes *Small Island*	Sara Ahmed publishes *The Cultural Politics of Emotion*
			Sara Mills publishes *Language and Sexism*
2006			Ariel Levy publishes her critique of 'raunch culture', *Female Chauvinist Pigs: Women and the Rise of Raunch Culture*
2007	A global banking crisis begins		
2009		Hilary Mantel publishes *Wolf Hall*	
2010			Marianne Liljeström and Susanna Paasonen publish their edited collection *Working with Affect in Feminist Readings* in response to the 'affective turn' in feminist scholarship during the 2000s
2011			Clare Hemmings publishes *Why Stories Matter: The Political Grammar of Feminist Theory* in the context of a major reappraisal of how we tell the story of feminism's recent past
2013			Victoria Hesford publishes *Feeling Women's Liberation*

2014		Eimear McBride publishes *A Girl Is a Half-Formed Thing*	Victoria Browne publishes *Feminism, Time, and Nonlinear History*
			Chimamanda Ngozi Adichie publishes *We Should All Be Feminists*
2016	Europe's refugee and migrant crisis reaches a new peak		

Introduction

Lynne Pearce and Catherine Riley

Since the 1970s a great many academic books have been written on both women's writing and on feminism, but what makes this one unique – and, we hope, timely – is that it seeks to capture the ways in which the political movement (and the theory and criticism to which it has given rise) inspired and shaped a truly magnificent archive of expressly feminist literature by twentieth-century and twenty-first-century female authors.

There are strong political arguments for why it is still necessary to ring-fence and promote the work of women writers (see discussion following), although the reason this particular project focuses exclusively on female authors – and, indeed, on fiction rather than other literary forms – is in large part due to its origins in the research that one of us (Catherine) has conducted on the history of the feminist publishing industry in the UK. Working closely with many of the women who set up the now legendary women's presses such as Virago and The Women's Press in the 1970s and 1980s, Catherine has gained many important insights into why these initiatives came about, how the presses evolved and, most importantly, how they responded – over time – to the changes and developments in the feminist movement itself. Although one of the presses, Virago, did publish some fiction by men (hence making the important political point that men can be feminists too), their collective mission was very much one of making women's writing newly visible (including a great many texts which were no longer in print), thus challenging the deeply patriarchal 'literary canon' that, even in the 1970s and 1980s, was overwhelmingly male (see Chapter 1).

While the situation is much improved for the majority of today's students at school and university, the gender balance of individual courses/syllabuses remains unpredictable, and there is still the possibility that one or more of the students on a university women writers course (such as the one taught at Lancaster University for over thirty years) will have studied *no* women authors for their high school exams. This said, 'gender', as a concept, is much more widely discussed at every level of the education system than it used to be, with 'masculinities' as well as 'femininities' a popular topic for consideration. This progress has, however, been something of a mixed blessing as far as the teaching of the history of feminism and women's writing is concerned. Post-millennium, there has been a tendency for (some) colleagues to assume that this is a battle that has now been won; they fail to register that new generations of students are not necessarily familiar with the journey that has brought us to where we are today, and/or that women's writing is still massively under-represented on many courses. 'Gender awareness' is seen to be enough. Needless to say, this book starts from the assumption that it is *not* enough, and that there are a great many student (and other) readers out there who want to know more about the history of the modern feminist movement – itself now over 100 years old – and how its principles and politics have contributed to a highly self-conscious and imaginative interrogation of gender across the many genres of women's writing. Contextualising, and historicising, the thematics of a work of fiction in this way is, we would argue, very different from simply being 'gender aware' when we read it.

As will be discussed in the section following, exactly what defines the feminist movement, and how that movement voices its concerns, varies from decade to decade and is in a process of constant renewal. Post-millennium, there has, for example, been a new groundswell of feminist activism in the Western world linked to the digital revolution and, in the UK, epitomised by initiatives such as Laura Bates's 'Everyday Sexism' website (<http://everydaysexism.com/about>). Following a couple of decades when feminism was seen to have retreated into the academy (i.e. to have become a largely intellectual struggle picked over by academics), this has been received as a welcome attempt to reconnect feminism's core principles – notably the respect for, and equality of, women – to women's experiences in everyday life. The volatile, and reactive, nature of social media sites and platforms such as Twitter has, however, allowed a good deal of strident backlash from men (and women) hostile to feminism, and the polarisation of the public's views via 'likes' and 'dislikes' has arguably undermined more complex debate (thus widening the gap between how issues of gender and sexuality are discussed in academia and how they are talked about 'on the street'). This said, there can be no doubt that digital media have been responsible for recruiting, and energising, a new generation of young feminists, including many students. At Lancaster University, where one of us (Lynne) works, the women writers course mentioned above (initiated by two feminist colleagues way back in 1984) was recently brought back onto the undergraduate syllabus by popular student demand (after it had been dropped in favour of a period course on contemporary literature), while postgraduate students requested the feminist literary and cultural theory lecture course that Lynne now convenes for the faculty. This lecture series, which has attracted a wide and enthusiastic audience, clearly speaks to the needs of a new generation of feminist scholars (including many international students) who feel that they have missed out on the training in feminist approaches and methodologies that previous generations enjoyed.

There is an important pedagogical principle here which this volume seeks to address: namely, that before any of us can take ideas forward and/or add new layers of complexity to current debates, we need a thorough grounding in what has gone before. Because many readers will not have been born when Judith Butler published her paradigm-shifting analysis of gender, over a quarter of a century ago (*Gender Trouble*, 1990) (see discussion following), it is, we feel, vitally important to provide some information about the feminist theorising and activism that preceded that moment, as well as the different directions in which both theory and fiction have travelled since. While the future is un-deniably the prime concern and responsibility of every new generation, meaningful progress always depends upon a good, grounded knowledge of the past. It is our hope that *Feminism and Women's Writing* will fill in some of the gaps in readers' knowledge and keep the dialogue between feminism's past, present and future alive.

Making waves/breaking waves

Exactly how feminists in the present relate to, and represent, their move-ment's past has been the topic of passionate debate since the millennium. A growing awareness of the importance of temporality in feminist theorising (see, for example, Elizabeth Grosz's *Time Travels*, 2005) has given rise to a new awareness of the temporalities of feminism itself, and several important books have been published since 2010 that have challenged the narratives traditionally used to characterise its trajectory (for example Hemmings 2011; Hesford 2013; Browne 2014; Withers 2015; McBean 2015).

For all those of us who have taught feminist theory and women's writing for many years (as Lynne has done), Clare Hemmings's book *Why Stories Matter* (2011) was a somewhat embarrassing wake-up call. Through its astute analysis of teaching resources and introductory student guides, we recognise only too well the 'narratives' (most notably the 'progress narratives') we use, repeatedly, to explain how – as feminist scholars – we got to where we are today:

> First, it is clearly a positive account, one told with excitement and even relish. It is a narrative of success and accomplishment and positions feminist theory and its subjects as attentive and dynamic. Second, it is a narrative with a clear chronol-ogy: we are taken from the past – via key shifts in politics, theory and feminism's subject, and towards a complex feminist present. The shifts represented are from singularity of purpose and perspective to understandings that emphasise multi-plicity, instability and difference. (Hemmings 2011: 35)

Implicit in this trajectory is the problematic assumption that the first and second waves of feminism, while politically laudable, were conceptually and intellectually flawed, with Hemmings's invocation of 'multiplicity, instability and difference' being code for the way in which scholars and writers from these earlier periods are now dismissed because of their supposed failure to recognise differences of ethnicity and sexuality; or, indeed, the way all of us, in the wake of post-structuralism, are seen to be 'subjects in process' rather than individuals with fixed identities or identifications. According to Hemmings, this has led to a vast archive of pre-1990s theorising being unfairly ignored or misrepresented; as Mary Eagleton has also observed, 'history has not been kind to the feminist literary criticism of the 1970s' (quoted in Sellers and Plain 2007: 111) – a prejudice that this volume will, we hope, help to redress.

This challenge to what is effectively an *evolutionary* model of feminism also includes a critique of the way the history of the feminist movement in the twentieth and twenty-first centuries has traditionally been carved up into consecutive 'waves'. These are typically categorised as follows:

- The first wave focused on the worldwide suffrage movement that campaigned for women's right to vote in democratic elections, from the 1880s through to the 1930s and 1940s (although for some countries, even in Europe, the vote came even later).
- The second wave originated in the 'modern' women's liberation movement in the US, itself linked to the civil rights movement of the 1960s (which sought equality for black Americans). The second wave extended through the 1970s and early 1980s (although national/cultural variations apply).
- The third wave was linked both to the rise of queer theory (and the self-conscious practice of both heteronormative and alternative sexualities) as well as to what was perceived, by some, to be a period of 'backlash' against second-wave feminism, through the 1990s and into the early 2000s.
- The fourth wave (ongoing) has been characterised, in particular, by the use of digital media to rekindle feminist activism and to reconnect feminist politics with everyday life. In academia, it is also associated with a challenge to 'evolutionary' temporalities of feminism (see above) and a reconnection with many second-wave debates.

What those theorists and critics who have challenged the 'wave' model are most concerned about is that it renders obsolete issues, debates and, indeed, human rights abuses that are still very relevant today. Such assumptions can all too easily play into the myth that the feminist movement, as a movement, is a thing of the past (i.e. twentieth century rather than twenty-first century) and that certain theoretical 'advances' (queer theory being the most notable) are incontestable and irreversible. As will be seen in the discussions of sexuality in Chapter 4, there are several writers and campaigners in the present who do not consider this to be the case and who are arguing for a reconsideration of older (i.e. pre-Butler) models of identity politics.

Given these compelling critiques of the ways in which the 'progress narrative' has problematically impacted on our understanding of feminism's recent past, readers may now be surprised to learn that we have nevertheless elected to retain the 'wave' model as part of our own presentation of the way in which the feminist movement and feminist fiction have informed one another over the years. This is, in part, because – as noted above – we strongly believe that new generations of readers need to share in the knowledge that we (the previous generation) were 'brought up with', but also because it is a nomenclature that the feminist publishing industry itself recognises and continues to use. Further, it can be argued that 'waves' constitute a highly appropriate imagery for the feminist movement precisely because they are suggestive of flux and circularity rather than linear progress, with each 'new' wave turning back and renewing itself in relation to previous waves. This said, we very much hope that this opening contextualisation will encourage readers to check out the work of authors like Clare Hemmings (2011), Victoria Hesford (2013), Victoria Browne (2014) and Sam McBean (2015) for themselves since these critiques of the stories traditionally told about how feminist theory – and, indeed, the feminist movement itself – have 'evolved' represent one of the most important developments in the field in recent years. We now proceed with a brief overview of how the four waves have typically been characterised, in advance of their invocation in the chapters that follow.

One of the first things that readers new to 'wave theory' need to be aware of is that the so-called 'first wave' should not be confused with the start of feminism as a movement. While colleagues working on the Renaissance/early modern period (a period which featured some memorable 'proto-feminist' writers and intellectuals such as Margaret Cavendish, Duchess of Newcastle) may well dispute this, the origins of the feminist movement as we know it today are usually sourced to the French Revolution (1789–99) and, in particular, the writings of Mary Wollstonecraft (1759–97). Wollstonecraft was one of a small group of men and women who campaigned for the equality of women in the wake of the French Revolution and who was especially concerned with women's education and their rights within marriage: issues she addressed both in her celebrated polemic *A Vindication of the Rights of Woman* (1792) and in her hard-hitting (and often heart-breaking) fiction writings such as *Mary* (1788) and *The Wrongs of Woman* (1798). Readers interested in the full history of the women's movement and its writings should undoubtedly start here.

The women's suffrage movement, meanwhile – which represented a wider campaign for women's rights (across issues such as health, education, property ownership and rights within marriage) – spanned the late nineteenth century and early twentieth century (in Britain, women of all classes were finally given the vote in 1928), but is notoriously difficult to sum up since it took so many different courses in countries across the globe – see for example, Purvis and Holton (2000) on British suffrage and Giardina (2011) on the suffrage movement in the US. Indeed, suffrage is arguably an issue about which it is very important *not* to generalise, given that women in some countries took far longer than others to get the vote, and the fact that there are still many nations/regimes in the world which still do not afford women full democratic rights. As far as literary feminism is concerned, the UK has a very particular story to tell, inasmuch as many of its leading feminist writers from the first wave (such as Virginia Woolf, Vera Brittain, Rebecca West and Storm Jameson, to name a few) 'grew up' with the suffrage movement and the upper/middle-class women such as Millicent Fawcett, Ethel Smyth and the Pankhurst sisters who sacrificed so much to achieve this fundamental equality. (On this point it should, however, be recognised that other demographic groups in the UK took a while to secure the right to vote – 1867 in the case of working-class men, and 1918 in the case of women over thirty years of age – before the so-called 'universal franchise' was achieved in 1928.) The writings of a number of women from feminism's first wave are discussed in the chapters that follow: see especially Chapter 2 (Charlotte Perkins Gilman), Chapter 4 (Radclyffe Hall), Chapter 9 (Vera Brittain) and Chapter 10 (Georgette Heyer, Naomi Mitchison and Mary Renault).

Second-wave feminism is no less difficult to summarise in a few words, not least because – and as discussed above – it represents our *recent* past and, according to some, our ongoing present. The stories told about its origins are equally contentious, especially in the US, where several recent feminist scholars (see Giardina 2011; Hesford 2013) are keen to challenge the assumption that it simply 'grew out of' the civil rights movement, given that a great many women writers and campaigners were already active before, and during, this watershed in US history. Nevertheless, it is evident in classic second-wave feminist studies such as Kate Millett's *Sexual Politics* (1969) that the intellectual and political arguments that underpinned the campaign for black equality were also mobilised to make the case for women's rights: indeed, one of the most memorable scenarios that Millett explores in her book directly compares the profound 'ego damage' experienced by blacks as a consequence of their internalised racism with the self-denigration perpetuated by women – with the consequence that women often distrust and/or look down upon other women (Millett 1997: 55). It is also important to remember that, before the publication of second-wave's two flagship polemics – Millett's *Sexual Politics* in 1969 and Germaine Greer's *The Female Eunuch* in 1970 – a rigorous analysis of women's patriarchal oppression had already been undertaken by Simone de Beauvoir in *The Second Sex*, in 1949, and, in the US, by Betty Friedan in *The Feminine Mystique*, in 1963. In the meantime, so-called 'French feminism' was taking shape in continental Europe (see Marks and de Courtivron 1981; see also Chapter 4), causing many scholars, subsequently, to argue that the Anglo-American feminist movement should never be viewed in isolation when telling the story of the second wave. Further, and perhaps even more importantly, feminist scholarship only rather belatedly recognised the role that the arts – including literature – played in paving the way for the theorising and activism that was to follow. A great many female artists, photographers and film-makers were interrogating the exploitation and oppression of the female sexual body years before commentators like Greer (1970), Firestone (1976) and Irigaray (1985) took up the cause (see Schor 2016 on feminist artists from the period), while novelists like Angela Carter and Margaret Atwood (whose work is discussed in the chapters that follow – see in particular Case studies 2.2 and 3.1, respectively) were actively 'deconstructing' femininity years before the advent of either post-structuralism or queer theory.

Many of the key literary critical authors and texts that are credited with initiating the second wave within the academy, meanwhile, are the subject of the chapters that follow: names like Elaine Showalter, Ellen Moers, Sandra Gilbert and Susan Gubar, Patricia Spacks and Lilian Faderman are now enshrined within the (admittedly very white, very Anglo-American) literary-critical canon, and their work – often focused on the recuperation of women writers from the past – still deserves our attention, as discussed in Chapter 1. In terms of methodology and textual practice, this second-wave criticism is associated with several models of reading and analysis that fell into disrepute in the wake of post-structuralism (discussed below). This included 'images of women' criticism, which critiqued male-authored texts for their 'sexist' representation of women, for example Kate Millett's (1969/1997) venomous attack on authors like Henry Miller, Norman Mailer and D. H. Lawrence (see Pearce in Mills and Pearce 1996: 23–55), as well as more sophisticated Marxist variants such as Penny Boumelha's book *Thomas Hardy and Women* (1982). It also included what was sometimes referred to as 'authentic realism': namely the sort of reading practice which purposefully embraced the reader's identification with the characters in a text as a means of 'consciousness raising'. During the 1970s this mode of reading also found a very particular social expression (which persists today, though typically in a less overtly political form): namely the women's book club. For decades now, women have been getting together in each other's homes to share their views and/or experiences of selected texts; in the early days, this was credited with changing women's lives in very material ways (e.g. women seeking more equality in their relationships with men and/or challenging their domestic and maternal roles). Needless to say, 'authentic realist' reading was also seen to be of great importance to lesbian women, black women and other minorities who were starved of representations of alternative lifestyles in mainstream culture (see Lynch in Jay and Glasgow 1990: 39–46; Mills in Mills and Pearce 1996: 56–90).

The other branch of feminist criticism which is synonymous with the second wave is that for which Elaine Showalter (1977, 1986) coined the term 'gyno-criticism'. Gynocriticism was distinguished both by its mission to celebrate and/or recuperate writing specifically by women (a project that the feminist presses discussed in this volume shared) and by a desire to prove that women write differently from men. The latter was to prove an elusive quest, however, with Showalter observing:

> Defining the unique difference of women's writing, as Woolf and Cixous have warned, must present a slippery and demanding task. Is difference a matter of style? Genre? Or experience? Or is it produced by the reading process, as some textual critics would maintain? (Showalter 1986: 249)

Showalter herself – in the essay 'Feminist Criticism in the Wilderness', from which the above extract is taken – ultimately decided that the 'unique difference of women's writing' was cultural, and proposed that women wrote differently from men on account of their access to life experiences that men could not share (she called this 'the wild zone' of female existence) (Showalter in Showalter 1986: 259–64). Not surprisingly, this was a claim vulnerable to all manner of challenges and qualifications, and very soon black and lesbian feminists were arguing for the specificity of their life experiences which would not necessarily apply to women in general (see for example Smith in Showalter 1986: 168–85). Such disputes were the start of what was probably the biggest debate that literary critical feminism has had to deal with: namely, how to avoid *essentialism* (i.e. the assumption that all women share the same qualities/experiences and that those qualities/experiences are necessarily different from men's) when arguing why, for example, we need to ring-fence and prioritise women's writing through dedicated courses, feminist publishing houses and, indeed, books like this one. The era of post-structuralism (see below) only increased scholarly anxieties around essentialism, and the 1990s opened with a flurry of articles and books, such as Diana Fuss's excellent *Essentially Speaking* (1990), which attempted to work through the issues essentialism presented for feminism. Simultaneously, however, Judith Butler's first publications (beginning with 'Performative Acts and Gender Constitution', 1988) started to emerge and, by the time *Gender Trouble* (1990) had worked its way into the feminist mainstream in the mid-1990s, the 'de-essentialisation' of the category 'woman' was complete; for Butler, not only gender but sex itself were positions in discourse rather than biological destinies (see further discussion of this in Chapter 2), with the consequence that it became impossible to make claims for the 'difference' of women's writing based on the biological sex of the author. According to Butler's new ('queer') paradigm of sexual difference, both men and women could, in theory, assume, and perform, identities traditionally associated with women if they so wished and, as she later qualified in *Bodies That Matter* (1993), *their circumstances allowed*.

In terms of our gendered lives in the material world, the case was (and is), of course, very different, and from the perspective of the 2010s it is clear that the critical perspective on so-called 'essentialist thinking' came with its own blind spots, one of which was a failure to recognise how vital the gynocritical project had been in recuperating the lives and writings of women who would otherwise have remained 'hidden from history' forever (Rowbotham 1973). While most of us would now agree that it is impossible to demonstrate any definitive difference between men and women when it comes to their writing (either stylistically or thematically), there clearly still *is* a case for recovering and valuing those texts that patriarchal institutions have excluded on account of their author's gender. In other words, sexual difference as a concept might be hard to pin down but patriarchy is not; and the exclusion of thousands of female-authored texts from mainstream, masculinist canons is arguably sufficient reason in itself to teach, and research, something called 'women's writing' (see Chapter 1).

Feminism's third wave, at least within the academy, clearly owes a great deal to Judith Butler and the branch of theory, known as 'queer', associated with

her. However, it is important to recognise that Butler's project had many ante-
cedents – notably, Michel Foucault's work on sexuality and power (Foucault
1976), Luce Irigaray's interrogation of sexual difference (Irigaray 1985) and
Joan Rivière's concept of 'masquerade' (1929) (which foreshadows Butler's
own focus on 'gender as performance') – as well as the wider post-structuralist
movement in general. The last had particular ramifications for feminism, on
account of the ways in which Ferdinand de Saussure's and Jacques Derrida's
linguistic theories, together with Jacques Lacan's psychoanalysis, came together
to destabilise the concept of the individual (now refigured as a 'subject' of
combined linguistic, cultural and psychoanalytic forces); while this radical
challenge to humanist thought was welcomed by some for its deconstruction of
what Lacan referred to as 'phallogocentrism' (the privileging of the masculine
'word of truth' in the construction of meaning), for others it was seen to scupper
the new-born feminist movement (which campaigned in the name of both
'women' and 'individuals') before it had properly got started (see Weedon 1987;
Waugh 1989). What Butler's theorising added to this new model of subjectivity,
however, was an account of how gendered identities, in particular, are *produced*
and (through repetition) *maintained* (with the implication that they could also
be 'performed' differently on other occasions). With echoes of Rivière's work on
masquerade, Butler drew on the figure of the drag artist to make visible how *all*
gendered identities (including the most superficially normative) are 'artificially'
constructed: 'In imitating gender, drag implicitly reveals the imitative structure
of gender itself – as well as its contingency' (Butler 1990: 137).

Outside the academy, meanwhile, Butler's theory chimed with a new politics
of sexual liberation that was already afoot in the wake of the AIDS epidemic.
The latter had brought together lesbians, gay men and celebrities – like the
singer Madonna – who were willing to renounce the privilege of their own
heteronormativity (and identify as queer) in order to support the gay men who
were being victimised. The notion that no one's gender and/or sexuality was
fixed, or given, but potentially fluid and a matter of 'choice' – but see Butler
on 'citationality' in *Bodies That Matter* for a qualification of this (Butler 1993:
241–3) – gradually entered the cultural mainstream of the Western world and,
twenty-five years on, has material expression in the huge range of sexual identifications that social media sites offer their users. As Chapter 3 demonstrates,
however, this further challenge to sexual orthodoxies may also be seen to have
gone hand-in-hand with the growth of both 'lad' and 'raunch' culture, whereby
heteronormative sexuality is given a queer (performative) twist and ramped up
into a new hyper-sexuality that some commentators (e.g. Whelehan 2000; Levy
2006) see as making its advocates acutely vulnerable to abuse.

For another group of prominent feminist commentators – most notably Susan
Faludi (*Backlash*, 1991) and Naomi Wolf (*The Beauty Myth*, 1992) – feminism's
third wave was characterised as the era of *post*-feminism and backlash (see also
Pearce 2004). As with all movements which have a 'post' ascribed to them, the
'change' implicit in the prefix is complex and means different things to different

people. This is certainly true of 'post-feminism', which is seen by some to indicate a new era that nevertheless builds on the former (the 'post' indicative of *continuity*) while, for others, it has been interpreted as an admission that the moment of feminism is 'over' or 'in the past'. With the benefit of hindsight, Faludi's argument that the 1990s heralded the beginnings of a public backlash against feminism seems problematic – and, indeed, anachronistic – inasmuch that this was the decade when feminist teaching (including masculinity studies) was becoming firmly established on school and university syllabuses, and the queer movement was opening doors for a new generation of gay, lesbian or other-identified men and women. Indeed, scholars like Imelda Whelehan (2000) have raised question marks about a troubling homophobia implicit in Faludi's thesis, which turns, in large part, on the idea that second-wave feminism – and its perceived rejection of *femininity* – alienated a great many heterosexual women who did not want to be mistaken for lesbians. While there will, of course, have been some truth in this as far as the heteronormative mainstream is concerned, what was especially concerning was the fact that Faludi was also referring to herself and other female academics and writers who identified as feminists. Therefore, although the post-feminist displays of newly liberated and empowered *heterosexuality* from this period – represented, most famously, by the girl band The Spice Girls – may be seen as progressive in some respects, as a statement it was, and remains, very context dependent: remove the frames that ensure that such overt celebrations of female sexuality are on *the woman's own terms*, and the 'performance' once more becomes the target of misogynist exploitation and abuse.

A realisation of the fact that women, the world over, continue to be denigrated and abused, despite the human rights and equality legislation now there to protect them, is also seen as one of the key instigators of what is now widely acknowledged to be a fourth wave of feminism. As noted above, the arrival of social media and other digital platforms has provided this generation's feminists (which also includes a great many women from the earlier campaigns) with a new means of reaching out, sharing experiences and taking a stand against the 'everyday sexism' in their lives. While it is still too soon to get a clear sense of how this most recent incarnation of feminism will establish itself and what particular values, and actions, will define it, it is clear that there is a widespread agreement (both within academia and without) that those who thought the second-wave struggles for respect, equality and justice were over were wrong. Further, as will be seen in several of the chapters that follow, 'ownership' of the female body and women's sexuality remains a particular concern, as women and girls realise that what they thought to be empowered expressions of their own desire continue to be interpreted very differently by predatory and exploitative men. In this respect, the fourth wave may well come to be defined as the moment when feminists recognise, once more, that meaningful change lies outside of the will of the individual: social and cultural values, and the discourses which circulate them, have to change too.

A short history of feminist publishing

The transmission of feminist ideas and ideology has always necessitated the exchange of writing. From the pamphleteering of the suffrage movement to the 'consciousness-raising' reading of second-wavers, to the academisation of women's theoretical texts in the 1990s, and through to today's online cyber-feminism, writing and reading have underpinned feminism's development and the proliferation of its ideas. Feminist publishers have produced fiction and non-fiction that have redefined the boundaries of the canon (see Chapter 1) as well as shaped debates about the body, identity, sexuality and the parameters of literature's many genres – as the following chapters will explore. In this book we have used the wave metaphor (with an understanding of its limitations) to plot out the changing aspects of feminist thought; but it can also be usefully applied to the history of feminist publishing, similarly in waves, each with its own fairly distinct set of characteristics and concerns.

During the first wave, pamphleteering and petitions were key to communicating feminist messages. The Women's Social and Political Union (WSPU) published its newspaper *Votes for Women* from October 1907, and *The Suffragette* from 1912 to 1915, for example, while the journal of the Women's Freedom League was called *The Vote* (Marlow 2001: 55). First-wave feminists set up publishing houses in considerable numbers before the outbreak of the First World War, as publishing scholar Simone Murray discovered (see Chapter 1). These feminist presses – which included among their number Virginia Woolf's Hogarth Press – enabled the dissemination of feminist arguments and ideas which fuelled the suffrage movement in the years up to the war, and whose impact can also be traced in the post-war fiction written by Rebecca West, Storm Jameson and Dorothy Richardson, for example (all of whose work, in turn, would be reprinted decades later for a new audience by the second-wave feminist presses).

The second-wave feminist publishing phenomenon was predicated on the idea that literature was a tool to gaining empowerment: the refrain 'this book changed my life' was central to its early consciousness-raising, as women read one another's writing in order to find the political in the personal, to recognise – and challenge – the shared structural inequalities they faced. The impact of feminist polemic by writers such as Sheila Rowbotham, Ann Oakley and Germaine Greer was felt not only in these moments of collectivising and organising, but also in the stories subsequently told by female fiction writers as the second wave took hold. Angela Carter, Jeanette Winterson and Alice Walker, for example, all made their names following their publication in the UK by the feminist publishing houses that sprung up here during the 1970s and 1980s. The emergence of Virago, The Women's Press, Sheba, Pandora and Onlywomen, to name just a few, gave an outlet for exciting new writing by women that explored, in fictional form, the debates around gender, the body and identity emerging from feminist politicking and theory.

These debates moved into the academy during the third wave, as feminist scholars established themselves throughout the university sector and courses were instituted on women's writing and, indeed, on 'women's studies' more generally. Feminism's increasingly complex and complicated agenda was a positive result of women's incursion into these intellectual settings, as well as the construction and deconstruction of successive ideas of feminist thought (as described above). The emergence of queer theory had – and continues to have – an electrifying effect on theoretical formulations of feminism and these, too, were played out in women's fiction at the turn of the millennium, for example in the writing of Kathleen Winter and Sarah Waters (see Chapter 2). But this latest 'sexual revolution' occurred synchronously with a mainstream disavowal of the 'f-word' and the cultural reification of individualism as the route to empowerment, at the same time as the corporatisation and conglomeration of the book industry saw radical changes in how books were produced and sold. Small-scale feminist publishers were priced out of a fierce market, and the rise of the 'star author' meant a writer's looks, as well as their books, determined sales (Moran 2000). In this context, new feminist fiction writers had to navigate the complexities of a book market less prepared to gamble on untried writers and unorthodox thematics. They could no longer rely on finding a home with a feminist publishing house; indeed, by the end of the 1990s, Virago was the only second-wave publisher still doing business (and even then, as an imprint within a multinational conglomerate).

Contemporary publishing continues to be driven more than ever by the bottom line, but there are new kinds of feminist publishing and feminist publishers. Fourth-wavers are exchanging ideas online, are self-publishing and are making use of social media to create movements and communicate ideas. The rise in technology has had a profound effect on feminism, from the ways that women's bodies are commodified in cyber culture (for example, through the epidemic of online pornography), the opportunities new technology presents for global communication (and conversely the disproportionate amount of online abuse directed towards women) and the exploration of these and other themes in fiction writing. Fourth-wave feminist publishing can take the form of a blog or a website as much as a novel or textbook; and while we limit our discussion here to the fiction that has been published in book format, we acknowledge the huge body of 'unpublished' writing generated by fourth-wave authors. In the mainstream industry, a commodified and celebrity-focused culture that valorises the individual has driven a shift towards publishing women's life-writing – a clever tactic in disseminating women's stories in a way that is acceptable to the marketplace, yet can transmit feminist ideas, and a return to the concept of the personal being political (see Chapter 9).

The practice and ongoing evolution of publishing, then, have been crucial for feminism. Feminist publishing is important for two main reasons – one, its dissemination of literature by and about women acts as a means to their gaining empowerment; and two, the act of publishing *itself* as a moment of feminist praxis – an enactment of feminist politics through an incursion into 'male' areas of economic and cultural authority. Critical evaluation of the important phenomenon of feminist publishing thus provides a perspective on the continuities and changes within feminism, as well as the resistances it has provoked. There were, for example, violent attempts to smash apart the suffrage presses, while, in the 1980s and 1990s, feminist publishers came under threat from mainstream houses that moved in to cream off their most successful authors once women's writing had proven itself a profitable 'product'. Feminist publishing throughout the twentieth and twenty-first centuries has had a profound impact on what has been both written and read, and has in great part shaped the body of work described in the chapters that follow.

The chapters

Part I of the book, Debates, looks at the way feminist ideas have affected the *content* of women's literature. Chapter 1 begins with an analysis of women's historical exclusion from the parameters of what has been considered 'great literature'. The establishment of a literary canon based upon Victorian ideals of male intellectual rigour and superiority of certain genres saw women's writing characterised as less meaningful and less valuable. The great body of work created by women writers at the end of the nineteenth and beginning of the twentieth centuries was subsequently largely overlooked and excluded from the canon that came to dominate school and university teaching in the first part of the twentieth century. Indeed, it was not until the start of feminism's second wave that women writers – and educators – demanded the record be set straight, and demonstrated that the themes upon which women wrote, and the genres through which they chose to express them, were as complex and sophisticated as those produced by men. There emerged, too, a much-needed critique of the institutional barriers that prevented women from achieving the same literary plaudits as men, such as a manifestly biased reviewing tradition and a literary prize system that was hugely weighted in men's favour. Chapter 1 sets out the feminist critique of the canon and expands upon the historical importance of feminist publishing as a vital conduit between women writers and readers throughout feminism's various waves.

Chapter 2 takes on what is perhaps the most central issue of contemporary feminism: gender. Since the first wave, feminists have sought to explain and expand on the differences between women's embodied sex and the identity/ identities they live out (as masculine or feminine or a combination of both) because of the cultural codes with which they have been raised. Throughout feminism's various waves there have been attempts to destabilise the masculine/ feminine dyad, both in theory and in fiction writing, and Chapter 2 looks at how these formulations of alternative gender identities have been played out by women writers. Fiction has allowed women to imagine worlds where gender does not determine behaviour, status and sexuality, and we can trace through the changing content of women's fiction writing since the first wave how the debates about what gender is, and what it does, have impacted on the female imagination.

Chapter 3, in turn, looks at the female body, and the ways in which an ideal body type has always been imposed onto women through cultural phenomena such as art, literature and the media. Although the form of that ideal has shifted during feminism's different waves, the scrutiny and policing of women's bodies have not altered, and this chapter shows the line of continuity, from the first wave to the fourth, as feminist writers have attempted to counter the gendered insistence that women 'perform' their femininity through their bodies. It also focuses on the sexed aspect of the female body, and the link between the imposition of a uniform bodily ideal and women's sexual objectification. The critique of this representation of women's bodies as sex objects has been central to feminist writing for more than 100 years. Today, in Western culture, the (over) sexed female body is more abundantly on show than ever before. In both fiction and theory, women writers have questioned and caricatured this prevalence of sexualised images of women, and the impact this has on women's physical and psychic well-being. Chapter 3 therefore includes examples of fiction texts in which women writers have sought to foreground, and undermine, the patriarchal construction of their bodies as objects for the male gaze.

This focus on the sexed body continues in Chapter 4, which explores the feminist engagement with LGBTI+ identities. The issue of sexuality has been a problematic one for the feminist movement, causing rifts between feminists of all genders, who have disagreed on the extent to which their sexuality can be defined as a political issue. From the first-wave preoccupation with androgyny to the second-wave 'political lesbian', to the contemporary rise of trans identity and trans pride, feminism has both defined and been defined by its attempts to resist heterosexual norms. Feminist critics have debunked myths about normative heterosexuality, have explored alternative formulations of sexual identity and have attempted to define sexual expression that is free from the constraints put upon women's bodies and minds by the highly gendered cultures in which we live. Fiction writing has, again, provided a space in which it has been possible to imagine new kinds of sexualities, and women writers have been at the vanguard of creating such content, and thus changing the way we talk about, and live out, our sexual lives.

The final chapter of Part I examines the issue of ethnicity, and questions the assumptions of a Western feminism that unavoidably contains within it the privileged perspective of its white, middle-class foremothers. The emergence of a new point of view that incorporated the intersections of ethnicity and feminism, and was sensitive to Britain's colonial and racist past (a past that defined the limitations of, for example, the suffrage movement), challenged not only white patriarchy, but also white women's racism as well as black men's sexism. The institution of a black British feminism during the second wave developed out of both theoretical writing by critics such as Mary Helen Washington (1989) as well as fiction writing by authors such as Joan Riley (1985). As diversity has gained increasing recognition in the UK, so too has the wealth of brilliant writing by black, Asian and minority ethnic women, and the parameters of British fiction and theory has so also grown, as these writers have helped interrogate the privileged site of literature itself. Chapter 5 examines their contributions, and shows the ways in which their texts have changed the face of of British fiction writing over the past fifty years.

Part II, Genres, looks at women writers' engagement with the different *genres* and *subgenres* of literature, examining the effect of feminist ideas on the *form* of women's writing. The derogation of certain subgenres of writing as 'low' literary forms – including romance, crime and science fiction – has historic- ally been used as a way of disregarding women's writing. Chapter 6 begins an interrogation of the ways in which female authors have attempted to contradict this prejudice, and have variously revised, expanded and revivified traditional generic forms through a focus on what is probably the most stereotyped of all categories of women's writing: romance fiction. There has long been a correla- tion between *all* women's fiction and romance fiction, with women's literary efforts dismissed as 'love stories' regardless of the narratives (and themes) they actually contain. Feminists have written about, and tried to live out, differ- ent formulations of the romance narrative: from first-wave experiments with extended families and polyamory as evidenced by the Bloomsbury set; to the second-wave insistence that heterosexual sex is intrinsically oppressive; to the contemporary critique of the marriage imperative and quest for 'Mr Right'. Notwithstanding the complex politics that continues to surround it, romance remains an enduringly significant genre for both women writers and readers: a crucial space in which the discourse of love and its attendant emotions can be explored and interrogated.

Chapter 7 moves from 'soft-centred' romance to 'hard-hitting' crime, and begins with a historical overview of this now phenomenally successful genre, which is widely recognised to have grown out of the gothic and sensation novels of the mid-nineteenth century (both of which were shaped by the contribution of women writers). As second-wave feminist literary critics began to excavate the genre's origins – finding, as they did, that the first 'proper' crime novel had in fact been authored by a woman – a renaissance of female crime writing simultaneously emerged. Women took on the generic conventions of crime fiction and reimagined them in ways that were explicitly feminist, for example through the construction of the hard-boiled female private investigator. This tidal wave of feminist crime writing – itself enabled by the second-wave feminist publishing phenomenon that provided an outlet for literally hundreds of such books – has subsided in recent times, but women remain well represented in the literary 'mainstream' that crime writing has now become. Indeed, it is unquestionable that female crime writers have continued to play a key role in shaping how the genre has developed in the twenty-first century.

As with the crime genre, science fiction writing has been shaped and changed by women's engagement with its generic conventions. Chapter 8 shows how science fiction's classic motifs – extra-terrestrial life, space and time travel, cyborgs and robotics – were given new meaning through feminist storytelling, as women writers used the conventions of the genre to explore radical re-formulations of gender and sexual identity. Feminist sci fi emerged and became established during the second wave, although literary critics such as Anne Cranny-Francis traced its roots as far back as Mary Shelley's *Frankenstein*, first published in 1818 (Cranny-Francis 1990). Certainly that novel's narrative of birth/parenthood, told through the story of its protagonist's monstrous creation, tallies with the feminist sci fi convention of showing the alien nature of everyday life through depiction of the otherworldly. Women writers helped shape the genre, while sci fi writing has in turn also helped shape feminist literary ideas: there arose a literary critical assessment of the genre which recognised its potential to radicalise the way we look at fertility and reproduction, for example, and which credited women's science fiction writing with creating new constructions of possible feminist futures (Haraway 1983; Hayles 1999).

Chapter 9 moves on to examine the genre of life-writing, which encompasses autobiography, epistolary writing, diaries, memoirs and other forms of personal narrative. Women have always written their own life stories as a way of instituting themselves as meaningful subjects in the patriarchal literary and cultural contexts in which their identities have been subsumed. Women have told their life stories in order to claim their experiences as worthy of telling – and in order to create a sense of commonality with their reader, to show their shared experiences. First-person narrative accounts written by women have, indeed, played a vital role in raising consciousness throughout feminism's various waves, most notably the second-wave consciousness-raising project of the 1960s and 1970s. At the same time, second-wave feminist literary critics also set about revaluing women's life-writing, rescuing the genre from centuries of perceived 'sub-literary' status: until this time, the only life-writing that was considered worthy of academic consideration was the published autobiographies of notable public figures, most of whom were, of course, men.

Since this time, women writers such as Jeanette Winterson have achieved popular success with their radical reinventions of the life-writing genre and now, post-millennium, the cultural shift towards ever-greater reification of the individual (along with the rise of celebrity culture) means that life-writing constitutes a growing proportion of published output. This outpouring of women's life-writing has allowed a return of the feminist tenet of 'the personal as political', as women continue to use the genre (albeit in a more obviously accessible and/or commercial way than literary feminists such as Winterson) to share with other women stories and experiences that would otherwise go unheard.

Finally, Chapter 10 looks at the ways in which changing feminist debates have intersected with women's writing of historical fiction. Women have contributed to the genre since the historical novel emerged in the seventeenth century as a category of writing that straddled history and storytelling. Throughout the twentieth century, women writers engaged with the genre as a way of *retelling* history, especially to include those (female and marginalised) voices that conventional historical narratives overlook. Women writers' engagement with the historical novel has thus allowed for a feminist interrogation of the parameters of 'history' itself, and a foregrounding of the inherent unknowability of the past. Its effect differs from that of life-writing: instead of making the personal political, historical fiction makes the political personal, using real events and people from the past to weave a fictional story with meaning for the present. Its potential for feminism is obvious – it allows women to write themselves back into the past, and to pose questions for the future; and it is for these reasons that women writers have been some of the keenest champions of the genre, as well as having contributed some of its most brilliant texts.

References

Boumelha, Penny. 1982. *Thomas Hardy and Women: Sexual Ideology and Narrative Form*. New York: Barnes and Noble.

Browne, Victoria. 2014. *Feminism, Time, and Nonlinear History*. London: Palgrave Macmillan.

Butler, Judith. 1988. 'Performative Acts and Gender Constitution'. In *Literary Theory: An Anthology*. Julie Rivkin and Michael Ryan (eds). Second Edition. Oxford: Wiley-Blackwell (2004), pp. 900–11.

Butler, Judith. 1990. *Gender Trouble*. London: Routledge.

Butler, Judith. 1993. *Bodies That Matter*. London: Routledge.

Cranny-Francis, Anne. 1990. *Feminist Fiction: Feminist Uses of Generic Fiction*. New York: St Martin's Press.

de Beauvoir, Simone. 1949. *The Second Sex*. London: Vintage Classics (1997).

Faludi, Susan. 1991. *Backlash: The Undeclared War Against Women*. London: Vintage (1993).

Firestone, Shulamith. 1976. *The Dialectic of Sex: The Case for Feminist Revolution*. London: Verso (2015).

Foucault, Michel. 1976. *The History of Sexuality Volume 1*. London: Allen Lane (1979).

Friedan, Betty. 1963. *The Feminine Mystique*. London: Penguin Modern Classics (2010).

Fuss, Diane. 1990. *Essentially Speaking: Feminism, Nature and Difference*. London: Routledge.

Giardina, Carol. 2011. *Freedom for Women: Forging the Women's Liberation Movement, 1953–1970*. Gainesville: University Press of Florida.

Greer, Germaine. 1970. *The Female Eunuch*. New York: Harper Perennial Modern Classics (2006).

Grosz, Elizabeth. 2005. *Time Travels: Feminism, Nature, Power*. Durham, NC: Duke University Press.

Haraway, Donna. 1983. 'A Cyborg Manifesto: Science, Technology and Socialist Feminism in the Late Twentieth Century'. In *The Cybercultures Reader*. David Bell and Barbara M. Kennedy (eds). London: Routledge (2000).

Hayles, Katharine. 1999. *How We Became Posthuman*. Chicago: University of Chicago Press.

Hemmings, Clare. 2011. *Why Stories Matter: The Political Grammar of Feminist Theory*. Durham, NC: Duke University Press.

Hesford, Victoria. 2013. *Feeling Women's Liberation*. Next Wave: New Directions in Women's Studies. Durham, NC: Duke University Press.

Irigaray, Luce. 1985 *This Sex Which Is Not One*. Cornell: Cornell University Press.

Levy, Ariel. 2006. *Female Chauvinist Pigs: Women and the Rise of Raunch Culture*. London: Simon and Schuster.

Jay, Karla and Joanne Glasgow (eds). 1990. *Lesbian Texts and Contexts: Radical Revisions*. New York: New York University Press.

Marks, Elaine and Isabel de Courtivron. 1981. *New French Feminisms: An Anthology*. Hemel Hempstead: Harvester-Wheatsheaf.

Marlow, Joyce. 2001. *Votes for Women: The Virago Book of Suffragettes*. London: Virago.

McBean, Samantha. 2015. *Feminism's Queer Temporalities*. Transformations. London: Routledge.

Millett, Kate. 1969. *Sexual Politics*. London: Virago (1997).

Mills, Sara and Lynne Pearce. 1996. *Feminist Readings/Feminists Reading*. Hemel Hempstead: Harvester-Wheatsheaf.

Moran, Joe. 2000. *Star Authors: Literary Celebrity in America*. London: Pluto.

Pearce, Lynne. 2004. *The Rhetorics of Feminism*. Transformations. London: Routledge.

Purvis, June and Sandra Stanley Holton (eds). 1999. *Votes for Women*. London: Routledge.

Riley, Joan. 1985. *The Belonging*. London: The Women's Press.

Rivière, Joan. 1929. 'Womanliness as Masquerade'. In *International Journal of Psychoanalysis*, 10, pp. 303–13.

Rowbotham, Sheila. 1973. *Hidden from History: 300 Years of Women's Oppression and the Fight Against It*. Third Edition. London: Pluto Classics (1992).

Schor, Gabriele. 2016. *The Feminist Avant-Garde of the 1970s: Works from the Sammlung Verbund Vienna*. New York: Prestel.

Sellers, Susan and Gill Plain (eds). 2007. *A History of Feminist Literary Criticism*. Cambridge: Cambridge University Press.

Showalter, Elaine. 1977. *A Literature of Their Own*. London: Virago.

Showalter, Elaine (ed.). 1986. *The New Feminist Criticism: Essays on Women, Literature, and Theory*. London: Virago.

Washington, Mary Helen. 1989. *Invented Lives: Narratives of Black Women 1860–1960*. London: Virago.

Waugh, Patricia. 1989. *Feminine Fictions: Revisiting the Postmodern*. London: Routledge.

Weedon, Chris. 1987. *Feminist Practice and Poststructuralist Theory*. Oxford: Blackwell.

Whelehan, Imelda. 2000. *Overloaded: Popular Culture and the Future of Feminism*. London: The Women's Press.

Withers, Deborah. 2015. *Feminism, Digital Culture and the Politics of Transmission: Theory, Practice and Cultural Heritage*. New York: Rowman and Littlefield.

Wolf, Naomi. 1992. *The Beauty Myth: How Images of Beauty Are Used Against Women*. London: Vintage Classics (2013).

Wollstonecraft, Mary. 1792. *A Vindication of the Rights of Woman*. London: Everyman (1992).

Wollstonecraft, Mary. 1788 and 1798. *Mary* and *The Wrongs of Woman*. Oxford: Oxford University Press (2009).

Part I. Debates

1 Gendering the canon

This chapter explores the historical formation of the literary canon, looking at the ways it has been defined and shaped, and examining the extent to which its boundaries have been drawn to exclude women. This incorporates discussion of the emergence in Victorian Britain of the concept of a canon of 'great literature', as well as its subsequent problematisation by feminist literary critics. It also examines the arguments made around literary 'gatekeeping' and the problems presented by a male-dominated review press, taking as a case study the Modern Classics Series published by feminist press Virago since the 1970s as an attempt to counter this masculinist bias as well as provide tangible evidence of a rich history of excellent female authorship.

The phenomenon of feminist publishing is itself investigated, since what we read is, of course, in part dictated by the production processes that lie behind the creation of any literary artefact. Feminism has always sought to empower women through the production, distribution and consumption of the written word. The emergence during feminism's first wave of a range of pro-suffrage presses was mirrored in the 1970s and 1980s by a raft of second-wave feminist publishers, who transformed the literary landscape and succeeded in 'mainstreaming' not only individual authors but also whole literary genres (about which I will say much more in Part II of this book). The role of the publisher is important in considering how a text becomes canonical, since the commissioning of any literary work is always culturally and temporally situated, and its 'value' is likewise produced in and by those specific paradigms. In contemporary culture, the roles of publicity and of the literary prize industry have come increasingly to define the relationship between literary and cultural capital, and canonicity, and so this chapter looks at the Women's Prize for Fiction as a case study in this context.

The canon

The contemporary formulation of the literary canon is built on a set of principles first explicated by the nineteenth-century schools inspector and poet Matthew Arnold (1822–88). Arnold's premise was that literary worth was located in a text's ability to communicate truth(s), and that the consumption of 'great' literature should illuminate moral certainties, leading to a more civilised society. In his book *Culture and Anarchy* (1869) he wrote:

> One must, I think, be struck more and more, the longer one lives, to find how
> much, in our present society, a man's life of each day depends for its solidity
> and value on whether he reads during that day, and, far more still, on what he
> reads during it. More and more he who examines himself will find the difference
> it makes to him, at the end of any given day, whether or no he has pursued his
> avocations throughout it without reading at all. (Arnold 2006: 5)

Arnold's writing reveals as much about his ideas of reading as a means of
adding 'value' to one's intellectual life as it does about the social, educational
and cultural paradigms of Victorian Britain. He is clear that the pursuit of
knowledge through the consumption of literature is a task for *men*, reflecting
the naturalised assumptions that women were intellectually inferior, current at
the time he was writing. This attitude is exemplified in other influential pieces
of writing of the era, for example that of psychiatrist Henry Maudsley. In *Sex
in Mind and Education* (1874) he argued:

> [it is] not a question of two bodies and minds that are in equal physical condition,
> but of one body and mind capable of sustained and regular hard labour, and of
> another body and mind which for one quarter of each month, during the best
> years of life, is more or less sick and unfit for hard work. (Maudsley 1874: 29)

Literary scholarship was deemed unsuitable work for Victorian women.

The idea of a 'canon' of great literary works was instituted at a time when
women were largely excluded from the academy, and from intellectual and
public life. Although Girton College, Cambridge, had been established for
female students in the same year in which Arnold wrote his treatise, it did not
allow women actually to receive degrees until 1948 (at Oxford women could sit
exams from 1884, but would not be allowed to receive a degree until 1920). The
University of London was the first to admit women to its degree programmes
(and actually allow them to graduate!), in 1878, followed by Durham in 1896,
the University of Birmingham in 1900 and the remaining 'redbrick' civic universities founded in the following decade. This limited incursion did not offset the
Victorian bias that was weighted heavily in favour of male academicians – and
for lower-middle and working-class women, even a rudimentary education was
often a privilege their families could not afford.

This, of course, had repercussions for the kinds of texts considered worthy
of canonical inclusion. The boundaries of the canon were largely drawn to
exclude women, with one or two honourable exceptions. George Eliot and Jane
Austen were given the nod, for example, in F. R. Leavis's *The Great Tradition*
(1948), in which the author took up Arnold's idea of literature as a civilising
tool, narrowing the focus of this approach to works of fiction; Arnold had also
included study of the classics and some philosophical texts when setting out
his original concept. Texts like Leavis's helped further define what the study of
English literature and the boundaries of the canon would encompass, so that
university and school syllabuses adhered to similar-looking lists of culturally
sanctioned 'great' writers.

Challenging the hegemony of this male literary canon became an important target of second-wave feminist activity as the women's movement emerged in the late 1960s and 1970s. A fledgling feminist literary criticism set about revealing the ways that the canon was not representative of *all* great literature. Two of its earliest – and most explosive – texts were premised on critiquing this male bias, with Kate Millett's *Sexual Politics* (1969) and Germaine Greer's *The Female Eunuch* (1970) both using literary analysis to show the confinement of women in culture, economics, politics and elsewhere. Greer indicated her contempt for the 'great tradition' set out by literary men such as F. R. Leavis:

> Dr Leavis believed that he could identify a woman writer by her style, even though necessarily all that she wrote must have been a parody of some man's superior achievement. After all, there was not much wrong with Virginia Woolf except that she was a woman. (Greer 1970: 104)

Millett's and Greer's were two of the foundation texts of second-wave feminism, published within a year of one another, and although both are inarguably polemical, and in many ways flawed, they were nonetheless the first texts to really chime with a new feminist audience. This is evidenced by the huge amount of attention they generated on publication, which helped situate them as 'important' – and, as Mary Eagleton has argued, polemic was a necessary tactic at the start of the 1970s (Eagleton in Sellers and Plain 2007: 107). Both Millett and Greer, trained in the discipline of English literature, pepper their texts with excerpts from a range of literary (as well as non-literary) sources to illustrate their arguments (see Mills and Pearce 1996: 51). These were texts that lobbied for material change, rather than theorised a concept, and one of their targets was the centrality of male writers and writing in the canon. They were a starting point for the new field of feminist literary criticism.

As the 1970s got underway, feminist scholars in the US also began to point out the omission of female writers from the canon: 'of all the reading and study material available for stylistic imitation, inspiration, and stimulation of ideas, *over ninety per cent is prepared and written by men*' (Mullen 1972: 80, original emphasis). Elaine Showalter, who would go on to become one of the most prominent feminist literary critics of the 1970s and 1980s, wrote that 'the very term "feminine", applied to literature, has been a pejorative' (Showalter 1971: 859). Her solution was to teach new syllabuses of female-authored texts, to act as a 'decontamination chamber' to counter this systematic devaluation of women's writing and women writers.

Feminist academic Cora Kaplan has pointed out that this emergence of a feminist critique of the canon began first in US institutions and took longer to establish a foothold in the UK (Greer was an honourable exception). In Britain, English literature and humanities departments were, according to Kaplan, the 'last bastion of resistance' against incorporating women writers into its teaching programmes (Kaplan in Carr 1989: 18). British works such as Ian Watt's 1957 study of 'the rise of the novel' bear out Kaplan's claim by reinforcing the stereotype that women's engagement with literature was only ever as readers, not writers; Watt's list of novelists is almost entirely male, and those women who do feature are described as imitators, not innovators (Watt 1957: 296). Against this long history of exclusion, then, texts like Sheila Rowbotham's *Hidden from History* (1973) were a vital first challenge to such received wisdoms. The conclusion she drew – that the literary records of women's lives had been lost or obscured – was a clarion call to second-wave feminist scholars, readers and writers. After a century of literary learning in which their efforts had been devalued, overlooked or deliberately omitted, women began to set the record straight.

Indeed, by the mid-1970s there was a groundswell of feminist critical writing from both sides of the Atlantic that interrogated the formation of the English canon of literature – indicative of the dynamic and symbiotic nature of UK and US feminism at that time. In 1975, American scholar Annette Kolodny echoed Showalter's demand that the literary record be put straight: 'one vital goal of feminist scholarship must be the rediscovery and unearthing of texts by women which have, for one reason or another, been either lost or ignored' (Kolodny 1975: 88). A year later Ellen Moers, another US academic, argued that 'literature is the only intellectual field to which women, over a long stretch of time, have made an indispensable contribution' (Moers 1976: xi). Somewhat counter-intuitively, she argued that women's limited role in public life through-out history had not limited their scope as writers, but had in fact allowed them to flourish. 'Denial of access to the Real made it fascinating to women', she argued, driving them to investigate a broad range of themes, and to overachieve in their imaginings (Moers 1976: 83). She cited the work of many innovative and brilliant female writers to back up her theory.

Rediscovering historical literature consequently became a vital task, a way of proving the validity of these arguments. One of the ways this was effected was through the republishing of 'lost' historical works by women (see Case study 1.1, 'Virago Modern Classics'), alongside new investigations into when and why these works had been allowed to go out of print. In setting out her theory of a 'female imagination' in writing, Patricia Spacks asserted that 'women wrote most of the novels of the eighteenth century (although few of those are now read for pleasure)' (Spacks 1976: 57), before exhaustive research by Betsy Dinesen and Dale Spender was published in the 1980s revealing the sheer numbers and names of these 'mothers of the novel'; as Spender observed:

> I had no idea that for more than 150 years before Jane Austen, women had been writing novels, and that to return to the early days of women's relationship to fiction meant to go back to the seventeenth, and not the nineteenth century. (Spender 1986: 1)

These lists of hundreds of female novelists, excavated from literary archives and libraries, evidenced what Moers had argued: women had always written, had written well, and had enjoyed success and some acclaim in doing so. Their disappearance from view, Spender argued, was because of this very success, a backlash against their dominance of the literary scene:

> it was not unknown during the eighteenth century for men to masquerade as female authors in the attempt to obtain some of the higher status (and greater chances of publication) which went with being a woman writer. (Spender 1986: 118)

Echoing Moers's idea that fiction provided female writers (and readers) with a way into the world of ideas, Spender argued that this had led to a deliberate suppression of women's literary efforts as a means to suppress their involvement in public life more generally. She found evidence, for example, that male critics in the seventeenth and eighteenth centuries drew parallels between female writing and prostitution in their attempts to discourage women novelists (Spender 1986). Meanwhile, Dale Spender's sister, Lynne, developed a theory of literary 'gatekeeping' to show that canonical inclusion was protected by reviewers and scholars whose interests were served by the texts they granted entry (Spender 1983). The feminist challenge to the 'review tradition', a lasting bastion of male judgement and privilege, was underway. For example, Jane Tompkins found evidence that one of the most important – and bestselling – works of US fiction of the nineteenth century had been deliberately miscast as 'sentimental' as part of a concerted effort to smother its influence. In spite of selling more than a million copies after its release in 1852, Harriet Beecher Stowe's novel *Uncle Tom's Cabin* was derided by male critics, ensuring its exclusion from serious discussion as a canonical text (Tompkins in Showalter 1986). And in the UK other female writers who had, in their day, been similarly successful were shown to have been consigned to obscurity by unfavourable review coverage (see Case study 1.1, 'Virago Modern Classics').

In 1987, a comprehensive investigation of this issue was undertaken by Women in Publishing – a networking and professional development group for women in the industry.* The resulting book, *Reviewing the Reviews*, gave a damning indictment of the nature and influence of review culture, highlighting the bias in favour of male writers and revealing 'a discrepancy between the apparent interest in women's books and the actual notice they receive in the press. A casual glance at the book pages will often show a much larger number of reviews of books by male authors' (Women in Publishing 1987: 1). The consequence of this sidelining of women's writing on the review page was to limit women's achievement of their rightful share of the market, as well as to perpetuate a general view of literature as 'male':

> literary editors may claim that their pages reflect society, but people in positions of responsibility who deal with the world of ideas are the best placed to influence

---

* This publication was commissioned in response to an identified lack of women's coverage in the reviewing media.

changes in attitudes. In producing pages biased against women, they are perpetuating existing prejudices and subtly shaping people's perceptions of reality.
(Women in Publishing 1987: 91)

On this point it is important to recognise that the bias in review coverage continues to impact on women in these ways, and to thus subtly affect the shape
of the canon. In 2010 US organisation VIDA analysed data from a range of
literary publications to show how much space in each was devoted to the work
of male and female authors.* Its scan of the *London Review of Books* showed
that 168 reviewers were men, compared to 47 women – less than a third. And of
the authors reviewed, 68 were women, 195 men. In the *Times Literary Supplement*, male reviewers outnumbered female by 900 to 341, and while 330 pieces
of writing by women were reviewed, the number of works by male writers was
more than treble this, at 1,036. The need to challenge this review bias continues.

In such an environment, making women's writing available – and endors-
ing its value – has been critical. New anthologies of women's writing such as
Sandra Gilbert and Susan Gubar's 1985 collection *The Norton Anthology of
Literature by Women* were among the first to give students a new set of literary
texts to counter the masculinist literary bias that had emerged and become
entrenched in the late nineteenth and early twentieth centuries. As observed in
the Introduction to the present volume, courses on women writers were also
gradually added to undergraduate English literature programmes, and school
syllabuses were rewritten to include more female authors and poets, although
the student experience in this regard remained patchy well into the millennium. This balancing of what was taught in schools and universities so that it
included a fairer (although by no means equal) representation of female writers
was symbolically important, as literary critic John Sutherland has described:

> there are, in fact, few better preservatives of a novel and its author's fame than to
> be set for examination, to be judged as suitable research material by the commit-
> tees which approve PhD topics, or to be approached by an American university
> offering the curatorship of manuscript material. (Sutherland 1981: 11)

Inclusion in these curricula meant female writers attained cultural authority
and influence – as feminist critic Nina Baym reasoned, canonising a book (or
set of books) inevitably sets in action an unbreakable cycle of literary 'value'
(Baym in Showalter 1986).

The canon was thus interrogated and altered by the emergence of the
second-wave feminist literary criticism in the 1970s and 1980s. The extent
to which its aims have been attained – school syllabuses continue to include
more male authors than female, courses on women writers have been cut from
university programmes, male authors continue to dominate literary book prize
awards (see Case study 1.2, 'The Women's Prize for Fiction') – is still limited,

---

* Reported at <http://www.vidaweb.org/the-count-2010> (accessed 3 July 2012).

but the challenge laid down by feminist critics has nonetheless seen a lasting change to the body of work now considered canonical for English literature in the UK. The incursion of women into the academy – as writers, readers, researchers and teachers – thus remains an ongoing challenge in continuing the project of achieving genuine canonical equality.

Case study 1.1 Virago Modern Classics

A vital element of the feminist critique of the literary canon was the re-printing of 'lost' female fiction, which gave the lie to the idea that women had not written, or had not written well, in the past (for more on the role of feminist publishers in challenging the formation of the canon see 'Getting into print: publishers, publicity and prizes' later in this chapter). The feminist publishing house Virago, established in London in 1973 by Carmen Callil, spearheaded this campaign.

In the UK, writer Sheila Rowbotham, a close friend of Virago's founding director Ursula Owen and member of Virago's Advisory Group, had in 1973 published *Hidden from History*, in which she concluded that the literary records of women's lives had been deliberately obscured. This book, as well as Callil's drive to emulate the success of Penguin's reprinted lists, led to the establishment in 1977 of Virago's reprint library: a selection of works of fiction by historical women writers. This was quickly developed into the Virago Modern Classics series, launched in 1978. The series challenged the bias that had consigned women authors – even those who had been a critical and commercial success in their day – to obscurity. One of its first reprinted authors, Rosamond Lehmann, was a case in point:

> Lehmann's reputation remains problematic. In her day, she was certainly considered an important writer, and she was popular, too; but still, to look back on some of the reviews she received is to be reminded that notions of what constitutes a 'serious' writer can be heavily weighted with assumptions; and also that the Virago Modern Classics project was (and remains) a necessary one. (Coe 2007)

Elaine Showalter's *A Literature of Their Own*, published by Virago in 1977, was a critical guide to the texts that were included in the early years of the series, as well as an influence on which texts were selected. The first Virago Modern Classic was *Frost in May*, by Antonia White, originally published in 1933 and reprinted by Virago on 15 July 1978. The Virago Modern Classics were 'branded' with a combination of green spines, an apple logo and classic artwork on the front cover (chosen by Callil), and put Virago at the centre of the feminist attempt to reinsert women writers into literary history, as author Hilary Mantel observes:

'I was living abroad when the list began,' says Hilary Mantel. 'When I came back briefly in the 1980s – not a published writer then – the green spines were everywhere. I remember thinking that the world had changed while my back was turned, and changed very much for the better, as if a subtle re-balancing was occurring. Probably young women won't realise what it was like before. The star names among women – Murdoch, Spark – were treated like honorary men. Older, less-known women writers were only to be found in tatty library editions [. . .] Suddenly, women had become powers in the publishing industry, and they were using that fact to publicise the vitality and enduring quality of women's writing [. . .] I remember a man sneering at me at a dinner party circa 1975: "Women have no tradition." Actually, they had, and here was some of it in print'. (Cooke 2008)

Echoing Moers's argument that 'confidence was the resource that women writers drew from the possession of their own tradition' (Moers 1976: xiii), Callil stated that she chose the books in the series based on a desire to 'reveal, and indeed celebrate, the range of female achievement in fiction, and to bury, if possible forever, the notion that women novel-ists are confined to this ghetto of the imagination' (Callil 1980: 1001). Following on from her creation of Virago, the 1970s and 1980s saw a remarkable explosion in feminist publishing, with new companies such as The Women's Press, Sheba, Pandora, Onlywomen, Stramullion, Feminist Books, Honno, Black Woman Talk, Aurora Leigh, Urban Fox Press and Scarlet all emerging onto the scene. Although their working method-ologies, published lists and target audiences were hugely varied (they variously prioritised black women's writing, lesbian writing, separatist principles, cooperative working and so on), together these new publishers helped strengthen the feminist campaign to enlarge the parameters of literary 'greatness' to include a fairer representation of female writers.

As well as Virago, The Women's Press – established in 1978, the same year as Virago's Modern Classics series – similarly set out from the start to reprint historical women's writing. It launched with a reprint of Jane Austen's *Love and Friendship* (originally published belatedly in 1922), followed by Kate Chopin's *The Awakening* (originally published in the US in 1899), Sylvia Townsend Warner's *Lolly Willowes* (originally pub-lished in 1926) and Elizabeth Barrett Browning's *Aurora Leigh* (originally published in 1857). This engagement with the past is evidenced too in the early output of some of the other new feminist publishers who reissued out-of-print women's fiction as well as publishing new writing that theorised the importance of these historical works. Taken together, these reprints helped to reinsert women writers into literary history.

Of all the fiction published during Virago's first decade (1973–83), 136 texts were Modern Classics, while only 24 were new works of fiction. This did not go without criticism, with some pointing out it was much cheaper and quicker to reprint a dead novelist than invest in a live one. Others argued that the Classics pandered to middle-class sensibilities, but Virago's directors were clear that the Classics were not simply a means of peddling historical versions of romantic genre fiction. Alexandra Pringle, who began editing the series in 1982, explained:

> it was a very straight reclamation of women's lives and publishing novels that deal with women's lives in all their aspects [. . .] it was looking at all sort of writers [. . .] and finding completely hidden voices like an Indian writer, Attia Hosain, or the lesbian writer Eliot Bliss, and so all the different aspects of women's lives were illuminated. (Interview with Alexandra Pringle, 28 October 2009)

The Virago Modern Classics helped reshape women's literary history, rescuing women's stories from the past and re-presenting them for a new audience. The 'rediscovery' of all these rescued texts provided evidence of the ways the parameters of 'great' literature had been drawn to deliberately exclude women.

Getting into print: publishers, publicity and prizes

The canonisation of a literary text is to a large extent dependent on academic endorsement, as discussed at the start of this chapter. There is, however, a range of more practical factors that affect the production and reception of a text, and subsequently influence the ways that it is received both in the academy and literary culture, as well as by a more general readership. The mechanics of the publishing industry – including marketing and publicity, the task of commissioning work, and book prizes – all have an effect on which books are chosen for production, as well as which of those get noticed once they've made it into print. Beginning with feminism's first wave, there have been attempts to circumvent the publishing traditions that have excluded women from these processes, starting with the suffrage movement's institution of a range of printing presses run by women, for women, at the turn of the nineteenth/twentieth century.

Simone Murray is one of only a few archivists of the feminist publishing tradition, and has researched both first- and second-wave printing and publishing enterprises, drawing a line of inheritance between the two. She found that 'there is evidence of at least eleven pro-suffrage presses in addition to the

Woman's Press operating in London' before the outbreak of the First World War (Murray 1998: 199). These early feminist presses were established in order to take control of the *means* of production, an important act in ensuring their messages could be conveyed without interference or censorship. Virginia Woolf, who co-founded the Hogarth Press in 1917, articulated the need for women to empower themselves in this way: 'to enjoy freedom, if the platitude is pardonable, we have of course to control ourselves' (Woolf 1932: 258).

Having the power to publish was thus figured early on as vital to feminism, an idea set out neatly by American second-wave feminist Charlotte Bunch in words that evoke Woolf: 'controlling our words corresponds to controlling our bodies, our selves, our work, our lives' (Bunch in Hartman and Messer-Davidow 1982: 140). The second-wave feminist publishers that emerged in the UK in the 1970s and 1980s were an important moment of feminist praxis: the very act of setting up a feminist publishing house was fundamentally political. Companies like Virago, The Women's Press, Sheba, Pandora and Onlywomen challenged the history, structures and practices of the industry in which they operated. They shifted the parameters of what was considered 'publishable' by proving there was a (considerable and eager) market for literature written by women, and they set out to show that this material had as much literary worth as fiction and poetry written by men.

They also changed perceptions of women in business, demonstrating formidable prowess as entrepreneurs while challenging the domination of the publishing industry by 'gentlemen in trousers', as Virago founder Carmen Callil put it (Simons in Simons and Fullbrook 1998: 190). One of the publishing world's grand dames, Diana Athill, recalled in her 2000 memoir *Stet* just how entrenched this domination had been:

> All publishing was run by many badly-paid women and a few much better-paid men: an imbalance that women were, of course, aware of, but which they seemed to take for granted. I have been asked by younger women how I brought myself to accept this situation so calmly, and I suppose that part of the answer must be conditioning: to a large extent I had been shaped by my background to please men, and many women of my age must remember how, as a result, you actually saw yourself – or part of you did – as men saw you, so you knew what would happen if you became assertive and behaved in a way which men thought tiresome and ridiculous. Grotesquely, you would start to look tiresome and ridiculous in your own eyes. (Athill 2000: 56)

In 1989, research commissioned by Women in Publishing and published as *Twice as Many, Half as Powerful?* revealed an industry still firmly demarcated along the gender lines Athill describes (Tomlinson and Colgan 1989). But the incursion of feminist presses began to have an effect, so that by the time the third wave gathered momentum in the mid-1990s, there was a glut of powerful female executives running not just feminist companies but also mainstream publishing houses. By the turn of the millennium, Gail Rebuck was 'routinely described as the most powerful figure in British publishing' (Wroe 1999). And in a 'digital dialogue' on the bookseller.com in 2003, publisher turned literary agent Clare Alexander argued that the appointment of Caroline Michel as managing director of Harper Press signalled the shattering, at last, of the glass ceiling:

> In the past, high profile female publishers would have reported to male managers (or suits), but Michel was hired by the MD of HarperCollins's general division, Amanda Ridout, who reports to chief executive officer and publisher of the UK company, Victoria Barnsley, who in turn reports to the American head of Harper-Collins publishing worldwide, Jane Friedman. (<http://www.thebookseller.com>, accessed 17 February 2003)

Women have progressed in the publishing industry in ways not mirrored in other professions:

> trade publishing has a largely female workforce, with women at the top of some of the UK's largest publishing houses – Helen Fraser at Penguin, Gail Rebuck at Random House and Victoria Barnsley at HarperCollins. (*The Bookseller* 2007)

This movement of women into the top publishing roles is not only symbolically important: it has an effect on which books are chosen for production. Lennie Goodings, Virago chair, explains:

> There's a very great anxiety not just from this publishing house but from all publishing houses about 'small' books because of the way bookselling is going now – the big books sell so much better and the little ones just disappear. [But I will publish even if the book is] small because I think it's an important book to do. (Interview with Lennie Goodings, 8 November 2004)

Installing women at the top of the industry is an immediate challenge to the 'great tradition' that helped shape a canon dominated by male writers. The blossoming of feminist publishing ventures during the second wave, and the incursion of women into mainstream companies during the third wave, have been crucial factors in shifting the parameters of the canon by including women's choices as editors and publishers. When women began to choose the books that were produced, they did not automatically reproduce the male bias that had for so long dictated what was published, reviewed and sometimes made 'canonical'. Former publisher Liz Calder sums it up:

> I'm sure there is a correlation: men and women tend to favour their own gender. When I went to Jonathan Cape in the early Eighties there were very few female authors on their list. It was always very much a male province, but maybe it was more open to raising the glass ceiling than other industries. (Quoted in Smith 2003)

Simply getting published is not, of course, an automatic guarantor of a text's literary worth, much less it being deserving of praise, study or inclusion within the limits of the literary canon – but it is an important first step.

Goodings's observation also touches on another increasingly important aspect of the publishing industry, one that has a powerful effect on book selection and production. The rapid corporatisation of the trade in the past twenty years has seen it come to be dominated by a small number of huge international conglomerates, containing the more distinct imprint names of smaller operations such as Virago (which now sits within the publishing house Little, Brown, which in turn sits under the overall print/media umbrella of Hachette Livre). It also sped the closure of a great number of the second-wave feminist publishing houses: cooperatives such as Sheba and Onlywomen could no longer compete with the corporate muscle of mainstream houses in an increasingly cutthroat market, while Pandora and The Women's Press, which had always been financed by larger umbrella groups, were deemed insufficiently profitable to continue operations. The inexorable shift towards consolidation and conglomeration over the past twenty years has seen the number of independent publishers more than halved (Squires 2007). The result, it is argued, is a 'dumbing down' of the books that are produced:

> The advance of publishing houses toward monolithic consolidation continues inexorably, leaving almost no independent companies of large dimension operating today. The result is the emergence of a system for producing literature that might best be likened to dairy farming, with authors forced into the role of domesticated cattle resignedly allowing themselves to be milked to satisfy the thirst of a mass market. That the product will inevitably become homogenized goes without saying. (Curtis 1998: ix)

This has an effect on the formation of the canon. As Lynne Pearce has argued in terms of black and Asian British writers, it is the same names that routinely make it on to schools and university syllabuses – authors like Monica Ali or Zadie Smith (Pearce et al. 2013). She puts this down to a complex interplay of factors, including the geographic location of these London-based writers. I would further argue that it is their marketability as what Joe Moran would call 'star authors' (Moran 2000) that has impacted on their sales, and subsequently enabled – in part – their becoming canonical. The cult of celebrity and its intersection with consumerism defines all aspects of contemporary UK culture – including literary culture. Authors have become desirable, consumable commodities to be marketed just as fiercely as the literature they produce. Literary agent Clare Alexander directly links the 'celebrification' of authors to their success in the marketplace: 'there has been a drive to get authors into the features pages and the glossy magazines. Obviously if they are young and gorgeous they have got a head start' (quoted in Gibbons 2001a).

As Moran argues, star authors 'have the potential to be commercially successful and penetrate into mainstream media, but are also perceived of as in some sense culturally "authoritative"' (Moran 2000: 6). The effect of this is to shift the parameters of literary judgement, what publishing analyst James F. English describes as a 'reshaping of the relationship between journalistic and cultural capital, celebrity and canonicity' (English 2005: 207). In a culture in which the celebrity figure has influence and authority, the power of the old guardians of literary culture – the network of newspaper reviewers, academics, publishers and editors – is diminished. For women readers and writers, this shift is more welcome, since they have historically been shut out of traditional literary networks. It is, of course, also problematic: focusing on good-looking and thus 'marketable' individuals will always be at the expense of other authors, regardless of the quality of their work. This is antithetical to the aims of a feminist women's political movement that has sought, throughout all its 'waves', to remove the focus on women's bodies and appearance and to institute a cultural order in which gender identity does not impact on authority.

Case study 1.2 The Women's Prize for Fiction

Literary prizes dictate not only what is read, but to a not inconsiderable extent what goes on to be taught and to be subsequently included in the canon of 'great' writing. It is difficult to overstate the influence book prize lists have on sales, and consequently on the way books are contracted, produced and marketed. Even those authors merely nominated for the Man Booker Prize or the Costa Book Awards, for example, can expect huge uplifts in sales. Titles that make the Booker shortlist are guaranteed thousands of extra hardback sales – though many consider this a very conservative estimate (Todd 1996). Historically, the literary press and the world of book prizes have been dominated by men who, as feminist critics have pointed out, 'found the contributions of their own sex immeasurably superior' (Spender 1989: 1). This resulted, unsurprisingly, in many more men than women being awarded literary prizes. The Booker Prize, for example, instituted in 1969 (as second-wave feminism emerged), has had twice as many male winners as female. This culture of privileging male writing led women writers, readers and publishers to think about ways of challenging the status quo, leading to the instigation of a prize in 1996 dedicated solely to women writers.

The Women's Prize for Fiction, an annual award originally sponsored by the mobile network provider Orange but now backed by the drinks company Baileys (it was initially to have been called Uni, with Mitsubishi agreeing to sponsor the award, but the company pulled its backing in 1994 after derisory press coverage), was catalysed by the exclusion of Angela Carter from the 1991 Booker Prize shortlist, an omission that was widely condemned in literary critical circles. Kate Mosse, one of the driving forces behind the Prize, had long noted a tendency among literary critics to view any Booker-shortlisted female writer as somehow representative of her sex, so that a female-authored text constituted a 'woman's entry', whereas male-authored texts were assessed on merit alone: 'writing by women is always "women's writing", to be understood and evaluated in terms of the special case of their gender. Writing by men is just writing' (quoted in Morris 1993: 46). Mosse and others thought the only way to address this was to institute a prize for which only women could be considered: 'paradoxically, the way to take gender out of the equation was for all the entrants to be women' (Mosse quoted in Bedell 2005).

The Women's Prize for Fiction was launched in January 1996 and Mosse was shocked by the vitriol that surrounded its inception: 'I thought everybody who was concerned about reading books would be happy that there was a new prize. The first question anyone asked was, "Are you a lesbian?"' (quoted in Bedell 2005). In spite of this prurient response, the prize had a clearly discernible effect on sales: five years after the award's inception, women writers outnumbered men in *The Guardian*'s Fastseller list, the definitive guide to the year's hottest paperbacks, for the first time (Gibbons 2001b).

The importance of the Women's Prize for Fiction, then, is not so much in attributing 'greatness' to a select group of writers or texts, but in boosting sales of women's writing – in today's literary culture, this in itself helps denote authority: 'in recent years we are, in fact, experiencing an intense politics of literary merit linked as never before to its economic value' (Ponzanesi in Görtschacher and Klein 2006: 116). The Women's Prize for Fiction allocates women writers the same kind of authority-through-sales that the mainstream prizes have long afforded (mostly) men's work. There is, of course, discomfort – among women writers themselves as much as anyone else – that there should be a dedicated women's prize:

> Anita Brookner, a Booker winner, has no mixed feelings. 'I'm against positive discrimination. If women want equality, which they do, and which they have largely achieved, they shouldn't ask for separate treatment. Publishing is an open forum. If a book is good, it will get published. If it is good, it will get reviewed. The whole idea of an award just for women fills me with horror.' She has backed her words with deed, refusing to allow her latest book to be put in for the award. (Quoted in Jeffreys 1996)

Brookner has stuck by her position, but the reality was – and still is – that mainstream review and prize cultures favour men. In the first thirty years of the Booker Prize, almost two-thirds of those shortlisted were men, while 'in the past nine years of the Booker, the pattern still has not changed noticeably: 33 men (61 per cent) have been shortlisted, compared to 21 women (39 per cent)' (Coe 2007). It is therefore arguable that the

Baileys Prize for Women's Fiction still has a role to play in combatting this unspoken and to a large degree unchallenged bias, bringing women's writing greater attention through greater sales. In a literary economy in which value and longevity are increasingly determined by numbers sold, women's incursion into the canon is only aided by the institution of awards that boost their sales figures.

Bibliography

Arnold, Matthew. 2006. *Culture and Anarchy*. Oxford: Oxford University Press. (1869)

Athill, Diana. 2000. *Stet: An Editor's Life*. London: Granta.

Bedell, Geraldine. 2005. 'Textual Politics'. In *The Guardian*, 6 March.

Callil, Carmen. 1980. 'Virago Reprints: Redressing the Balance'. *Times Literary Supplement*, 12 September, p. 1001.

Carr, Helen (ed.). 1989. *From My Guy to Sci Fi: Genre and Women's Writing in the Postmodern World*. London: Pandora.

Coe, Jonathan. 2007. 'My Literary Love Affair'. In *The Guardian*, 6 October.

Cooke, Rachel. 2008. 'Taking Women Off the Shelf'. In *The Guardian*, 6 April.

Curtis, Richard. 1998. *This Business of Publishing: An Insider's View of Current Trends and Tactics*. New York: Allworth Press.

English, James F. 2005. *The Economy of Prestige: Prizes, Awards, and the Circulation of Cultural Value*. Cambridge, MA: Harvard University Press.

English, James F. (ed.). 2006. *A Concise Companion to Contemporary British Fiction*. Malden: Blackwell.

Gibbons, Fiachra. 2001a. 'The Route to Literary Success: Be Young, Gifted But Most of All Gorgeous'. In *The Guardian*, 28 March.

Gibbons, Fiachra. 2001b. 'Women Lead the Way in "Hottest" Books List'. In *The Guardian*, 29 December.

Gilbert, Sandra M. and Susan Gubar (eds). 1985. *The Norton Anthology of Literature by Women: The Tradition in English*. New York: Norton.

Görtschacher, Wolfgang and Holger Klein, in association with Claire Squires. 2006. *Fiction and Literary Prizes in Great Britain*. Vienna: Praesens Verlag.

Greer, Germaine. 1970. *The Female Eunuch*. London: MacGibbon and Kee.

Hartman, J. and E. Messer-Davidow (eds). 1982. *Women in Print II: Opportunities for Women's Studies Publication in Language and Literature*. New York: Modern Language Association of America.

Jeffreys, Susan. 1996. 'Women Caught in a War of Words'. *Sunday Times*, 21 April.

Kolodny, Annette. 1975. 'Some Notes on Defining a "Feminist Literary Criticism"'. In *Critical Inquiry*, 2 (autumn), pp. 75–92.

Leavis, F. R. 1948. *The Great Tradition*. London: Chatto and Windus.

Maudsley, Henry. 1874. *Sex in Mind and Education*. New York: C. W. Bardeen.

Millett, Kate. 1969. *Sexual Politics*. New York: Simon and Schuster.

Mills, Sara and Lynne Pearce. 1996. *Feminist Readings/Feminists Reading*. Second Edition. Hemel Hempstead: Harvester-Wheatsheaf.

Moers, Ellen. 1976. *Literary Women*. New York: Doubleday.

Moran, Joe. 2000. *Star Authors: Literary Celebrity in America*. London: Pluto.

Morris, Pam. 1993. *Literature and Feminism: An Introduction*. Oxford: Blackwell.

Mullen, Jean S. 1972. 'Women Writers in Freshman Textbooks'. In *College English*, 34:1 (October), pp. 79–84.

Murray, Simone. 1998. '"Books of Integrity": The Women's Press, Kitchen Table Press and Dilemmas of Feminist Publishing'. In *European Journal of Women's Studies*, 5:2, pp. 171–93.

Murray, Simone. 2004. *Mixed Media: Feminist Presses and Publishing Politics*. London: Pluto Press.

Pearce, Lynne, Corinne Fowler and Robert Crawshaw. 2013. *Postcolonial Manchester: Diaspora Space and the Devolution of Literary Culture*. Manchester: Manchester University Press.

Rowbotham, Sheila. 1973. *Hidden from History: 300 Years of Women's Oppression and the Fight Against It*. London: Pluto.

Sellers, Susan and Gill Plain (eds). 2007. *A History of Feminist Literary Criticism*. Cambridge: Cambridge University Press.

Showalter, Elaine. 1971. 'Women and the Literary Curriculum'. In *College English*, 32:8, pp. 855–62.

Showalter, Elaine. 1977. *A Literature of Their Own: British Women Novelists from Brontë to Lessing*. London: Virago.

Showalter, Elaine (ed.). 1986. *The New Feminist Criticism: Essays on Women, Literature and Theory*. London: Virago.

Simons, Judy and Kate Fullbrook (eds). 1998. *Writing: A Women's Business. Women, Writing and the Marketplace*. Manchester: Manchester University Press.

Smith, David. 2003. 'Women Celebrate a Turn-Up for the Books'. In *The Observer*, 21 September.

Spacks, Patricia Meyer. 1976. *The Female Imagination: A Literary and Psychological Investigation of Women's Writing*. London: George Allen and Unwin.

Spender, Dale. 1986. *Mothers of the Novel: 100 Good Women Writers Before Jane Austen*. London: The Women's Press.

Spender, Dale. 1989. *The Writing or the Sex? Or Why You Don't Have to Read Women's Writing to Know It's No Good*. New York: Teacher's College Press.

Spender, Lynne. 1983. *Intruders on the Rights of Men: Women's Unpublished Heritage*. London: Pandora.

Squires, Claire. 2007. *Marketing Literature: The Making of Contemporary Writing in Britain*. Basingstoke: Palgrave Macmillan.

Sutherland, John. 1981. *Bestsellers: Popular Fiction of the 1970s*. London: Routledge and Kegan Paul.

The Bookseller. 2007. 'Men – An Endangered Species?' (Editorial). In *The Bookseller*, 21 May.

Todd, Richard. 1996. *Consuming Fictions: The Booker Prize and Fiction in Britain Today*. London: Bloomsbury.

Tomlinson, Frances and Fiona Colgan. 1989. *Twice as Many, Half as Powerful? Report of a Survey into the Employment of Women in the United Kingdom Book Publishing Industry*. London: Polytechnic of North London/Women in Publishing.

Watt, Ian. 1957. *The Rise of the Novel: Studies in Defoe, Richardson and Fielding*. London: Chatto and Windus (1974).

White, Antonia. 1978. *Frost in May*. London: Virago.
Women in Publishing. 1987. *Reviewing the Reviews: A Woman's Place on the Book Page*. London: Journeyman Press.
Woolf, Virginia. 1932. 'How Should One Read a Book?' In *The Common Reader Second Series*. London: Hogarth Press.
Wroe, Nicholas. 1999. 'Success is a Feminist Issue'. In *The Guardian*, 31 July.

2 Gender

This chapter begins with an overview of feminism's articulation(s) of gender – starting with first-wave explorations of female identity and fictional explorations through the image of the 'New Woman' during the *fin de siècle*, before a critical understanding of gender had been defined. It then moves forward through Simone de Beauvoir's famous epithet 'one is not born, but rather becomes, a woman' to critical conceptualising of gender during the second wave, and the subsequent feminist problematisation of the construction of femininity, in particular the naturalisation of the roles of mother, house-wife, sex object. Next, it looks at Judith Butler's important intervention in these debates in *Gender Trouble* (1990), and the subsequent 'queer' focus on alternative/subversive genders, before moving onto more current discussions of gender constructs.

On this point it is, indeed, important to recognise that 'post-Butler' there have been attempts to move beyond/through queer theory to examine gender – and indeed feminism – in new ways. Bruce Bawer (1996), for example, has attempted to wrest back gay/lesbian identities from 'queer' culture to state the specificity of those identities as *political*, lived positions. Other critics, such as Clare Hemmings, have argued that gender, like feminism, has not developed in a sequential way, linking back to the ideas set out in the Introduction to this book about the validity of the feminist 'waves' construct (Hemmings 2011). Our understanding of gender, like feminism itself, thus continues to evolve – both through the formulation of new concepts and strategies, and through a process of continual turning back and revision, thereby incorporating aspects of earlier formulations alongside these new ones.

Having performed this brief overview of the evolving critical formulations of gender, there follows a reflection on Charlotte Perkins Gilman's 1915 text *Herland* (Case study 2.1) – an early and radical interrogation of normative gender – before the chapter then moves on to consider how interrogations of gender manifest themselves in women's fiction. In fact, the impact of gender's articulation and explication is a theme throughout this book, whose focus is on how feminism has altered women's writing, which is conceptually underpinned by the articulation of a concept of gender. This chapter begins to explore, then, the way 'gender' is problematised and/or radicalised by women writers, intro-ducing some of the writers who will be looked at in greater detail in subsequent chapters, and showing how the feminist project of critically defining gender had an immediate and electrifying effect on female fiction. As with other aspects of feminist theory that will be explored later in this book, women's fictional explorations of gender anticipated and, in several instances, tested out the key ideas being put forward in critical texts. This dialogue between theory and fiction can be seen as a thread running throughout feminism's various 'waves'.

What is 'gender'?

The category 'gender' is a relatively recent construct, as is reflected in contemporary dictionary definitions where its 'cultural constructedness' is brought to the fore. In the *New Oxford Dictionary of English*, for example, gender is defined as 'the state of being male or female (typically used with reference to social and cultural differences rather than biological ones)' (Pearsall 2001). Indeed, the category 'gender' helps us distinguish biological differences between the sexes from those which are cultural, psychological, political, economic or other. Arriving at this useful category definition was the result of a feminist exploration and theorisation of women's status in culture, beginning with examinations of the figure of the 'New Woman' during what we now call the 'first wave' of feminist politicking.

The figure of the New Woman emerged in the UK at the end of the nineteenth century as suffrage activity gained momentum. As Victorian Britain changed radically under the influences of a new socialism, imperialism, industrialisation and urbanisation, there emerged new spaces (both literal and intellectual) in which women could construct and enact new attitudes and behaviours. With the approach of the *fin de siècle*, some shifts in women's status arising from these societal changes could be observed. The Married Women's Property Acts of 1870 and 1882 finally ended the system of 'coverture', the legal doctrine that had subsumed women's identities – and thus rights – under that of their husbands' (Bland 1995). This legal reinstitution of married women's individual identities meant they were allowed to own and inherit money and property and this, coupled with the Matrimonial Causes Act 1878, which reformed divorce law (to a limited extent), was both the result of and a contributing factor to women's new interrogation of their role in culture. The distinction between sex and gender was not fully articulated until well into the following century, but the New Woman figure was a launching point for the debates around cultural constructions of (especially female) identity that fed into its articulation.

Other changes were occurring beyond the legal system that similarly challenged the traditional construction of the category 'feminine', with its emphasis on motherliness, domesticity and docility – some in unlikely places. The establishment, for example, of the Aerated Bread Company (ABC) chain of tearooms in 1864 established a new 'reputable' space for women, free from the connotations of bars and restaurants in which a woman dining alone was a provocation for scandal. The invention of the bicycle gave women new freedom of movement and was enthusiastically adopted by New Women (as is evidenced by popular depiction of her on two wheels). In 1881 the Society for Rational Dress was formed in London by a group of women who argued that 'feminine' garb – tight corsets, high heels and unwieldy skirts – was absurd. This early critique of 'gendered' clothing was spearheaded by Sarah Grand, the writer and activist who helped coin the term 'New Woman', and who would provide some of the earliest literary evidence of the emergence of 'gender' debates in women's writing.

Grand, along with other British writers like Ella Hepworth Dixon, Mona Caird, Maria Louise Ramé (under the pen name Ouida) and Olive Schreiner (although South African-born, Schreiner's parents married in England and she was based in the UK for almost a decade during the 1880s) established the New Woman figure in their fiction writing. Alongside similar representations of alternative versions of womanhood by US writers like Charlotte Perkins Gilman, Willa Cather and Kate Chopin – as with aspects of later feminist 'waves', this early contestation of gender norms was a transatlantic phenomenon – these novels provide the first literary examples of feminism's exploration of gender constructs before the term itself had fully been enunciated. The bicycle-riding, 'bloomer'-wearing, strident caricature so derided in Victorian publications like *Punch* magazine bears little resemblance to the independent, opinionated but ultimately socially and economically *restricted* women portrayed in New Woman fiction texts like Schreiner's *Story of an African Farm* (1883), Grand's *The Heavenly Twins* (1893) and Dixon's *The Story of a Modern Woman* (1894). This early literary engagement with troubling the gender order illustrates the prominent role fiction has always played in interrogations of gender, as well as the deep unease such interrogations have always elicited, as shown through the exaggerated response and stereotyping of the figure of the New Woman.

Following on from New Woman fiction, and the wider first-wave attempt to articulate the concept of gender and to traduce traditional binary notions of masculine/feminine, the modernist writer Virginia Woolf similarly explored the possibility of a new kind of female identity that was not bound by such binaries. Drawing on the emerging theories of sexologists such as Havelock Ellis and Richard von Krafft-Ebing, who posited new categories of (sexual) identity, Woolf proposed an androgynous ideal by which men and women were made up of both masculine and feminine qualities, rather than being mistakenly assigned to one physiology and category of behaviours or the other.* In her fictional exploration of androgyny *Orlando* (1928), the tale of a time-travelling transgender eponymous protagonist, Woolf demonstrates the limitations imposed on both sexes by the culturally sanctioned behaviours demanded of sexed bodies. Orlando's transformation through the process of inhabiting first a male body and then a female one allows Woolf to illustrate how the behaviours we would now describe as 'gendered' serve to falsely contain men and

---

* For an introduction to the 'science' of sexology, see Bland and Doan (1998).

women alike. In *A Room of One's Own*, published a year after *Orlando*, Woolf reflected upon this fictional experiment in her critical writing:

> it is fatal for anyone who writes to think of their sex. It is fatal to be a man or woman pure and simple; one must be woman-manly or man-womanly [. . .] for anything written with that conscious bias is doomed to death. (Lee 1984: 97)

Woolf's fiction writing thus allowed her to explore the possibilities of her androgynous ideal, predating by several decades the theoretical and fictional engagement with gender made by feminist writers of the second wave and beyond.

Defining gender was a crucial aspect of second-wave feminist theory. Although pre-dating its emergence by several years, Simone de Beauvoir's 1949 text *The Second Sex* was an important influence on this articulation of gender. De Beauvoir describes the processes by which women are made 'feminine' by being assigned this gender at birth on the basis of their physiology and then taught to regard it as natural because of its deep entrenchment within cultural institutions: 'one is not born, but rather becomes, a woman', as she neatly put it (de Beauvoir 1949: 295). The subsequent work of Robert Stoller also examined the differentiation of sex and gender, providing another foundation stone for increasingly complex interrogations of these terms. In his 1968 text *Sex and Gender* Stoller argues that 'one can speak of the male sex or the female sex, but one can also talk about masculinity and femininity and not necessarily be implying anything about anatomy or physiology' (Stoller 1968: ix). Sex and gender, then, 'are not at all inevitably bound in anything like a one-to-one relationship'; rather, gender is culturally determined so that girls learn from birth to act in a 'feminine' way, boys in a 'masculine' way, yet we all have degrees of both masculinity and femininity within us (Stoller 1968: ix). Another important early text in this regard was Kate Millett's *Sexual Politics* (1969), which drew upon the US civil rights movement and its challenge to the 'race' binary to launch an attack on patriarchy's imposition of a gender binary (Pearce in Mills and Pearce 1996).

In the UK, these ideas fed into the second-wave articulation of gender, with texts such as Ann Oakley's *Sex, Gender and Society* (1972) further differentiating between sex as the anatomical differences between women and men, and gender as a set of cultural assumptions and psychological attributes. Gayle Rubin, meanwhile, coined the concept of the 'sex/gender system' as the locus of women's oppression in her celebrated 1975 essay 'The Traffic in Women: Notes on the "Political Economy" of Sex'. 'Gender is a socially imposed division of the sexes', she stated (Rubin in Reiter 1975: 170). This separation of sex from gender became a cornerstone of second-wave politicking, providing a basis from which women could examine the ways in which specific roles and behaviours had come to be ascribed to them. In particular, the imposition of the roles of housewife, mother and passive sexual object as idealised forms of 'femininity' were problematised both through this polemical writing and, increasingly, in fiction too (see under '(Re)telling gender in fiction' later in this chapter).

Problematisation of the housewife role for women had earlier – and perhaps most famously – been articulated by US writer Betty Friedan in her 1963 text *The Feminine Mystique*. In this investigation of the 'problem that has no name', as Friedan put it, she shows how the idealisation of the housewife led to abject misery for the millions of women constrained in the role: 'in 1960 the problem that has no name burst like a boil through the image of the happy American housewife [. . .] the actual unhappiness of the American housewife was suddenly being reported' (Freidan 1963: 19). Texts like Eva Figes's *Patriarchal Attitudes* (1970) followed in the UK, in which the author argued that women's confinement to the domestic was an economic inevitability: 'the concept of marriage makes women unable to be really independent, and her inability to be independent makes it necessary to try to protect her with marriage' (Figes 1970: 184). In *Woman's Estate* (1971) Juliet Mitchell similarly argued that women's 'oppression is experienced in the most minute and specific area – in the home', and is maintained there due to a lack of viable alternatives (Mitchell 1971: 21). Feminist analysis of media and advertising showed how these industries reinforced the image of the housewife as both normative and desirable, linking economic and cultural discourses into the propagation of gendered norms. Accordingly, countering these prevailing discourses became an important element of second-wave critical thinking and activism.

The critique of motherhood was interlinked with the problematisation of women's role as housewife. Germaine Greer argued early on that:

> there is no reason, except the moral prejudice that women who do not have children are shirking a responsibility, why all women should consider themselves bound to breed. A woman who has a child is not then automatically committed to bringing it up. (Greer 1970: 262–3)

Combating these dual assumptions – that women ought to bear children and then ought to be mainly responsible for raising them – was a central tenet of second-wave politics, and this was reflected in both the critical and the fiction writing that emerged during the 1970s and 1980s. Shulamith Firestone argued in 1970 that reproduction was itself the basis of women's and men's unequal status. She imagined a utopia in which conception and gestation occur artificially, free from the human body, as the end goal of feminism: 'not just the elimination of male *privilege* but of the sex *distinction* itself: genital differences between human beings would no longer matter culturally' (Firestone 1970: 11–12). This radical thesis influenced a raft of feminist sci fi writing that examined the possibility of parthenogenesis* and other forms of artificial reproduction (see Chapter 8) – it also marks a line of inheritance back to

---

* Parthenogenesis is the process of reproduction from an ovum without fertilisation – in other words, reproduction from the female only.

first-wave feminism, replicating the ideas explored in, for example, the fiction writing of Charlotte Perkins Gilman (see Case study 2.1, 'Herland').

This gendering of the domestic – the unquestioning allocation of the roles of wife and mother to women – is not only a theme that we can trace back, but also one that projects forward from the second wave. In many parts of the world today, and across many cultures, women continue to be defined by domestic duties that reinforce the 'feminine' gender role. The theoretical approaches I outline above reveal a kind of Anglo-centrism in mainstream feminist approaches that has, at times, served to overlook other cultural discourses, and so to exclude these subject positions. Nevertheless, the problematisation of the housewife/mother dyad was part of the development of a definition of gender in UK (and US) feminism, on which this book is focused. There is much more to be said about the ongoing battles to dismantle the naturalised imposition of these gender roles in other cultures – but this remains outside the remit of this text.

The figuring of women as *objects* in sex, never *subjects*, was the third element in the gender category 'feminine' to come under feminist interrogation. Female bodily objectification was an important catalyst for the emergence of the women's liberation movement of the late 1960s and early 1970s (as arguably it has been for the current re-engagement with feminism in the 'fourth wave'). In spite of the so-called 'free love' era of the 1960s, women were still socially and psychologically constrained to one of two sexual categories – the active, desiring 'whore' or the passive, inhibited 'virgin' – both of which imposed on them a limited and inauthentic model for sexual expression. This imposition was exposed in texts such as Germaine Greer's *The Female Eunuch* (1970), which called for women to embrace a more liberated, even promiscuous sexuality (but on their own terms), and in Kate Millett's *Sexual Politics* (1969), which argued that 'sex has a frequently neglected political aspect' (Millett 1969: xiii). There was an outpouring of critical and autobiographical material examining women's relationship to their sexuality, with texts such as Nancy Friday's *My Secret Garden* (1975), a collection of women's sexual fantasies, seeking to enable a freer and more truthful exchange of stories of sexual experience and desire.

This interrogation of the sex object role that normative gender imposes on women retains its urgency, and its effect on *both* sexes remains a central aspect of contemporary feminist discussion. Feminist emphasis has moved beyond demonstrating that the sexual gender binary of male = active, female = passive limits women, to show more recently the ways that it limits *all* sexual beings. As this chapter will shortly go on to show (see '(Re)telling gender in fiction', below), interrogation of the sex object role was central to many of the works of fiction written during the 1970s, 1980s and 1990s. Indeed, storytelling was a key element in the feminist exploration – and contestation – of women's figuring as sex objects.

In 1990 the interrogation of gender took on a radical new formulation that effected a paradigm shift in the way gender is now understood. Emerging out of her immersion in post-structuralist theory (and, in particular, a focus on the works of Michel Foucault), Judith Butler posited in her text *Gender Trouble* that both gender *and the sexed body itself* were 'created' through a process of repetitious re-enactments of culturally sanctioned behaviours.

> Gender is not to culture as sex is to nature; gender is also the discursive/cultural means by which 'sexed nature'" or 'a natural sex' is produced and established as 'prediscursive', prior to culture, a politically neutral surface *on* which culture acts.
> (Butler 1990: 11, original emphasis)

Butler thus articulated a *performative* concept of gender, emphasising the ways we produce our gender identity through both speech and action. In this, she built on the 'speech-act theory' posited by the linguist J. L. Austin, which demonstrates how we use language to enact things, not simply to describe or assert them; for example, in the marriage ceremony the statement 'I do' is not merely an utterance, but an act that confers a new social status on the couple concerned. What we say, as well as what we do, are performances that produce our reality, as well as our identities.

Butler's theories thus shifted focus to the ways both sexes are constructed within cultural discourses, and put centre stage the overarching paradigm of consumerism that has increasingly come to define cultural constructions of all identities – male, female or other. Arising in part from Butler's theoretical intervention, a new 'queer theory' emerged which built upon the feminist interrogation of gender's construction to critique sexual and other identities and, in particular, hegemony's reliance on, or troubling of, normative and deviant categories.

Third- and fourth-wave understanding of the concept 'gender', then, incorporates the second-wave critique of the mother/housewife/sex object triad as well as a more nuanced, Butlerian conception of the ways that all identities are in some way culturally contingent and potentially fluid. In her feminist re-articulation of gender, Cordelia Fine emphasises anew the emphasis still placed on 'natural' differences between the sexes, and how these continue to be used as evidence to support the idea that fundamental gender differences exist. 'The sheer audacity of the over-interpretations and misinformation is startling', she asserts (Fine 2010: 237). In her important text *Delusions of Gender* she describes the 'relentless gendering' of everything in our culture, making gender 'norms' impossible to avoid and difficult not to assimilate even when the 'theory' is there to tell us we should know better. 'Our minds, society and neurosexism create difference. Together, they wire gender. But the wiring is soft, not hard. It is flexible, malleable and changeable' (Fine 2010: 239). Contemporary feminism is now engaged with this battle to unseat the still deeply entrenched, as well as culturally and psychologically reinforced, assumptions about how gender should be enacted.

Case study 2.1 *Herland*

Although the term 'gender' as we now understand it had not been articulated when Charlotte Perkins Gilman wrote *Herland* in 1915, her text is nonetheless a radical interrogation of gender constructs. I acknowledge here that there have been alternative interpretations of Gilman's text by feminist scholars – for example, Bernice Hausman (1998) argues that Gilman distinguishes not between sex and gender, but between those aspects of the sexed body that can be altered and those that cannot – but *Herland* is nonetheless prescient in its critique of the housewife/mother/ sex object categories that discussions of gender were centred on during the second wave and beyond.

In Herland, a woman-only utopia set somewhere beyond the limits of charted civilisation, there is no distinction between masculinity and femininity, since there is no differential of male/female sex onto which to map gendered behaviours. In Gilman's novel three male characters unwittingly stumble across this all-female society and, through their eyes, we see how arbitrary and often absurd the rules that govern gender are. The women of Herland defy categorisation as 'feminine'. They sport sensible, shapeless garb designed to be practical rather than fashionable, and likewise keep their hair cut short. This makes it difficult for the three male intruders into Herland to relate to them as women, since they have no model for understanding 'femininity' in this form. Gilman's depiction of the men's struggle to accommodate this version of femaleness, and their different approaches to sexualising Herland's women, constitutes an excoriating critique of the 'sex object' role. Gilman's text evidences her feminist idea that (hetero) sexuality oppresses women because female sexuality must be enacted within the confining strictures that 'gender' imposes. She uses *Herland* to problematise the construction of gendered sex as masculine/aggressive and feminine/passive, anticipating both later articulations of this same idea in feminist discussions, as well as the use of fiction to explore alternatives.

In Gilman's utopia, women have adapted to reproduce without sexual intercourse, with the consequence that they do not understand sexual desire. This conflation of sexual behaviour with procreation situates Gilman's text historically, written as it was at a time when female sexuality could only be imagined in the context of reproduction. *Herland* also contains a feminist critique of gendered expectations of motherhood, radically unshackling women from the category 'mother'. Herland's women have evolved a way of reproducing through parthenogenesis, and allocate the responsibility of raising children to those in the group best suited to the task, rather than leaving it to 'birth' mothers. Gilman thus interrogates the naturalised link between anatomical femaleness and 'nurturing' maternity, proposing (as Firestone and other radical feminists would in the 1970s) that the emphasis on women's role as mother was a tool in maintaining inequality between the sexes.

Finally, *Herland* also contains a critique of the construction of work as 'masculine' and the gendered expectation, current at the time Gilman wrote, of women's economic dependence on men. In Herland all work is (necessarily) undertaken by women, and the effect of successive generations of employed women is shown to be their evolving aptitude for work of all kinds. Gilman's female cast are removed from the domestic sphere and re-engaged in a range of physically and mentally demanding roles. Gilman uses her fiction to imagine alternative realities, and to illuminate the ways in which the working roles described as 'suitable' for men have become so simply because men have undertaken them. This problematisation of the link between masculinity and work has continued to occupy feminism and has remained a key target of feminist campaigning, as well as a subject in much female writing, critical and fictional. In the Western world, working women are undoubtedly more ubiquitous now than in the early twentieth century, but those organisations which manage and control the world's finances (e.g. global corporations and the banks) are still overwhelmingly in the control of men.

A century after Gilman's utopian story was first told, then, its themes remain remarkably current: women's confinement to the roles of housewife, mother and sex object – also set out at the start of second-wave feminism as key issues to target – continue to occupy feminist thinkers and female writers. Contemporary fiction undoubtedly contains portrayals of women that defy these gendered categories, but it also continues to demonstrate an engagement with them and the ongoing ways in which normative gender is constructed. In fiction by authors as diverse as Helen Fielding (author of the *Bridget Jones* books) and Gillian Flynn (who wrote *Gone Girl* and other recent bestsellers), female characters struggle with negotiating multiple messages about what 'femininity' should look like and how it should be lived. Gender's power to direct behaviour and to dictate thought remains a pressing issue for women and men alike.

(Re)telling gender in fiction

Formulating a definition of gender – and articulating the ways that gendered assumptions naturalised the roles of housewife, mother and sex object – was one of second-wave feminism's earliest achievements. Once the distinction had been made between sex as the anatomical difference between women and men, and gender as a set of cultural assumptions and psychological attributes, critical explorations gave way to ever more fictional ones. The challenge of even imagining alternatives to the status quo is eloquently put by feminist publisher Ursula Owen:

> until the late 60s, women's territory was still fundamentally seen to be confined to the domestic – birth, death, marriage, motherhood, children – and the emotional – love, friendship, nurturing, caring, with most of the feminine stereotypes still firmly in place – passivity, irrationality, compliancy, formlessness. Indeed it is hard to convey to young women today how marginal women felt. (Interview with Owen, 5 February 2009)

This cultural imposition of gender norms had an effect upon literature: women writers were expected to concern themselves with the domestic, the maternal and the emotional – and, in a cunning twist of logic, were disparaged when they did so. As Atwood put it, 'when a man writes about things like doing the dishes, it's realism; when a woman does, it's an unfortunate feminine genetic limitation' (Atwood 1982: 199).

The feminist critique of gender created a framework for women (writers) to envisage and describe female identity differently. Novelists like Margaret Atwood, Angela Carter, Marilyn French and Marge Piercy, who began writing in the 1960s and 1970s, Joan Riley and Jeannette Winterson, in the 1980s, Sarah Waters and Jackie Kay, in the 1990s and 2000s, and Ali Smith and Kathleen Winter, post-millennium, have all created strong and subversive fictional characters who defy categorisation as housewives or mothers or sexual objects, and/or who allowed exploration of alternative constructions of gender. Atwood's first novel, for example, takes on gendered stereotypes to show how they strangled women's potential and suffocated their desires. *The Edible Woman*, written in 1965 and published in 1969, critically examines the cultural imposition of gendered stereotypes on women, building on influential texts that pre-dated the second wave (for more analysis of this text see Chapter 3). Atwood acknowledges their influence in her introduction to the 1980 UK edition of her book: 'like many at the time I'd read Betty Friedan and Simone de Beauvoir behind locked doors' (8) (see 'What is gender?' earlier in this chapter for more on de Beauvoir and Friedan).

The Edible Woman deftly illustrates the social and psychological confinement of women within gender norms, and Atwood uses the central protagonist, Marian, to demonstrate the frustration with the very norms that gave rise to second-wave feminism. Coming out of, as well as helping institute, this new feminism were other novels, such as Erica Jong's *Fear of Flying* (1973), an exploration of sexual politics and female gender roles, and Marilyn French's 1977 novel *The Women's Room*, which deals with a female character's confinement – and escape from – normative enactments of gender. These texts manifested a new kind of feminist fiction, the telling of stories that revealed the extent of women's deep unhappiness with how their gender had been constructed for them, and how it constricted them.

In interview Ursula Owen recalled the proliferation of this kind of women's writing, noting the move from polemic and non-fiction to novels: 'what happened in the early 1980s is that a lot of feminist ideas got written in the form of fiction'. Along with Atwood, whose output has continued to interrogate gender, British women writers including Angela Carter, Jeanette Winterson, Marge Piercy, Joan Riley and Jackie Kay published novels that presented new perspectives, including the intersections of race and sexuality to create particular gendered experiences (for more on Carter see Case study 2.2, 'Angela Carter', at the end of this chapter, and for more on the specificities of these intersections see Chapters 4 and 5). These novelists use their work to explore multiple, unconventional and often contradictory representations of gendered – and non-gendered – selves, moving from *The Edible Woman*'s focus on the three stereotypes of femininity to more diffuse and complex gendered identities, echoing the way gender itself was being articulated.

Winterson's novel *Written on the Body* (1993), for example, utilises a gender-less narrator in order to destabilise the love story told through the course of the text: what appears to be romantic heroism (gendered 'masculine') in Winterson's protagonist might in fact be heroine-ism – a contradiction of appropriate 'femininity'. Since the narrator's sexed identity is never revealed, Winterson's novel unsettles fixed ideas of gender, while also allowing the narrative to be read as a lesbian love story – evoking Willa Cather's short story 'On the Gulls' Road' (1908), which radically undertook the same experiment at a time when gender and 'queer' ideas had not been articulated. Winterson's novel exemplifies the feminist shift, post-Butler, from defying categorised behaviours to defying the category of 'body' itself.

Jackie Kay's novel *Trumpet* (1998) similarly evokes Butler's performative concept of gender formation, using a range of categories, including biography, sexuality, race and (trans)gender, to unsettle assumptions about 'naturalised' identity traits. *Trumpet* also evokes the critical formulations of drag and trans identities put forward by Butler, who argued that these manifestations undermined the notion of an 'original' or primary gender identity: '*in imitating gender, drag implicitly reveals the imitative structure of gender itself – as well as its contingency*' (Butler 1990: 174, original emphasis). The protagonist of Kay's *Trumpet* constitutes a literary example of Butler's thesis, whose drag disguise destabilises normative constructions of gender. Similarly, Sarah Waters' *Tipping the Velvet* (1998) illustrates the liberatory potential for women of donning a male appearance and garb. Waters depicts the cross-dressing rituals of Victorian music hall culture to reveal, through her character Nan, how transgressing gender-prescribed dress codes allows the experience of new freedoms, and enables exploration of new feelings, behaviours and even places:

> London, for all my weeping, could never wash dim; and to walk freely about in it at last – to walk as a boy, as a handsome boy in a well-sewn suit, whom the people stared after only to envy, never to mock – well, it has a brittle kind of glamour to it, that was all I knew, just then, of satisfaction. (Waters 1998: 195)

The appearance of these cross-dressing characters in fiction reflects the shift in feminist theory from problematising the norms of 'femininity' to destabilising the very concepts of masculinity and femininity, male and female. Contemporary women's fiction reflects an evolving understanding of the concept of gender, with women writers exploring the effects of gendered stereotyping, as well as imagining alternatives to the masculine/feminine binary. Along with male writers like Iain Banks and Jeffrey Eugenides, female authors such as Kathleen Winter have created characters that trouble and tease the normative formulation of gender that continues to structure how we think, act, read and write. Winter's novel *Annabel* (2010), for example, is centred on a character whose gender is in flux throughout the narrative. The intersex condition of the protagonist, Wayne/Annabel, allows the author to explore the various and subtle ways gender identity is enforced in the small community of Croydon Harbour, Canada, where he is raised. Winter shows through hermaphroditism how arbitrary the rules of 'gender' are, and how their imposition onto a body that contains both sexed identities leads to crisis. There is no model in which Wayne can live as both masculine and feminine, since culture, medicine and psychology allow for only one choice. The conclusion of the novel, and Wayne's decision to attempt to live authentically as both male and female, points hopefully to contemporary assimilations of trans identities in culture, and to current understandings of how gender can be lived more fluidly.

The feminist project of defining, and refining, what gender means, then, is evidenced in novels such as those by Atwood, Winterson, Kay, Waters and Winter. Feminist criticism and women's writing have combined to fundamentally alter concepts of gender, and the cultural, economic, psychological and medical impositions of binary notions of sexed identity. Defining and describing gender, and understanding its effects on all aspects of culture, including literary culture, is one of feminism's most powerful and lasting legacies. The rest of this book will show the various ways that this evolving concept of gender, and its articulation by feminist critics and scholars, has changed the way women write, as well as what they write about.

Case study 2.2 Angela Carter

If deconstructing gender was one of second-wave feminism's most complex and compelling tasks, Angela Carter was, arguably, its most innovative and imaginative proponent. Her fiction writing constitutes a sustained interrogation of the boundaries of masculinity and femininity, as well as the ways in which these binary classifications are constructed and maintained. Although Carter wrote six novels as well as some poetry and short story collections in the 1960s and early 1970s, the influence of feminism on her writing exploded into life with her 1977 novel *The*

Passion of New Eve, her most radical treatment of gender politics and a text that captures the fervour of second-wave politics as well as the ingeniousness of Carter at the peak of her writing powers.

The Passion of New Eve tells the story of Eve/lyn, who at the start of the text is a biological male. His casual objectification, abuse and subsequent abandonment of nightclub dancer Leilah is shown as stereotypical of the behaviours and attitudes that constitute 'masculinity'. In the course of Carter's novel, Eve/lyn is forcibly changed from male to female through a castration/reassignment operation performed by the character Mother. Eve/lyn's 'gender reassignment' from Evelyn to Eve, the original and primary woman, is at first only skin deep: 'when I looked in the mirror, I saw Eve; I did not see myself' (Carter 1977: 74). But gradually, through her experiencing the world within and through a female body, in particular via her brutalisation at the hands of Zero, she acquires a sense of her new feminine gender. Carter thus exemplifies de Beauvoir's epithet that 'one is not born [even artificially], but rather becomes, a woman', using Eve/lyn to subvert the construct of physiologically determined gender.

Eve/lyn allows Carter to trouble the naturalisation of the feminine gender roles of mother/housewife/sex object. Her critique encompasses the reductive correlation of female/feminine with life-giving and parenthood, showing through her depiction of the mother-goddess civilisation named Beulah that any such veneration of women's role as mother – even one which attempts to free itself from the biological imperative by invoking a technologically engineered 'motherhood' – is both limited and limiting. Later in the novel, through Eve's encounter with Zero, Carter devastatingly conflates hyper-masculinity with the confinement of women in the home, showing through the drudging servility of Zero's harem how women are duped into domestic aspirations that serve only to imprison them. And, of course, Eve/lyn's experiencing of his/her sexuality from within a changing body allows Carter to explore the different ways gender affects sexual behaviour and attitudes. As a man, Evelyn's approach to sex is predatory, aggressive and based on objectification of a specific construction of a feminine ideal. As a woman, Eve *becomes* that construct, and then must mitigate the ways in which this limits her – as well as the potential she finds for empowerment and pleasure within her female body once it is freed from gendered expectations. Carter's friend and fellow writer Margaret Atwood pays testament to this ability to unsettle accepted sexual norms. Carter, she argues, uses her writing to show the ways that women – and men – can be both 'tiger' and 'lamb', predator and prey: 'lambhood and tigerishness may be found in either gender, in the same individual at different times' (quoted in Easton 2000: 121–2). Carter also uses her fiction to show that sex has the potential to create spaces where gender binaries can be broken down, and boundaries moved. The pursuit of pleasure has the power to unseat certainties.

Two years after publishing *The Passion of New Eve*, Carter followed up with *The Sadeian Woman* (1979), her examination of the works of the Marquis de Sade and a continuation of her interrogation of gendered norms, especially in regard to sexual desire. In this text, Carter explores de Sade's representation of male and female sexual behaviours, troubling the masculine/feminine structure imposed on sexual roles by revealing the ways in which de Sade's work, which covers the range of sexual behaviours to its very extreme, allows women as well as men expression of an (albeit perverse) aggressive, active sexuality. Although a work of non-fiction, this book shows Carter once again using storytelling to defy the hypocrisy of sexual morality, and giving pleasure and agency back to women in the act of sex. And this was the message she repeated in her fantastical re-scripting of traditional fairy tales, *The Bloody Chamber*, published in the same year.

Carter published only two more novels before she died in 1992, aged just fifty-one. These, too, contained wild and wayward women, exemplary in their defiance of gendered norms and intended as an inspiration for those who read her work. In *Nights at the Circus* (1984) Carter recasts the active, acting hero of romance narratives as a woman. In her story, her heroine, Fevvers, is in control, and controlling, of her lover, Walser: She takes the initiative in her storytelling, as well as in her seduction:

> 'Is there some place we can be alone?' Fevvers had suggested, batting her eyelashes in an unequivocal fashion. Walser, whose head was clearing minute by minute, seized her hand and ran her to the Shaman's house but lost the initiative immediately as she pinned him cheerfully to the bed and told him to wait while she freshened up. (Carter 1984: 293)

In contrast, Walser must undergo a radical transformation in order to become a man worthy of Fevvers' attention. *Nights at the Circus* describes the education of Jack Walser, who learns in the course of a journey that takes him from London to Siberia to question everything he knew of himself. Gender norms are turned upside down through the course of their romance, as Walser's love for Fevvers is portrayed as one of equals. Carter writes into life a remarkable character who defies the category of sex object – although she is certainly sexual – and embodies instead an active, desiring and desired subject in her revolutionary romance narrative.

In her last novel, *Wise Children* (1992), Carter's heroine, Dora Chance, is a performer, an actor/showgirl/dancer who spends her long life taking on different roles (dutiful sister, beautiful starlet, daughter, mother, lover) with what Carter portrays as great ease. 'The Chances in *Wise Children* are exemplary postmodern heroines who take control of their own performances and manipulate their self-stagings for their own advantage' (Britzolakis in Easton 2000: 175). Carter's tale evokes Judith Butler's work in demonstrating that life is, indeed, a series of performances and repetitions. For example, Melchior Chance, the father of Dora and her twin sister Nell, spends his entire life acting, ironically as part of a studied attempt to convince others (and himself?) that he is something – anything – other than merely an actor. Like their father, the Chance twins themselves spend their long lives taking on every kind of role, 'performing' their own histories. They also act out their sexuality in an entirely free and open way – even to the point of 'performing' as each other in their sexual liaisons. Throughout the novel, this performativity is something that the twins revel in. Unlike their tortured father, Carter grants Dora and Nora an empowerment in their take-up of multiple, fluid and sometimes conflicting roles so that we see them enjoying their shape-shifting, deriving pleasure from it: 'we'll go on singing and dancing until we drop in our tracks, won't we, kids. What a joy it is to dance and sing!' (Carter 1992: 232).

This text, then, may be seen as an example of exactly the kind of gender 'troubling' Butler calls for, in that it exemplifies the ways in which identity is profoundly performative and iterative, an enactment of prescribed behaviours. This theme runs throughout Carter's fiction, which contains a vivid array of unconventional and radical characters and relationships: 'she deals in polymorphous perversity with a youthful vitality and rebelliousness' (Barker 1995). Marina Warner explains that Carter's writing 'helped establish a woman's voice in literature as special, as *parti pris*, as a crucial instrument in the forging of an identity for post-imperial, hypocritical, fossilised Britain' (Warner 1992: 25). Carter intended her writing to show alternatives to the essentialising notions of gender that governed women – and men – and the social and psychological construction of 'feminine' and 'masculine'. Her work sits comfortably with current formulations of feminism that seek to include men, showing that both sexes (as well as individuals who evade male/female categorisation) must join the fight for equality, and must benefit from it.

As noted in the Introduction, in many respects Carter's fiction anticipated and pre-empted Judith Butler's theories as she played with notions of drag and disguise to show the arbitrariness of gender's *accoutrements*. Her writing was a challenge to cultural as well as literary norms, refusing categorisation and resisting the notion of a unified self, or a linear narrative. In her writing Carter imagined liminal spaces where transgressions could be enacted, and with her stories she leaves us a cache of questions about, and solutions to, the problem of gender. Speaking through her hero/ine Eve/lyn, she observes:

> Masculine and feminine are correlatives which involve one another. I am sure of that – the quality and its negation are locked in necessity. But what the nature of masculine and the nature of feminine might be, whether they involve male and female, if they have anything to do with Tristessa's so long neglected apparatus or my own factory fresh incision and engine-turned breasts, that I do not know. Though I have been both man and woman, still I do not know the answer to these questions. Still they bewilder me. (Carter 1977: 149–50)

Bibliography

Atwood, Margaret. 1969. *The Edible Woman*. London: Virago (1980).

Atwood, Margaret (ed.). 1982. *Second Words: Selected Critical Prose*. Toronto: Anansi.

Atwood, Margaret. 2005. *Curious Pursuits: Occasional Writing 1970–2005*. London: Virago.

Barker, Paul. 1995. 'The Return of the Magic Storyteller'. In *The Independent on Sunday*, 8 January.

Bawer, Bruce (ed.). 1996. *Beyond Queer: Challenging Gay Left Orthodoxy*. USA: Free Press.

Bland, Lucy. 1995. *Banishing the Beast: English Feminism and Sexual Morality 1885–1914*. London: Penguin.

Bland, Lucy and Laura Doan. 1998. *Sexology Uncensored: The Documents of Sexual Science*. Cambridge: Polity Press.

Butler, Judith. 1990. *Gender Trouble: Feminism and the Subversion of Identity*. New York: Routledge.

Carter, Angela. 1977. *The Passion of New Eve*. London: Virago (1982).

Carter, Angela. 1979. *The Sadeian Woman*. London: Virago.

Carter, Angela. 1984. *Nights at the Circus*. London, Virago.

Carter, Angela. 1992. *Wise Children*. London: Virago.

de Beauvoir, Simone. 1949. *The Second Sex*. London: New English Library (1962).

Easton, Alison (ed.). 2000. *Angela Carter*. Basingstoke: Macmillan.

Figes, Eva. 1970. *Patriarchal Attitudes: Women in Society*. London: Virago (1978).

Fine, Cordelia. 2010. *Delusions of Gender: The Real Science Behind Sex Differences*. London: Icon Books.

Firestone, Shulamith. 1970. *The Dialectic of Sex: The Case for Feminist Revolution*. London: Jonathan Cape.

French, Marilyn. 1978. *The Women's Room*. London: Sphere.

Friday, Nancy. 1975. *My Secret Garden: Women's Sexual Fantasies*. London: Virago.

Friedan, Betty. 1963. *The Feminine Mystique*. London: Victor Gollancz.

Greer, Germaine. 1970. *The Female Eunuch*. London: MacGibbon and Kee.

Hausman, Bernice. 1998. 'Sex Before Gender: Charlotte Perkins Gilman and the Evolutionary Paradigm of Utopia'. In *Feminist Studies*, 24:3, pp. 488–510.

Hemmings, Clare. 2011. *Why Stories Matter: The Political Grammar of Feminist Theory*. Durham, NC: Duke University Press.

Jong, Erica. 1973. *Fear of Flying*. London: Vintage (1998).

Kay, Jackie. 1998. *Trumpet*. London: Picador.

Lee, Hermione (ed.). 1984. *Virginia Woolf: 'A Room of One's Own' and 'Three Guineas'*. London: Hogarth Press.

Millett, Kate. 1969. *Sexual Politics*. New York: Simon and Schuster.

Mills, Sara and Lynne Pearce (eds). 1996. *Feminist Readings/Feminists Reading*. Second Edition. Hemel Hempstead: Harvester Wheatsheaf.

Mitchell, Juliet. 1971. *Woman's Estate*. Harmondsworth: Penguin.

Oakley, Ann. 1972. *Sex, Gender and Society*. London: Temple Smith.

Pearsall, Judy (ed.). 2001. *New Oxford Dictionary of English*. Oxford: Oxford University Press.

Reiter, Rayna R. (ed.). 1975. *Toward an Anthropology of Women*. New York: Monthly Review Press.

Stoller, Robert. 1968. *Sex and Gender: On the Development of Masculinity and Femininity*. London: Hogarth Press.

Warner, Marina. 1992. 'Obituary'. In *The Independent*, 18 February.

Waters, Sarah. 1998. *Tipping the Velvet*. London: Virago.

Winter, Kathleen. 2010. *Annabel*. London: Jonathan Cape.

Winterson, Jeanette. 1993. *Written on the Body*. London: Vintage.

Woolf, Virginia. 1928. *Orlando*. London: Hogarth Press.

3 Body/image

In the last chapter I looked at the emergence of a definition of gender, and the feminist attempt to identify – and then undo – the cultural, psychological, political, medical and economic imposition of gendered norms. This focused on behaviour, specifically with regard to three main facets of acceptable 'femininity': housewife, mother and sex object. In this chapter I move on to consider the female body, and the construction of an (unattainable) ideal body type in both popular and literary culture, and then to focus in more detail on the ways in which the female body has been figured as a sexualised object.

In 1994 feminist psychologist Lynne Segal wrote that 'the place of the body in feminist theory is probably more confusing today than it has ever been' (Segal 1994: 226). Over twenty years later, this statement has never been more true, and the debates that have been played out around women's bodily empowerment and disempowerment remain unresolved. The bodily ideal has shifted form during the different feminist waves, according to the vagaries of fashion and culture, but the emphasis on female self-presentation and policing of the female body has remained constant. I look at these themes using the example of Margaret Atwood's debut novel *The Edible Woman* to show how women writers have, throughout contemporary feminism, tackled these themes in their fiction (Case study 3.1).

Despite second-wave feminism's attempt to challenge the 'Barbie doll' stereotype which has dominated Western culture since the 1950s, unrealistic bodily ideals remain a pervasive and pernicious influence on women's self-perception. There have been shifts in this ideal – from the 'power babe' of the 1980s, to 'heroin chic' in the 1990s, the sporty/thin body of the 2000s and today's surgically crafted female form – but throughout these various incarnations of the sexed female body, feminist writers have sought to fight back against such dehumanising and reductive portraitures of women. I will look at the evolution of all these sexed body types, as well as how fiction and critical writing have sought to offer an alternative, including Lucy Ellmann's 1988 text *Sweet Desserts*, which connects second- and third-wave thinking on this concern (Case study 3.2). The chapter will show how women's bodies in the Western world continue to be policed and scrutinised in both popular and literary culture, as part of the gendered insistence that women 'perform' their femininity (see Chapter 2). It will also show how the feminist resistance to these discourses has been written through stories and non-fiction throughout feminism's various waves.

Case study 3.1 *The Edible Woman*

Margaret Atwood's *The Edible Woman* was one of the earliest works of second-wave feminist fiction, written in 1965 and published in 1969. It established the parameters of feminism's problematisation of the way women's bodies were figured, highlighting in often comic ways the difference gender made to women's self-stylings, and indeed their sense of self. Atwood's protagonist, Marian, endures a slow breakdown through the course of the novel, sliding into a somnambulant depression upon accepting a proposal of marriage from her boyfriend Peter: '*The Edible Woman* depicts Marian's transformation into the consumable female object that Peter desires' (Bouson in Bloom 2000: 81). In this, the novel very much evokes Freidan's 'problem that has no name' (see Chapter 2), as Marian is shown to lose her sense of self in the face of her impending nuptials and the assumption of the roles of housewife/mother, and decorative accessory to her fiancé, which must follow. Peter's pleasure in the prospect of marriage is presented in stark contrast to Marian's desperate gloom: 'now that she had been ringed he took pride in displaying her' (Atwood 1969: 90).

Marian's growing sense of panic is compounded by her awareness of its impropriety – within the culture of the 1960s, in which the novel is set, she is achieving 'every woman's dream'. This, coupled with her inability to identify the cause of her malaise, leads to her sense of alienation from herself, made manifest in the novel's form through Atwood's switching from a first-person to a third-person narrative. As Marian becomes more and more estranged from herself, her story is told not from her perspective but from an outside point of view, with Atwood portraying her protagonist's search for selfhood as a search for something satisfying to eat – which, in the end, turns out to be an effigy of herself made from cake. *The Edible Woman* thus examines women's relationship to food and eating in the context of a sexist culture within which women are objects, not subjects:

> In her novels eating is employed as a metaphor for power and is used as an extremely subtle means of examining the relationship between women and men. The powerful are characterised by their eating and the powerless by their non-eating. (Parker in Bloom 2000: 113)

Marian's body is often described as something alien to her, a decorative thing for others to admire. Atwood thus critiques the cultural positioning of women as sexual objects, and in switching Marian's narrative to the third person she reinforces this sense of dislocation between selfhood and embodiment. In one of the novel's final scenes, Marian and Peter throw a party, for which Marian dons a feminine 'mask' of makeup, shoes and red dress. It is her final – failed – attempt at inhabiting the ideal body, her garb and her demeanour as attentive hostess, providing food and drinks for Peter's friends, depicted as quintessentially feminine. Tellingly, some of the friends who show up fail to recognise her in this guise (including her would-be lover, Duncan), as Atwood shows Marian's extreme discomfort – psychological as well as physical – with becoming the 'ideal woman'. The stereotype of attractive femininity is revealed to be a miserable masquerade, and one that Marian must escape from.

At the end of the novel, Atwood uses Marian's cake-baking to represent a gesture of complicity in the domestic myth and the tyranny of women's policed bodies. Marian addresses her cake-self with pity, recognising that it, too, is a decorative object for consumption by others: '"You look delicious," she told her. "Very appetizing. And that's what will happen to you; that's what you get for being food"' (Atwood 1969: 270). Marian's liberation comes with the symbolic consumption of her former powerless self, which is shown as an act of literal consumption: 'the baking of the cake is her mute and "feminine" act of protest which also bears the seeds of potential liberations: she will, henceforth, refuse to be consumed' (Waugh 1989: 181). This task completed, she resumes speaking to the reader through a first-person address, indicating the re-emergence of her selfhood and subjectivity – and her growing confidence: 'I was irritated with him for not wanting to discuss what I was going to do myself. Now that I was thinking of myself in the first person singular again I found my own situation much more interesting than his' (Atwood 1969: 278). *The Edible Woman* constitutes, then, an early and powerful feminist depiction of the limited and limiting figuration of the female body in patriarchal culture, and the policing of women's food and sexual appetites. It set the scene for the raft of criticism and fiction that would make the issue of women's bodies, and their presentation as sexed objects, central to feminist discourse around subjectivity and selfhood.

The ideal body type

Many books have been written on the changing form of the ideal body type, its temporality and cultural specificity. The idealised image of woman is a culturally prescribed one and, thus, as culture changes so will that ideal. Over the past 120 years, the various waves of feminism(s) have highlighted the ways this ideal is constructed, received and resisted, beginning with the first wave's championing of the New Woman image – athletic, strong and strident – as an antidote to the historical idealisation of the curvaceous female form. At the start of the second wave, Germaine Greer argued in *The Female Eunuch* (1970) that, historically, the most popular image of woman was 'all boobs and buttocks, a hallucinating sequence of parabolae and bulges' (Greer 1970: 33). This, she argued, was because all repressed, indolent people in history have been fat, and thus women were encouraged to aspire to this curvaceous ideal since they, too, were repressed and indolent. She notes the beginnings of a move towards (self) regulating the female figure, a shift in the ideal type towards thinness, control, tailoring – although for the desired 'pneumatic boobs', the goal was always more, bigger, harder, higher, regardless of waist size (Greer 1970: 34).

There began a feminist critique of the focus put on women's weight. Susie Orbach's landmark text *Fat Is a Feminist Issue*, first published in the US in 1978 and reprinted in the UK a year later, took up this issue to show the many ways that, as with gender itself, the ideal body type was culturally, psychologically, economically and in other ways imposed on women. Her focus was women's psychological attachments to eating, and her text set the boundaries for now-mainstream discussions around body image, control and food. In *Femininity* (1984), Susan Brownmiller wrote that 'the ideal feminine shape has always been subject to change, not only structurally by means of foundation garments, but by the amount of flesh that has been considered desirable in a given age' (Brownmiller 1984: 29). She, too, points out the pressure on women to 'achieve' a specific weight in order to embody – literally – the womanly ideal.

In literary terms, the size of the 'ideal woman' was discussed in a range of critical texts from writers such as Marilyn Lawrence, Sheila MacLeod and Kim Chernin – many of these published by the feminist presses that sprung up in the UK during the 1970s and 1980s (see Chapter 1). In her text *The Hungry Self* (1986), published by Virago, Kim Chernin writes that 'a troubled relation to food is one of the principal ways the problems of being female come to expression in women's lives' (Chernin 1986: ix). The inexorable rise of eating disorders in young women (and now, increasingly, young men) bears witness to the pervasiveness of these messages about ideal size, and the perniciousness with which they are reinforced within a consumer culture that has much to gain from exploitation of bodily insecurities.

The imposition of a specific body size and shape as part of the feminine ideal remains a focus of feminist attention. Towards the end of the twentieth century, women's 'ideal' weight was revised ever downwards. In *The Beauty Myth* (1990) Naomi Wolf argued that this was a response to women's breaking out of the home and of domesticity, and entering en masse into male terrain – in the privacy of their homes, she reasoned, women were permitted to enjoy the fullness of their bodies, but as they moved into the public sphere their bodies were made into the prisons their homes used to be (Wolf 1990: 184). Certainly consumer culture exerts unrelenting pressure on (especially) women to be thin. Wolf concluded that, since a thin woman is a weak woman, in a sexist and sexualised culture, thinness is idealised. Capitalism as well as sexism underpins this body type, as the diet and health industries have much to gain from exploiting the image of thinness as desirable: 'women do not eat or starve only in a succession of private relationships, but within a public social order that has a material vested interest in their troubles with eating' (Wolf 1990: 189). Feminist critics began to focus on women's corporeality and the tyranny of a bodily ideal, with texts from Elizabeth Grosz, Judith Butler, Susan Bordo, Alison Jaggar and Sarah Sceats in the 1990s all making this their focus. In *Unbearable Weight* (1993), for example, Bordo shows how women's destructive self-limiting of food is at once both an attempt to resist dominant cultural and psychological constructs of the female body, and also a deadly reinforcement of that construct, writ large on their own corporeality.

Sarah Sceats has written extensively on the issues of women, power and food, arguing that 'power relations in their broadest sense can be seen to operate, and fluctuate, in all activities associated with food and eating' (Sceats in Sceats and Cunningham 1996: 117). She invokes Freud to reason that eating is a model for desire, since consuming food psychologically mirrors the same pleasures, frustrations, anxieties and controls as we experience in our sexual appetites. She also explores the centrality of food in women's writing, showing its engagement with, and reflection of, culture:

> because of the close cultural association between women and food, or because of feminism's politicization of the domestic, or because of the advance of a material culture, the work of women writers in the latter half of the twentieth century is particularly fruitful for an examination of the relations between power and food. (Sceats in Sceats and Cunningham 1996: 117)

She cites Angela Carter's work as the ultimate example of this exploration of huge, predatory and insatiable appetites, and also points to the work of Doris Lessing, Margaret Atwood and Michèle Roberts, who investigate women's many and varied appetites through the course of their writing.

The triumvirate that Sceats describes – women's association with food and the domestic, feminism's politicisation of this association, and increasing consumerism – persists. In spite of feminist attention, discussion and disapprobation, the thin ideal has endured across several decades. More so than ever, it is reified and reinforced by a powerful and pervasive media: 'the images we see of women, on billboards, in magazines, are more uniform than ever. You really will not see the hint of a bulge anywhere – that would be too much like real life' (Viner in Walter 1999: 20). The characterisation of this thin ideal might have changed over the years – from 1990s 'waif' to today's 'gym-honed go-getter' – but the insistence on a flat stomach and the policing of women's bodies remains. Recent modifications include a new glorification of the female posterior, pointing to the influence of black and Latino culture in the US, and its knock-on effect in an increasingly Americanised UK youth culture. What this also reveals is the white bias of the construction of the ideal body type, as feminist critics (particularly in the US) have pointed out. The mainstream model of beauty is Caucasian, and this new emphasis on bigger bottoms is its only concession to the different physiology of black, Hispanic, Latino and Asian women.

This uniformity of the female bodily ideal – in terms not only of ethnicity, but also of disability, age, gender identities and so on – means that all kinds of women are not represented in standard images of female 'beauty'. Along with bigger women, it is rare to see older women, trans women, butch women, disabled women or any other woman belonging to a 'minority' group represented as aspirational beauty types. Feminists have critiqued time and again the ways in which popular culture promotes a uniform image of the female body, but popular imagery remains focused on a toned, hairless figure that represents the literal embodiment of female success.

The removal of hair from the ideal female body is arguably another modern, and demoralising, adjustment. Again, it is one inextricably linked to consumer culture, with Gillette marketing its first razor for women in 1915 – with the consequence that shaving armpit, leg and pubic hair fast became the norm. Germaine Greer problematised this trend in 1970, arguing that since sexuality is (falsely) associated with animalistic, bestial imagery, so women must rid themselves of the hair on their bodies, as it suggests a link to furriness and thus a 'masculine' sexuality they are not permitted to enjoy. She returns to the issue in her 1999 text *The Whole Woman*, stating that 'however much body hair she has, it is too much' (Greer 1999: 19). In 2007 Karin Lesnik-Oberstein edited a collection of essays looking at this issue, entitled *The Last Taboo*, which also concluded that female body hair threatens the binary masculinity/femininity, and thus represents a threat to gender norms, hence its annihilation in mainstream culture. It is also, of course, a way of returning the adult female body to an appearance of pubescence, or even pre-pubescence, at once infantilising it while also reinforcing an unattainable ideal. There have been recent – and often humorous – feminist subversions of this, such as the 'Armpits4August' campaign, but the cultural insistence on women removing their body hair persists.*

The associated insistence on nubility is, in addition, a 'symbolic statement about the value our society attaches to youth and beauty' (Romaine 1999: 253). Women (and men, to a lesser extent) are compelled by a consumer culture in which youth is the ultimate commodity to continually invest in, in trying to look young(er). The ideal body for women is eternally youthful. Feminist critique has pointed to the threat posed by older women, who are less compelled to obey the rules of the 'beauty myth'. As Wolf puts it: 'ageing in women is "unbeautiful" since women grow more powerful with time, and since the links between generations of women must always be newly broken' (Wolf 1990: 14). As second-wave feminists grew older, there appeared new critical material pointing to the uniformity of youthful bodily ideals, and to the silencing of

---

* Armpits4August is a month-long charity event begun in August 2012, whose participants grow underarm hair for one month, raising sponsorship money for polycystic ovary syndrome.

the voices of older women. As journalist Amelia Hill observes: 'we still only see images of highly glamorous young women despite the fact that the largest group of people in this country [the UK] is over 45, female and not glamorous at all' (Hill 2005).

The rarity of positive representations of older women was the provocation for Nikki Read to establish a publishing house in April 2005 dedicated to providing books for women aged over forty-five. Read claimed that 'until now there hasn't been an identifiable body of fiction that mirrors the experiences of today's 45+ woman – and yet we make up almost forty per cent of the female population in the UK.'* Her intention with her publishing venture, named Transita, was to provide a balance to the dominant cultural and literary invisibility of older women. However, after only two years in business, Transita stopped publishing new material. Its failure points to the overwhelming power of the discourses around women's corporeality and age, as well as to the power of trends in consumer culture to drive trends in literature.

There has been a recent literary re-engagement with the ageing woman. Some of the *grand dames* of second-wave feminism, including Lynne Segal, Angela Neustatter and Germaine Greer, have written from a critical as well as an autobiographical perspective on the relative invisibility of older women, while feminist critics of popular and literary culture such as Imelda Whelehan and Jeanette King continue to examine the reasons why older women are figured as undesirable, problematic or tragic – or a winning combination of all three (see King 2012; Whelehan and Gwynne 2014). King looks in particular at the effect of this on women's fiction writing in the twentieth century and up to the contemporary, noting the ambivalence with which women writers have portrayed older or ageing female characters. This ambivalence relates to their sexual identities and desires, which are often portrayed as conflicted or uncertain, as well as ambivalence about their cultural and psychological status becoming more or less assured with the onset of age. King concludes that it is Angela Carter (again!) who provides an exemplary – and rare – textual exploration of the ageing *and* empowered woman, in her 1992 novel *Wise Children*. Carter, says King (2012), manages to provide a feminist discourse on ageing without relying on essentialist concepts of gender or female identity and, indeed, while recognising and highlighting the constructed nature of both. She also provides, through the characters of the Chance twins, a rich and multi-faceted portrayal of older women which glories in the ageing body and so provides a rare counterpoint to the uniform images of youthful desirability so prevalent in mainstream culture.

Feminist criticism of the imposition of a uniform body type thus continues, and has perhaps become more urgent with the rise of modern phenomena such as plastic surgery, as well as the proliferation of the diet and health industries

---

* 'Welcome to Transita', Transita Publishing website, at <http://www.transita.co.uk/index_about.htm> (accessed 17 June 2015) (para. 2 of 9).

(see Case study 3.3, 'I'm a Barbie girl'). These have all emerged within an increasingly commodified culture in which the body is an 'asset' to be sold, and to be sold to. The imposition of a bodily ideal through the commodification of the body itself is deeply entrenched in our culture, and in our psychology. Rolling back the influence of powerful corporations invested in this exploitation of derivative images of the perfect body is one of contemporary feminism's biggest challenges.

Case study 3.2 *Sweet Desserts*

Lucy Ellmann's debut novel *Sweet Desserts* (1988) is a chronicle of sexual dissatisfaction, bodily insecurity and the quest for happiness. It centres on two sisters, Suzy and Fran, and their various (often disastrous) relationships, as well as their familial bond both with each other and with their father. The novel is full of details of the food eaten by its protagonists, and the narrative is also interspersed regularly with snippets of magazine household hints and advice columns, reinforcing the sense of domesticity that so clearly limits as well as compels Suzy and Fran's behaviour. The story is also set between the US and the UK, providing interesting comparisons between the two different cultures' attitudes to food, eating and the body.

The story begins from the perspective of two-year-old Fran, as she contemplates – unhappily – the arrival of her sister. The narrative continually shifts between Fran and Suzy in the early part of the text, but towards its conclusion remains more with Suzy as she attempts to navigate her way through a post-divorce dating landscape. Suzy's marriage to Jeremy is depicted as loveless and without passion – indeed, appetites of all kinds are subdued or concealed in their household, with Suzy hiding her consumption of forbidden food as a counterpoint to Jeremy's lack of desire for her. One of their rare moments of intimacy comes only after Suzy has suggested to Jeremy that they should end their relationship:

> He was soon fucking me (I didn't attempt to get my cap for fear of his losing interest). Immediately afterwards, he got off me, turned on the light, opened a carton of yoghurt he'd brought with him, and a thriller. I went back to sleep slowly, feeling envious of the yoghurt. (Ellmann 1988: 39)

Throughout the story, Ellmann explores appetites, in both their excess and their lack, in ways that show her female protagonists to be less powerful that the male characters. There is continued, and casual, reference to denial of eating and/or bulimic behaviour, as Ellmann exposes Suzy and

Fran's insecurities about their bodies, and thus the damaging and pernicious cultural imposition of a fallacious bodily ideal.

It is only when Suzy's body is no longer entirely her own – when she
falls pregnant – that she can begin to assert her own desires, and finally
to end her relationship with appetite-less Jeremy. It is interesting that
Ellmann locates the pregnant body as one that is free from the cultural
imposition of a specific ideal, no longer someone else's to observe,
critique and/or desire:

> I saw in pregnancy a chance to feel Normal. I went to ante-natal clinics and
> had blood tests and urine analyses. I was asked questions about myself, I
> was scanned with ultra-sound and saw my child's back through technologi-
> cal mists. My body could do this incredible thing, just like everybody else.
> I talked with strangers about pregnancy and discovered that I had physical
> and emotional experiences in common with other women. (Ellmann
> 1988: 69)

Being pregnant, because pregnancy is deemed not 'sexy' and the pregnant
body is somehow outside the parameters that control women's bodily
form, allows Suzy the freedom to finally be at ease with her physicality, as
well as to find commonality with other women. Experiencing her body as
in some way 'unsexed' through pregnancy gives Suzy the chance to enjoy
her appetites as well as her sense of solidarity with other women – albeit
temporarily.

The death of Suzy and Fran's father gives Ellmann another opportunity to expose the complexity of her female characters' relationships
with food and their bodies: 'As my father wasted away, I ate. Once I knew
he was dying, I ate and ate for two weeks solid, until I felt as solid as he'd
once seemed' (Ellmann 1988: 119). In contrast to the extremely controlled
eating that underpinned Suzy's attempts to feel desired, and desiring,
this determined intake of food shows another aspect of the psychology
of eating: that it is a comfort. Suzy and Fran revisit the gastronomy of
their childhood, eating 'slabs of salt beef and two long pale pickles', a re-
emphasis of this link between eating and contentment, safety and security
(Ellmann 1988: 118). In the moment of her absolute grief at her father's
passing, Suzy no longer polices her body, but rather releases herself from
the everyday restrictions she places on her appetites, and indulges in a different kind of compulsive behaviour around food.

Ellmann's novel thus explores the psychology of women's relationship
to eating and their bodies, in particular in relation to self-image and sexuality. She also examines corporeality in relation to death, portraying the
bodily decay of Suzy and Fran's father and his daughters' responses to his
declining physical condition:

it's like showing your cunt to a doctor, having to tell strangers your father is dying. You feel so grateful if they're kind about it, since you're showing them something much more important to you than to them. You feel so soft and pathetic. (Ellmann 1988: 133)

Suzy equates the emotional exposure of losing her dad with the feeling of physically exposing her sexed body – the intimacy of grief is likened to physical intimacy. Ellmann's novel succeeds in relaying the various and complex ways in which culture influences women's psychology, and the effect this has on their bodies and their relationship to their own sexuality. It thus both reflects and contributes to discourses of the body within contemporary feminism.

The sexed body

The imposition of a uniform female bodily ideal – slim, shaven, busty – is inextricably linked to women's sexual objectification. Women's representation as sexed bodies has been a key aspect of feminist critique for more than forty years and yet the prevalence of sexualised images of women has never been greater. Women's figuring as sex objects has been the focus of a raft of feminist writing and activism, as I describe in Chapter 2. Here, I will consider specifically the figuring of the female *body* in ways that have reduced it to nothing more than a thing to be acted upon, as well as the reflection and repudiation of this in women's writing.

During feminism's first wave, in Victorian Britain, the female body was not for show. The sexual double standard meant 'respectable' women were covered, and contained to the domestic, and sexual appetite was cast as strictly masculine. The emergence of the New Woman figure, in bloomers and astride a bicycle, shifted to some extent the way femininity was figured (see Chapter 2), with women's writing reflecting this shift – more than 100 novels were written between 1883– and about the New Woman figure, coinciding with the peak of the suffrage movement's activity (Ledger 1997). But the female body remained taboo, and was kept largely under wraps throughout the first half of the twentieth century. It wasn't until the so-called 'free love' era of the 1960s that women's bodies began to come out from under their clothing, in particular in the images of a new consumerism that has, since then, come to dominate cultural discourse and create powerful and controlling images of women's (sexed) bodies.

Feminist publisher Marsha Rowe recalled in interview (15 July 2004) that, in spite of the libertarian ideology of 1960s counter-culture, the overriding paradigm of patriarchal attitudes meant it was only *women's* bodies that were displayed sexually: 'what had been quite freeing to the underground press [. . .]

all that had been rather rebounded and become over-determined so I was beginning to feel really uncomfortable with the images of the underground press'. In the mainstream, this portrayal of the sexed female body was just as prevalent, a fact that galvanised the burgeoning women's movement and its subsequent problematisation of this issue. The dominant, mainstream representations of the female body as seen through the media, advertising and in popular culture showed it to be reducible to its sexual parts.

The 1970s and 1980s saw important texts by Helen Baehr, Julienne Dickey, Annette Kuhn, Michele Mattelart, Lorraine Gamman and Margaret Marshment, among many others, institute a feminist critique of media and advertising. There were also offbeat interventions such as Jill Posener's photobooks, capturing the witty undercutting of advertising images by feminists armed with spray cans (Posener 1982). In the intervening years, feminist critique has shown that the female body has been shaped – *literally* shaped – by cultural, economic, psychological and political discourses that have mainstreamed a sexed ideal of the female body. These images of women, described as a 'demography of demi-goddesses', have a huge influence on women's self-regard and subsequent self-presentation (Lazier and Kendrick in Creedon 1993).

The female body on display has been inscribed into culture via the intersections of a sexist media, normative ideas of gender that continue to be culturally and psychologically reinforced, and the powerful influence of consumer enterprises that have reaped huge economic gain from the creation and maintenance of sexed images of women. These images, described by Baehr as 'submissive, passive and [. . .] portrayed largely in terms of their sexuality or domesticity', are so prevalent that they contribute to women's own self-presentation (Baehr in Baehr 1980: 30). In seeing themselves perpetually represented as sexed bodies, women inevitably present themselves in these terms and shape their bodies accordingly. This explains the exponential rise in breast augmentations, liposuction, laser hair removal and other 'beauty' procedures that began in the 1970s and have grown steadily since. Women's bodies are being moulded into an ideal that enhances their sexual characteristics and obliterates difference.

In literary terms, this is reflected in the 'bonkbuster' genre, whose popularity is borne out in book sales and on shop shelves, alongside the feminist attempt to present alternative images of women's bodies. Jackie Cooper, Barbara Cartland and Jackie Collins dominated sales lists in the 1980s and 1990s with their derivative but hugely popular stories of beautiful women snaring handsome men. The only woman (writing *adult* fiction – J. K. Rowling, Jacqueline Wilson and Enid Blyton were also in the top ten) to make Nielsen's top ten bestselling author list for the first decade of this millennium was Danielle Steele, who writes romantic fiction in which women's bodies are shown as sexualised weapons in the snaring of a man (MacArthur 2009). Arguably the biggest literary phenomenon of this decade has been E. L. James's 'Fifty Shades' trilogy, another tale – actually, four tales and counting – in which a woman's sexed body is central to the plot. Indeed, it *is* the plot. The wild success of the 'Fifty Shades' books points also

to the ambiguity of contemporary women's status in terms of sexual empowerment – one of feminism's long-standing goals – and there has been much
written about their problematic and/or anti-feminist intent and/or reception.
Women's writing such as James's, read by millions, reveals the contradictions
and failures of feminism, by showing that romance narratives and the representation of women's bodies as sexual objects remain compelling, in spite of
a sustained feminist attempt to counter them (for more on the romance genre,
feminism and women writers, see Chapter 6). While women readers may be
capable of negotiating the complexity of the representations and messages they
read, see and hear, and are aware of the normative and ideological effect of
these representations and messages, they remain very hard to resist.

Other women writers have used their fiction to interrogate the sexed female
body. Jacqueline Susann's 1966 novel *Valley of the Dolls* is an early example of
a fictional response to the imposition of sexed stereotypes on the female body.
In it, Susann's character Jennifer sees her value as so inextricably linked to her
perfect breasts that the threat of losing them (through mastectomy), even in
order to become well, drives her to her death. Her literal as well as psychic annihilation by the sexist discourses that locate a woman's worth in her bodily sex
characteristics reflects Susann's awareness of the feminist critique of the female
body, positioning her text as an exemplary fictional response to these issues.
The ubiquity of women's representation as sexed bodies is also highlighted in a
pithy passage from Margaret Atwood's novel *Lady Oracle* (1976) – and, indeed,
is a theme in most of her novels:

> 'Ah but the mystery of man is of the mind,' Paul said playfully, 'whereas that
> of the woman is of the body. What is a mystery but a thing which is remaining
> hidden? It is more easy to uncover the body than it is the mind. For this reason, a
> bald man is not looked upon as an unnatural horror, but a bald woman is.'
> 'And I suppose a moronic woman is more socially acceptable than an idiot
> man,' I said, intending sarcasm.
> 'Just so,' said Paul.
> (Atwood 1976: 166)

Atwood effectively lampoons the woman-as-sexed-body stereotype, making
a joke of the attitudes underpinning this ubiquitous image. Other women
writers have used their work to spotlight the brutality arising from it, with
stories by, for example, Sarah Kane and Camilla Gibb revealing the devastating
violence enacted on women's bodies that are figured as mere sexual objects.
Helen Zahavi's 1991 novel *Dirty Weekend* is a different kind of response, a
rape revenge narrative which describes a violent three-day spree enacted by a
young woman named Bella. Zahavi's cast of male characters get their come-
uppance for sexually objectifying the protagonist, who reacts murderously and
is rewarded with a sense of peace and empowerment at the story's denouement.
The text communicates a palpable sense of rage at the ways in which women's
bodies, because of their figuring in sexual terms, are continually under threat.

At the end of the twentieth century feminist critics were refocusing their attention on the sexed female body. Greer argued in 1999 that women's sexuality
had come to be all that defines them: 'to deny a woman's sexuality is certainly
to oppress her, but to portray her as nothing but a sexual being is equally to
oppress her' (Greer 1999: 319). The portrayal of women's bodies as sexed and
sexual is reinforced by powerful consumerist influences, which have succeeded
in making desirable, even empowering, the strip club, sex toy and topless model
image. In this culture (our focus here is on Anglo-American culture rather than
an international perspective, which, of course, would be hugely more complex)
younger women have increasingly co-opted sexualised imagery in their construction of an empowered new identity:

> while retaining the critique of the beauty culture and sexual abuse from the sec-
> ond-wave, young women have complicated the older feminist critique of the male
> gaze as a weapon to put women in their place, and instead exploit the spotlight
> as a source of power and energy. Thus girls do not see a contradiction between
> female power and assertive sexuality. (Rowe in Hollows and Moseley 2006: 64)

While this may, on the one hand, appear to echo the sexual emancipation
promoted by Angela Carter in *The Sadeian Woman* (1979) and *The Bloody
Chamber* (1979) (as discussed in Chapter 2), there is a crucial difference – not
always easy to distinguish on the surface – between genuine sexual agency in
which women – and men – negotiate power and pleasure on their own terms
and sexual relationships that are mediated and defined by values and ideologies
that remain profoundly misogynist.

As noted in the Introduction, the attempt to lay claim to a greater empowerment through self-display is undermined by the role sexist consumer culture
plays in directing these 'freedoms'. This was explored in detail in 2006 with
the publication of Ariel Levy's *Female Chauvinist Pigs*, which examines and
critiques the commodification of women's bodies and their sexual depiction.
Levy argues that women have been sold a lie, and that the idea of liberation
through exhibition of an aggressive sexuality and sexualised bodily ideal plays
into the hands of a sexist commodity culture. She writes:

> The freedom to be sexually provocative or promiscuous is not enough freedom;
> it is not the only 'women's issue' worth paying attention to. And we are not even
> free in the sexual arena. We have simply adopted a new norm, a new role to play:
> lusty, busty exhibitionist. There are other choices. (Levy 2006: 200)

This problematisation of 'raunch' showed that sexual expression cannot simply
be equated with empowerment (a line of argument Greer had made nearly forty
years earlier in *The Female Eunuch*).

> [Levy] can see that the problem is that women's liberation hasn't gone far enough.
> While women may congratulate themselves for smashing sexual ceilings, they
> seem to have forgotten to smash employment ceilings. And while they are still so

much less powerful than men, can they ever really have the freedom to play up to their own sexual fantasies, rather than men's? (Walter 2006).

Natasha Walter described her despair at this regressive portrayal of women, and of their bodies, in her 2010 text *Living Dolls: The Return of Sexism*, where she reflects on the hypersexualisation of culture generally, and of young women in particular.

As the third wave and its pro-sex agenda gave way to the fourth, there was thus a renewed attempt to resist women's representation as sexed bodies, and a growing awareness of sexual inequality within consumer and popular culture. Young women are now being driven towards feminist engagement by the hyper-sexualisation of culture, replacing the embracement of sex that marked some third-wave manifestations with a strong critique of the limits such a culture places on (especially) women. Women's portrayal as sexed bodies has never been more prevalent, as the proliferation of digital porn culture means such imagery is more readily and widely available than ever before. In fiction, women are responding with literature that interrogates, illuminates and undermines this one-dimensional depiction of women's bodies in sexual terms. Clever literary innovations such as Ali Smith's *How To Be Both* (2014), which portrays a fifteenth-century cross-dressing Casanova whose female body is hidden but still sexual, give us textual alternatives to the cultural status quo. And Eimear McBride's devastating *A Girl Is a Half-Formed Thing* (2014) depicts the annihi-lation of a young woman's sense of self, and eventually her own body, because of the ways it entraps her as a sexed 'thing'. These kinds of novels, and the ways they problematise and radicalise the presentation of women's bodies, are an important tool in the continued feminist attempt to counter women's sexual objectification.

Case study 3.3 I'm a Barbie girl

> To care about feminine fashion, and do it well, is to be obsessively involved in inconsequential details on a serious basis. There is no relief. To not be involved is to risk looking eccentric or peculiar, or sloppy and uncared for, or mannish and man-hating, or all of the above. (Brownmiller 1984: 56)

So wrote Susan Brownmiller in her 1984 text *Femininity*, a study of the ways in which the female form is historically, socially and psychologically constructed. The requirement for women to concern themselves with the 'inconsequential details' of fashion has long affected judgement of their bodies. Those women who refuse this engagement leave themselves open to disdain, as their bodies are made emblematic of their characters in ways never paralleled for men. Julie Burchill describes the way that larger, hairier, 'unfeminine' women who do not fit the ideal category

> have committed one of the most heinous modern crimes a woman can: they do not care whether or not they are physically attractive. Whereas a woman might once have been disapproved of merely as sloppy, today her appearance calls into question her sexual orientation, morals and even sanity. (Burchill 2000)

There exists a kind of 'ultimate' (or rather, extreme) female body type that I am going to describe here as a 'Barbie girl' – fashionable, feminine and formed from hours of attention and craft. Today, perhaps more than ever, we can see examples throughout UK popular culture of the pervasiveness of the Barbie girl image, and its power to persuade women into enacting a specific form of bodily 'femininity'. The Barbie girl must dedicate (a great deal of) time and money to the construction and maintenance of her body, and while she exists as a prototype for ideal femininity, other women risk being unfavourably compared, as Brownmiller and Burchill describe. The power of consumer culture to enforce this ideal, through books, magazines, TV, music and other media, means that the Barbie girl is an important emblem in the feminist fight against the limitations placed on women's bodies.

The Barbie doll was introduced in 1959, and so has existed alongside – and in many ways in antagonism to – contemporary feminism. The doll's physical attributes have always been controversial, with Barbie's vital statistics estimated to be a thirty-six-inch chest, eighteen-inch waist and thirty-three-inch hips, extrapolated from the doll's construction at one-sixth of human size. Barbie's physiology represents an unachievable 'ideal', an ideal that persists – for real women – in spite of decades of feminist critique. In spite of feminist awareness-raising of the imposition of false ideals of female beauty, the stereotype represented by bodies like Barbie's persist. Further, the rise of cosmetic surgery now makes her previously unattainable vital statistics a possibility – and for a growing number of women, a reality. In 2007, 91 per cent of all cosmetic surgical procedures in north America were performed on women, while eight out of nine cosmetic surgeons are men (Heyes and Jones 2009: 2). The proliferation and normalisation of body-modification procedures that enable women to 'become' Barbie are manifestations of a particular form of 'choice' rhetoric within consumer culture, coupled with the insistence within this culture on a specific, male-defined body ideal.

Susan Bordo has written extensively on plastic surgery and feminism, and has argued that popular culture falsely presents a rhetoric of choice while steering women towards homogenisation (Bordo 1993: 117). She is pessimistic that the trend towards more cosmetic surgery – the numbers of women opting for some form of procedure continue to rise year on year – will be reversed, as the cultural and economic discourses that normalise them, and make their outcomes appear attractive, are too powerful. Natasha Walter, too, points to the influence of popular culture in perpetuating the Barbie ideal: 'plastic surgery has been boosted in recent years by the rise of stars such as Victoria Beckham or Jordan who are obviously reliant on the needle and knife for their transformations' (Walter 2010: 68). The persuasiveness of cultural discourses that embody 'success' such as large breasts, small waist, long legs and little else is hard for young women, especially, to ignore.

Jordan, or Katie Price, is perhaps the ultimate contemporary mani-festation of the Barbie ideal. One of her many franchises has been as an 'author' (all of her books are ghost-written), where she has presented in literary terms a positive representation of the Barbie type – impressive sales figures for her four autobiographies and five adult novels pay testa-ment to her success in this. There is currency (literally and metaphorically) in presenting the Barbie girl as a success: a fact that is deeply troubling for feminism. Feminism's exhortation to women, particularly during its third-wave manifestations, to embrace and be empowered through bodily display and self-fashioning has been perverted under consumerism into figuring female 'success' in this way. The Barbie girl ideal resonates with so many women in the UK because of the prevalence and power of popular cultural and consumer narratives that posit it as in some way aspirational. Refutation of the Barbie ideal seems a feminist no-brainer – and as sales of the doll began to seriously decline in 2014, it also seemed attain-able – but the complex interplay of commerce and 'post-feminist' claims of empowerment through embodiment trouble this automatic assump-tion. The new generation of brasher, brattier dolls snapping at Barbie's high heels – all liberated self-confidence in their fishnet stockings – shows exactly how confusing the issue of the female body in feminism still is.

Bibliography

Atwood, Margaret. 1969. *The Edible Woman*. London: Virago (1980).
Atwood, Margaret. 1976. *Lady Oracle*. London: Virago (1982).
Baehr, Helen (ed.). 1980. *Women and Media*. Oxford: Pergamon Press.
Baehr, Helen and Gillian Dyer. 1987. *Boxed In: Women and Television*. London: Pandora.

Bloom, Harold (ed.). 2000. *Modern Critical Views: Margaret Atwood*. Philadelphia: Chelsea House Publishers.

Bordo, Susan. 1993. *Unbearable Weight: Feminism, Western Culture, and the Body*. Berkeley: University of California Press.

Brownmiller, Susan. 1984. *Femininity*. New York: Simon and Schuster (1986).

Burchill, Julie. 2000. 'Nagging Doubts'. In *The Guardian*, 8 July.

Carter, Angela. 1992. *Wise Children*. London: Virago.

Chernin, Kim. 1983. *Womansize: The Tyranny of Slenderness*. London: The Women's Press.

Chernin, Kim. 1986. *The Hungry Self: Women, Eating and Identity*. London: Virago.

Creedon, Pamela J. (ed.). 1993. *Women in Mass Communication*. London: Sage.

Davies, Kath, Julienne Dickey and Teresa Stratford (eds). 1987. *Out of Focus: Writings on Women and the Media*. London: The Women's Press.

Ellmann, Lucy. 1988. *Sweet Desserts*. London: Virago.

Gamman, Lorraine and Margaret Marshment (eds). 1988. *The Female Gaze: Women as Viewers of Popular Culture*. London: The Women's Press.

Greer, Germaine. 1970. *The Female Eunuch*. London: MacGibbon and Kee.

Greer, Germaine. 1999. *The Whole Woman*. London: Transworld.

Grosz, Elizabeth. 1995. *Space, Time and Perversion: Essays on the Politics of Bodies*. New York: Routledge.

Heyes, Cressida J. and Meredith Jones (eds). 2009. *Cosmetic Surgery: A Feminist Primer*. Farnham: Ashgate.

Hill, Amelia. 2005. 'Sisters Just Ain't Doing It For Themselves'. In *The Guardian*. 30 January.

Hollows, Joanne & Rachel Moseley (eds.). 2006. *Feminism in Popular Culture*. Oxford & New York: Berg.

King, Jeanette. 2012. *Discourses of Ageing in Fiction and Feminism: The Invisible Woman*. Basingstoke: Palgrave Macmillan.

Ledger, Sally. 1997. *The New Woman: Fiction and Feminism at the Fin de Siècle*. Manchester: Manchester University Press.

Lesnik-Oberstein, Karin. 2007. *The Last Taboo*: women and body hair. Manchester: Manchester University Press.

Levy, Ariel. 2006. *Female Chauvinist Pigs: Women and the Rise of Raunch Culture*. London: Pocket Books.

MacArthur, Brian. 2009. 'Bestselling Authors of the Decade'. In *The Telegraph*, 22 December.

Mattelart, Michele. 1986. *Women, Media and Crisis: Femininity and Disorder*. London: Comedia.

McBride, Eimear. 2013. *A Girl Is a Half-formed Thing*. London: Faber and Faber.

Posener, Jill. 1982. *Spray It Loud*. London: Routledge.

Romaine, Suzanne. 1999. *Communicating Gender*. Upper Saddle River: Lawrence Erlbaum Associates.

Sceats, Sarah and Gail Cunningham. 1996. *Image and Power: Women in Fiction in the Twentieth Century*. London: Longman.

Segal, Lynne. 1994. *Straight Sex: The Politics of Pleasure*. London: Virago.

Smith, Ali. 2014. *How To Be Both*. London: Hamish Hamilton.

Susann, Jacqueline. 1966. *Valley of the Dolls*. London: Cassell.

Walter, Natasha (ed.). 1999. *On the Move: Feminism for a New Generation*. London: Virago.

Walter, Natasha. 2006. 'Still One of the Guys'. In *The Guardian*, 18 February.

Walter, Natasha. 2010. *Living Dolls: The Return of Sexism*. London: Virago.

Waugh, Patricia. 1989. *Feminine Fictions: Revisiting the Postmodern*. London: Routledge.

Whelehan, Imelda and Joel Gwynne (eds). 2014. *Ageing, Popular Culture and Contemporary Feminism: Harleys and Hormones*. New York: Palgrave Macmillan.

Wolf, Naomi. 1991. *The Beauty Myth*. London: Vintage.

Zahavi, Helen. 1991. *Dirty Weekend*. London: Flamingo.

4 Not straight sex

In this chapter I will explore the feminist engagement with LGBTI+ identities and fiction's role in describing as well as interrogating the complexities and sheer variety of women's sexual experience. Throughout feminism's multiple waves, some women – including those who were born male but identify as women, and those who reject that label entirely – have resisted the paradigm of normative heterosexuality. Through both fiction and theory, women writers have explored the many and multiple manifestations of female sexuality, debunking myths about normative heterosexuality, female pleasure and 'appropriate' sex roles, and constructing their own spectrum of sexual behaviours and identities, distinct from but always connected to gender identity. The correlation between gender and sexual identity is itself hugely varied: the 'butch' heterosexual woman, for example, rejects normative femininity but nevertheless lives as a highly conventional straight woman. Conversely, a lesbian-identified woman may mark out a gender identity that is conventionally 'feminine' and apparently heterosexual, while choosing to have sex with women.

The chapter begins with an analysis of how non-heterosexual sexual identities were figured at the turn of the twentieth century, as women's intense 'romantic attachments' with one another were described – and dismissed – in strictly non-sexual terms. First-wave feminism did not politically organise around the issue of resisting heterosexuality, although many of those involved in the fight for women's enfranchisement were in fact in lesbian relationships. The Victorian taboo around lesbian sexuality – indeed, female sexuality in its entirety – made discussion of such issues almost impossible, however much the New Woman espoused the idea of sexual freedom. As the first wave drew to a close, the scandal surrounding the publication of Radclyffe Hall's *The Well of Loneliness* (1928), which tells the story of lesbian protagonist Stephen Gordon's quest for love and acceptance, certainly put lesbian existence in the spotlight, but simultaneously served to further silence discussion of female desire and alternative sexualities – a silencing that was broken by the emergence of feminism's second wave. The woman-centred politics of the early second wave, during the 1960s and 1970s, brought a new blossoming of lesbian narratives, with US texts by Rita Mae Brown, Jane Rule and Kate Millett finding an eager audience with UK readers discovering feminism for the first time (Brown 1973; Rule 1964; Millett 1976). They were followed by a number of British writers who began to describe lesbian experience and existence in both fiction and non-fiction. The first section of this chapter explores this material, and the ways it politicised the personal. Lesbian identity morphed during the 1970s and 1980s into a de-sexualised 'political lesbianism' – an identity based not on sexual preference but on the conscious choice to refrain from sex with men since straight sex was figured as inherently oppressive. I will examine this, and the effect of the problematised of hetero-sex on feminist politicking, and on the feminist movement itself in the latter years of the second wave.

The chapter then turns to examine in Case study 4.1 the hugely influential ideas of French feminists, including Julia Kristeva, Hélène Cixous and Luce Irigaray. Their theories of *parler-femme* and *ecriture feminine* – the quest for a new 'feminine' language and/or writing style through which women's sexuality, in particular, could be authentically expressed – had a huge impact on both creative and critical writing in Western Europe and America. The effect of their ideas can be clearly discerned in the work of, for example, Angela Carter and Jeanette Winterson, whose playful use of language and interrogation of traditional sex roles run throughout their writing (although Carter's first novels pre-date the emergence of French feminism). The French feminist search for ways in which women could explore and express their pleasure, or what they termed *jouissance*, was centred on a retreat from normative, 'missionary' hetero-sex and its related binary ideas of active/passive, male/female, subject/object. Instead, they emphasised the pluralistic, non-genital aspects of female sexual pleasure.

The emergence of the third wave in the 1990s and 2000s coincided with a gradual, and limited, mainstreaming of gay identity in the West, and a post-Butlerian pride in queerer constructs of the self. This, of course, was also supported by political change in the UK, as it moved from Conservative to Labour rule in 1997, and Tony Blair's government repealed the oppressive Section 28 clause in 2003 (Section 28 of the 1988 Local Government Act had criminalised the 'promotion' of homosexuality in schools). In contrast to the political lesbianism of the second wave, third-wave formulations of lesbian identity emerged as a proudly and explicitly *sexual* choice. Now, in the fourth wave, there are debates around the 'heterosexualising' of lesbian identity as more and more gay and bisexual women enter the institutions of marriage and parenthood, following further changes in the law to allow gay couples to marry, foster, adopt and undertake fertility treatment. I will look at the extent to which non-heterosexual lifestyles have been 'mainstreamed' in the section of this chapter, 'Resisting heterosexuality – third and fourth waves', which also considers the role fiction and theory by women writers have played in presenting this, and even enabling it.

Finally, this chapter will examine in Case study 4.2 the rise in trans identities and visibility, and the extent to which these, too, are in the process of being mainstreamed. I include here a broad range of subject positions in my definition of 'trans identities', from cross-dressing to 'genderqueer' rejections of the male/female binary to sex reassignment – everything that marks out a distance and difference from the 'cisgender' position in which one's birth-assigned gender matches with bodily and personal identity. I will look at the development of trans identities through literature, and the impact that a feminist critique of trans identity has had on what is written as well as how trans lives are lived and also the different ways in which the adoption of a trans identity then impacts upon the subject's sexual identity.

Resisting heterosexuality – first and second waves

During the first wave of feminism, female sexuality was an issue only inasmuch as it was linked to women's relationships to men. In Chapter 2, I described the impact of the Married Women's Property Acts of 1870 and 1882, which legally instituted married women's individual identities, meaning they were allowed to own and inherit money and property. I also described the New Woman of this period, whose concept of an emancipated sexuality was riddled with contradictions. The New Woman was often figured as an advocate of 'free love', which in reality was not a sexual but a theoretical position: the decision to live beyond the traditional marriage structure. But while the New Woman figure was associated with the rejection of marriage, the disadvantages – politically and economically – for women of actually doing so were such that few in reality made this choice.

During this period there was also campaigning around the Contagious Diseases Acts, passed during the 1860s to try to curb the spread of sexually transmitted diseases, in particular among military men. These Acts allowed the arrest and incarceration of women suspected of being sex workers, who could be forcibly examined and detained for up to three months to be 'treated' for infection – leaving infected men free to continue having sex. Following a long campaign, including efforts by writers such as Sarah Grand and Harriet Martineau, the Acts were repealed in 1886. All this feminist activity focused on the problematic aspects of heterosexuality – there was no sense of an articulation of alternatives to this, or of a politics of homosexuality or trans identity.

However, there were, of course, lesbian, bisexual and what we might now describe as trans individuals conducting, and writing about, their different sexual lives during the first wave. Willa Cather's sexuality, for example, has been the subject of much academic discussion and, while it remains oblique, what is agreed on is that her most significant adult friendships were with women (Rolfe 2004; Sharistanian 2006). Although American, her writing resonated with the 'New Woman' movement in the UK, and her example of sharing her life with women, and working as a professional writer, certainly marked her out as a 'New Woman' type. Cather's short story of 1908, *On the Gulls' Road*, is therefore important in its ambiguous treatment of sexuality, a radical intervention during feminism's first wave. In it, the narrator – whose gender and identity we never know – describes their passionate love for a married – and terminally ill – young woman:

> I leaned forward and looked at her. 'We could live almost forever if we had enough courage. It's of our lives that we die. If we had the courage to change it all, to run away to some blue coast like that over there, we could live on and on, until we were tired'. (Cather 1908: 18)

This doomed affair is in many ways indicative of the book's temporality. When Cather wrote it, there was little awareness, much less understanding, of lesbian lives and loves, and the thwarting of the love story in the book thus points to contemporary attitudes to homosexuality. But Cather nonetheless suggests a gay narrative by leaving the reader the option to ascribe either a male or female identity to the narrator. One can read into her novella's denouement Foucault's assertion that homosexual identities were instituted only once the categories themselves had been named: at the time Cather wrote her story, the term 'invert' was a catch-all for those who did not fit the heterosexual paradigm, and lesbian identity was vague and amorphous. In this context, it is no wonder her lesbian love story was doomed to fail.

As Lillian Faderman has discussed, the category 'lesbian' was instituted only at the turn of the twentieth century (Faderman 1981). She argues that it is the articulation of the *sexual* category 'lesbian' that led to the stigmatisation of women having sex with women – prior to this, many women had shared intense, passionate 'romantic attachments', but since female sexuality was in general so silenced, these had not been figured as sexual, and thus escaped censure. As the science of sexology, emerging in the time of Victorian Britain's obsession with categorisation, set out sexual classifications, 'romantic attachments' between women lost their innocence. In spite of Queen Victoria's denial of the specificity of lesbian identity and desire, both were suddenly made explicit.

In this context, one book above all others brought attention to this 'new' lesbian identity (although I will also look later in this chapter at ways of reading the same text as a trans narrative). Radclyffe Hall's *The Well of Loneliness* caused a scandal upon its publication in 1928, in spite of initial positive reviews. The text was published with a foreword by sexologist Havelock Ellis, whom Hall had approached with the intention that his endorsement would give her novel legitimacy. She wanted the story of her protagonist, Stephen Gordon, to act as a catalyst to greater public sympathy and understanding for non-heterosexual relationships, and her narrative is an appeal for legitimising lesbian love through marriage. However, due to the determined efforts of James Douglas of the *Sunday Express* newspaper, the novel's publication in fact led to a notorious obscenity trial and its eventual prohibition. It remained out of print until after the Second World War.

The character of Stephen Gordon in the novel can be described as 'butch', and indeed many lesbians have since disidentified with the text because of its butch/femme dynamic (see Case study 4.2, 'Trans identities', for other readings of Gordon's masculinity). But at the time Hall wrote her novel, understanding of lesbian existence was predicated on exactly this dynamic: that lesbians were either masculine or else were feminine women who were 'available' to butch women. Hall's appeal through her novel was to show that Gordon's female masculinity was not perverse, but rather entirely natural and unbidden, and she thus sought to show that marriage between Gordon and her lover(s) was as legitimate as any heterosexual union. This points to the time at which Hall was writing, when marriage was still perceived as being central to any 'proper' relationship. But it also shows that active female sexuality could not be expressed in terms other than masculine ones: in order for Hall to portray a lesbian female sexuality that made sense to her readership, that sexuality had to be coded male. Desire was still absolutely in the domain of men.

Hall's text was published in the same year that full female enfranchisement was achieved (1928), bringing an end to feminism's first wave. The vitriol surrounding the court case and the text's subsequent prohibition – Douglas said he would rather let children drink prussic acid than read it – no doubt had a profound effect on women writers following Hall. Critical surveys of the interwar years have tended to focus on lesbian love stories which described an unhappy end for their female protagonists, with one or two notable exceptions (the lesbian pulp fiction genre that emerged during the 1950s provides many – amusing – examples of the prowling lesbian getting her well-deserved punishment). Nonetheless, a whole subculture of lesbian romance also flourished around this time but, as with so much other women's writing, it has remained part of a subculture, and been rejected as canonical or even simply literary. It was not until the emergence of feminism's second wave that lesbian identity was once again articulated and examined, resulting in a blossoming of women's writing that explored alternatives to heterosexual identity.

The second wave emerged in part from women's dissatisfaction with the roles allotted them within the so-called sexual revolution of the 1960s. Changing attitudes to sex had certainly freed men's behaviour in the West, but the disassociation of sex with reproduction as the result of the introduction of the pill did not mean quite the same thing for women. For several decades, moral attitudes lagged behind sexual behaviours, so that while women could now enjoy sex without the fear of becoming pregnant, those who did so outside marriage might still be censured. The women's liberation movement set out to address women's lack of sexual agency by putting them in charge of their own sexual choices: 'putting women first was a basic organising principle for an autonomous women's movement' (Eisenstein 1983: 48). The emergence of early feminist writers like Kate Millett and Germaine Greer, who foregrounded the need for women to take ownership of their own sexuality and decisions concerning reproduction as one of the routes to female emancipation, meant that for the first time there was discussion of the ways that women could free themselves of the sexual identities that were forced onto them and culturally policed. Anne Koedt's *The Myth of the Vaginal Orgasm* (1968) likewise troubled the corollary between sexual pleasure and a heterosexual paradigm. This freeing of ideas around female sexuality not only led to women taking control in heterosexual contexts, it also led many women to consider enacting their sexuality outside of this context altogether. This was reflected in the literature that women began to write in the 1970s, much of it enabled by the establishment of feminist publishers such as Virago, The Women's Press and, especially, Onlywomen, dedicated to lesbian fiction and non-fiction writing.

It was Onlywomen that published Adrienne Rich's influential 1981 text *Compulsory Heterosexuality and Lesbian Existence*, in which she argued that heterosexuality was itself socially and psychologically imposed rather than a natural inclination, and thus created the category of 'political lesbianism'. Rich contended that all forms of sociability and solidarity between women are part of a 'lesbian continuum', and advocated lesbianism as part of every woman's emotional, if not necessarily physical, experience. 'Political lesbianism' was posited as a way in which women might reject their historical construction as mere 'object' in sexual terms and instead attain a more empowered form of sexual expression – choosing sex with other women was figured as a political rather than a sexual act. The articulation of political lesbianism coincided with the pornography debates of the late 1970s and early 1980s, in which feminist writers Susan Griffin, Catharine MacKinnon and Andrea Dworkin articulated an unequivocal opposition to pornography, arguing that it represented a disturbing indicator of the reality of women's oppression. Following their argument that heterosexual sex was innately oppressive to women, lesbian separatists defined their sexuality – which could mean anything from a refusal of sexual relations with men, to bisexual activity, to having sex with women – as an act of feminist praxis, an evasion of these imposed norms.

As the second wave progressed, political lesbianism served to fracture the feminist movement, as lesbians objected to the representation of their sexual identity as a *political* identity, and heterosexual women objected to a definition of heterosexuality that figured them as inherently oppressed. Writers such as Lynne Segal articulated a female sexuality that could include men without necessitating subordination: 'transforming the meanings attaching to sexuality is a political task which men and women can share' (Segal 1990: 216). At the same time, lesbian writers showed that it was possible to resist normative heterosexuality without necessarily ascribing a political meaning to their sexual desires and identity. During the 1980s authors such as Jeanette Winterson, Sara Maitland and Val McDermid used their fiction to imagine desire in new ways, distancing their non-heterosexual narratives from the radical separatism that had hijacked lesbian identity (for more on McDermid and women writing crime fiction, see Chapter 7). There was a determined attempt to wrest back the personal from the political in lesbian storytelling with, for example, feminist bookshop Silver Moon publishing its range of 'lesbian pot-boilers' – 'a conscious decision on the part of Silver Moon's publishers, Jane Cholmeley and Sue Butterworth, to "do 'fun' lesbian books"' (Duncker 1992: 41).

Winterson in particular emerged from the discord of political feminism as a swaggering, confident teller of lesbian tales. Following her debut, the quasi-autobiographical *Oranges Are Not The Only Fruit* (1985), her novels told of a series of remarkable, gender-bending, time-travelling women (and men) whose sexual exploits with other women (and men) denoted a radical new style in lesbian storytelling. In *The Passion* (1987), for example, she narrates her love stories through both male and female characters, sometimes describing heterosexual and sometimes homosexual encounters. All are shot through with intensity: 'passion will not be commanded. It is not a genie to grant us three wishes when we let it loose. It commands us and very rarely in the way we would choose' (Winterson 1987: 144). In marked contrast to the selfless and ultimately tragic heroine of Hall's *The Well of Loneliness*, Winterson's lesbian lovers are strident, sensuous and sometimes selfish. She portrays these characters as desiring and desirous, very different from the asexual 'political lesbianism' of the early 1980s feminist movement. Winterson's tall tales instituted a new kind of literary lesbianism, providing eroticised and empowered – as well as empowering – narratives of non-heterosexual desire. They anticipate, in many ways, the queerer storytelling of third- and fourth-wave lesbian narratives that incorporate a Butlerian destabilisation of fixed gender identity in their portrayals of gender and masquerade, as I will go on to discuss later in this chapter (and for more on Winterson see the section 'Resisting heterosexuality – third and fourth waves' below). They also, vitally, began the process of putting lesbian storytelling into the mainstream, as the success of Winterson's novels in both literary and commercial terms created a market for the proud, uncompromising non-heterosexual narratives that followed in the third and fourth waves. Sales of middlebrow mainstream author Joanna Trollope's lesbian story *A Village Affair* (1989) confirmed the trend, prompting the novel's adaptation into a TV series aired on ITV and proving that lesbianism had well and truly entered the mainstream.

Case study 4.1 French feminism and sexuality

Gender politics, and in particular the construction of the 'feminine', was the key focus of a particular school of feminist thought – widely referred to as 'French feminism' – that emerged in the 1970s and 1980s and which facilitated a radical re-appraisal of female sexuality. Spearheaded by Julia Kristeva, Hélène Cixous and Luce Irigaray, this group of writers refused the hierarchised and reductively gendered binaries upon which culture, they argued, was built. They drew upon the work of the psychoanalysts Sigmund Freud and Jacques Lacan to show how hetero-patriarchy works to stereotype the sexes and how we think about them in ways that privilege the masculine and negate the feminine. One of Cixous's key arguments was that this language of patriarchy – or *phallogocentrism* as it is referred to by Lacan – conceptualises the world in terms of binary pairings that are always structured in terms of superior/inferior elements (e.g. masculine/feminine, active/passive, singular/plural). By revealing the extent to which Western thought is indebted to this binary system – and how it stems from the superior status afforded to all things masculine – they also discovered a means by which the existing hierarchies could be challenged and overthrown: that is, by exposing and undermining the structuring principles of phallogocentrism itself.

Julia Kristeva's theories of female identity and sexuality were also based upon psychoanalytic and post-structuralist models of subject development (Kristeva 1984). Drawing upon Lacan's work to conceptualise a 'subject in process' – constituted by both the repressed (pre-linguistic) *semiotic* and the (phallogocentric) *symbolic order* (for a full discussion see Kristeva in Moi 1986: 99–100) – she posits that women (and other marginalised subjects) maintain a special relationship with the semiotic as a result of their exclusion from the 'symbolic order' and their difficulty in fully inhabiting the first-person 'I' of spoken and written discourse. According to Kristeva, the interaction between the semiotic and the symbolic constitutes language as a site both of (repressive) order and potential disruption. She also argues that the expression of these pre-linguistic semiotic rhythms is most clearly identifiable in poetry, a literary form that is permitted to deviate from the linguistic structures of spoken and written prose. The semiotic is revealed in 'genotexts' which escape the rules of language, while traditional prose writings, 'phenotexts', work actively to repress the semiotic. Kristeva's analysis of the gendering of language use within phallogocentric Western culture is then linked, in her other writings, to the materialities of the female body, where similar repressions/'eruptions' may be seen to have a bearing on how women experience their sexuality. One of Kristeva's concepts in this regard is *jouissance*: a term for the female sexual pleasure(s) that, like the semiotic of language, can erupt spontaneously and in defiance of the symbolic power afforded to the phallus (Kristeva 1977).

Hélène Cixous developed Kristeva's formulation of the semiotic to advocate a *sortie*, or 'exit', from the controlling domain of the symbolic order and its resulting imposition of fixed binaries on both gender and sexual identity. Cixous argued that a woman's complex libidinal economy, including her capacity for *jouissance*, defied patriarchal sexual classification. She also advocated a bisexual sexuality that would collapse the binaries of male/female, masculine/feminine, subject/object, and free women from their imposed gender and sexual identities. Like Kristeva and Irigaray, Cixous made an explicit – and, for many subsequent critics, problematic – connection between the female sexual body and women's use of written language, as is famously captured in her definition of *écriture feminine*: 'a woman's body, with its thousand and one thresholds of ardor [. . .] will make the old single-grooved mother tongue reverberate with more than one language' (Cixous in Marks and Courtivron 1981: 256). Her *écriture feminine* was thus figured as a rebuttal to the formal structures of masculine language and thought, playing with puns, metaphors and ellipses in order to destabilise meaning and trouble established ideas of language, even though the very self-consciousness with which this is done has caused critics to question in what sense this manner of writing necessarily belongs to women writers (see Mills and Pearce 1996).

Like Cixous, Luce Irigaray proposed a new language, *parler-femme*: a spoken equivalent of Cixous's literary *écriture féminine*. Her *parler-femme* also refused the logic and linearity of masculine discourse, and was characterised in terms of the female sexual body, which – in contrast to the male phallus – is multiple and polymorphous in terms of its pleasure: '*woman has sex organs more or less everywhere*. She finds pleasure almost anywhere' (Irigaray 1985: 28, original emphasis) and argues that since women can experience sexual pleasure all over their bodies, they should be able to speak in ways that reflect this fluidity, ambiguity and provisionality:

> if we don't invent a language, if we don't find our body's language, it will have too few gestures to accompany our story. We shall tire of the same ones, and leave our desires unexpressed, unrealised. Asleep again, unsatisfied, we shall fall back upon the words of men. (Irigaray 1985: 214)

French feminism, then, made central the polymorphous nature of female sexual pleasure sited across the entire body – a phenomenon associated with *jouissance* – and the refusal of a singular, phallus-focused sexuality that was associated with genital sex, both discursively and in practice. Such ideas were also in dialogue with writers and artists of the late 1970s and early 1980s. Angela Carter's novels, for example, use magic and metaphor to subvert the patriarchal imposition of rigid gender roles, and explore the potential of female sexual agency to challenge normative sexual practices. As observed in Case study 2.2, in *The Passion of New Eve*, Carter's hero(ine) Eve(lyn) explores and embodies a range of sexual and gender identities, allowing Carter to highlight the insufficiency of existing conceptual models. In the words of her central protagonist, Eve/lyn, who began life as a man, but who is now a woman in love with another 'woman', Tristessa, (herself a man in drag):

> what the nature of masculine and the nature of feminine might be, whether they involve male and female, if they have anything to do with Tristessa's so long neglected apparatus or my own factory fresh incision

and engine-turned breasts, that I do not know. Though I have been both man and woman, still I do not know the answer to these questions. Still they bewilder me. (Carter 1982: 150)

Similarly, Jeanette Winterson's depiction of a range of gender-fluid and sexually ambiguous characters refuses the patriarchal imposition of a phallus-centred pursuit of pleasure and constructs revolutionary narratives that dispel the concept of a unified self. Both writers subvert the sexist imagining of a kind of mythical ideal 'woman', and position their readers as active players in the construction of their works' meanings. In this, they show the influence of French feminist theory, and also anticipate many of the ideas and applications of queer theory and practice. Indeed, the legacy of French feminism can be clearly discerned in the rise of queer theorising, with Judith Butler's work being more indebted to Irigaray's than is often acknowledged (see Butler 1990; Pearce 1994). Both French feminism and queer theory regard gendered and sexual identity as, foremost, a position in discourse, and both have demonstrated how we can assume different positions/sexualities at different times. This conceptualisation of gender and sexuality as 'fluid' is one that was to have a huge influence as feminism moved out of its second wave, as I will now go on to examine.

Resisting heterosexuality – third and fourth waves

The shift from second- to third-wave feminism arose in no small part from the fractures caused by the 'identity politics' debates of the 1980s, where identity was defined by the specificities of race, class, sexuality and disability intersected with gender. For many, this insistence on difference left too little room for commonality, both among women and between women and men. Simultaneously, Judith Butler's important text *Gender Trouble* (1990) was destabilising the very category of gender, arguing that it – and indeed biological sex itself – was culturally contingent, a manifestation of repeated enactments of certain behaviours (see Chapter 2). Third-wave feminism, then, incorporated this queerer understanding of the ways that all identities were in some way culturally contingent and potentially fluid, alongside the second-wave critique of the gendered categories of mother/housewife/sex object. It also, as I argue in Chapter 3, contained a focus on female sexuality, its 'pro-sex' agenda incorporating heterosexual as well as alternative narratives of female desire and sexual freedoms.

Through the 1990s and into the 2000s, more complex ideas of gender entered the mainstream – accompanied as ever by a stubborn discourse of homophobic hate, particularly in online communities – as the strengthening of gay pride, in defiance of legislative restraints such as Section 28, resulted in a renewed expression of sexual freedom and more diverse and multiplicitous formulations of sexual politics. New images of male and female identity emerged that played with the limits of masculine and feminine norms: the sexually precocious 'ladette' (and its more masculine form, the lesbian 'boi'), the feminine metrosexual man and the ironic 'girly girl' all took up Butler's troubling of gender as 'natural', shifting the emphasis from a focus on women to a focus on the ways *both* sexes are constructed. In mainstream culture, celebrity figures such as the Spice Girls, Marilyn Manson, Eddie Izzard, models Kate Moss and Agyness Deyn, and even footballer David Beckham, all transgressed the boundaries between masculine and feminine, manifesting a shift towards a more androgynous, queer figuring of identity. As Helen Wilkinson observed in 1994:

> in many respects through figures like Sigourney Weaver and Madonna, kd lang and Sharon Stone, popular culture has been far ahead of politics in thinking through the blurring of the boundaries of male and female identity, and the potency of female sexuality. (Wilkinson 1994: 9)

Jeanette Winterson, again, used her literature to explore this gender-troubling, and to imagine a queer telling of sexual desire that resists a normative heterosexual framework. In *Written on the Body* (1993), she uses the same tactic as Willa Cather in her 1908 novella, leaving the reader to ascribe a gender to the narrator of the story. This destabilising device means Winterson's novel can be read as a heterosexual romance, or a homosexual one, or both. In this, it is a quintessentially queer text, playing with the categories of male and female, gay and straight, and thus showing us the arbitrariness of the ways in which these categories are constructed. Winterson's novel coincided, too, with the emergence in popular culture of a new kind of 'lesbian chic', which, for the first time, made lesbian identity commercially desirable, indeed fashionable. As celebrities like Madonna and Cindy Crawford played with lesbian iconography, 'women desiring women' were radically refigured within mainstream culture as 'cool'.

Lesbian author Sarah Waters came to fame as a result, in part, of this new lesbian chic, her debut novel *Tipping the Velvet* (1998) – and its subsequent TV adaptation – striking a chord within the context of this new fashionability of lesbian lives and loves. *Tipping the Velvet*, Waters' romping tale of show-business, cross-dressing, politics and betrayal threaded throughout with plenty of sex provides a literary example of the confident lesbian romantic narrative from this period. Waters is clear that she writes about lesbian sex – the title of the book itself is a euphemism for cunnilingus – for a reason:

> Despite embracing the lesbian writer label, Waters is bemused by what remains a somewhat prudish attitude to the sex scenes in her novels. 'I think that's

something about being a woman writer,' she says. 'People still think it's notice-
able if a woman writes about sex'. (Interview in Thompson 2015)

In making explicit her portrayals of lesbian sex, Waters ensures her text chimes
with the third-wave pro-sex agenda. Her writing is also a reclamation of lesbian
erotica and eroticism from both the political lesbianism of the 1970s and 1980s,
and the heterosexist pornification of 'girl-on-girl' sex: 'I think lesbian writers
had traditionally felt uneasy about what might happen if they wrote very explicitly about sex. There was a fear it might be consumed for titillation by a
male readership' (interview in Merritt 2000).

In addition, the cross-dressing narratives within *Tipping the Velvet* encourage queer readings of Waters' novel, and indeed the term 'queer' is
self-consciously repeated throughout the novel to draw the reader's attention
to its gender-destabilising intent. Waters' writing sits comfortably within third-
wave feminism's explorations of queer subcultures, her heroine Nan donning
various male guises and garbs en route to establishing her own sense of self: 'to
walk as a boy, as a handsome boy in a well-sewn suit, whom the people stared
after only to envy, never to mock – well, it has a brittle kind of glamour to it'
(Waters 1998: 195). Through her character Nan, Waters explores a Butlerian
destabilisation of gender and its performance, situating her text firmly within
the queer discourses taking place in popular and literary culture at the end of
the twentieth century.

Tipping the Velvet and Waters' subsequent novels are important in instat-
ing lesbian lives into written history, establishing in fiction the experiences of
women who have resisted heterosexual matrices. Along with other writers such
as Emma Donoghue, this deliberate attempt to rewrite history to include lesbian
experience is expressly political, redressing the historical silencing of alternative
sexualities (see Chapter 10 for a full discussion of feminism's engagement with
historical fiction). It also shows a continuity with the project of the feminist
publishing houses established during the second wave (see Chapter 1), which
similarly sought to reinsert women's experiences into literary history. Indeed,
the feminist publishing phenomenon did much to mainstream both women's
writing generally, and lesbian fiction specifically, with, for example, Jeanette
Winterson being first published by Pandora and Sarah Waters by Virago. As
Elaine Hutton observed in 1998: 'in the last three decades, representations of
lesbians in fiction have proliferated, since the explosion in feminist printing and
publishing as a result of the women's movement' (Hutton 1998: 1).

In the last decade, however, sexual politics have moved on again, and the
novelty of lesbian chic has given way to an unprecedented mainstreaming of
gay culture and identity. As feminism has moved into its fourth wave, female
sexuality has been put firmly at the centre of political engagement as a new
demographic of (especially young) women find themselves still battling sexist
and sexually objectifying cultural and political paradigms, decades after the
women's movement first set out to combat them (see Chapter 3). In this context,

then, it is remarkable that one of the most notable shifts in UK culture since the turn of the millennium has been the mainstreaming of gay and trans 'lifestyles' and identities, with trans celebrities now part of everyday discourse, and gay marriage made legal in England, Wales and Scotland (2014) if not yet Northern Ireland. This is in marked contrast to many other countries in Europe, several states in the USA, and swathes of both Asia and Africa, where homophobic and transphobic positions are not only tolerated but encouraged by the state. While correlations are still made between feminism and lesbianism in order to 'naturalise' the idea that feminists hate men (as evidenced by the vitriolic assaults – in particular in online communities – on women who speak out for women, and who are inevitably homophobically abused, regardless of their actual sexual identities), it is notable that UK culture has changed in its assimilation of non-heterosexual identities. Lesbians have never been as visible – or as accepted – as now, and we can see evidence of this not only in popular culture but in literary culture too.

Contemporary women writers like Ali Smith, Emma Donoghue and Stella Duffy are now producing fiction that, while it often contains lesbian thematics, does not make central to the plot this aspect of their characters' identity. In other words, resisting heterosexuality is now so mainstream that it does not warrant a plotline of its own. For example, in her Booker-shortlisted, Baileys Women's Prize for Fiction-winning novel *How To Be Both* (2014), Ali Smith conspires to chronicle the exploits of a cross-dressing lesbian Renaissance artist in such a way that her character's sexual identity is one of the least-discussed aspects of the novel (this is in no small part down to its innovative and ingenious formal properties). Similarly, Duffy and Donoghue are 'out' lesbians whose work can often contain portrayals of non-heterosexual sexualities but is just as likely to focus on other aspects of their characters' identity. This new visibility of lesbian writing and writers is reflective of a general shift towards a mainstreaming of what once would have been considered 'alternative' identities.

Writer Val McDermid explored this in an interview she gave to *The Independent* in 2010, noting that both her books and those written by Sarah Waters were no longer considered 'lesbian fiction' but simply 'fiction':

> I think there's been an opening up of British culture and a relaxing of British society. Our novels have done well at the same time as we've made legal gains; civil partnerships have come along. There's been a bit of a sea change that would have been unimaginable even 10 years ago. (McDermid 2010)

She also notes the contrast with her earlier experience of publishing novels featuring 'the UK's first openly lesbian detective, Lindsay Gordon', arguing that these novels were only considered viable by a feminist publisher (she was initially published by The Women's Press):

> Something has changed in the past seven years. My latest novel, *Trick of the Dark*, is probably the most lesbian book I've ever written in terms of the number of its

gay female characters. And not an eyebrow has been raised at my publisher, Little, Brown. The sales and marketing effort that has been put into this book is, as far as I can gauge, exactly the same as any other book with my name on it would have received. (McDermid 2010)

In popular as well as literary culture, contemporary women are resisting the heterosexual paradigm, with celebrities like Cara Delevingne, Miley Cyrus and Kristen Stewart making lesbianism visible and fashionable all over again. But there is a new complexity to current formulations of non-heterosexual sex. Terms like 'genderqueer' have emerged, proponents of which refuse assignation to the gender binary, instead ascribing neither to masculinity nor to femininity, but to both, or to a combination of the two (for more on this, see Case study 4.2, 'Trans identities'). This current formulation of (non)-gendered identity is contemporary culture's response to changing attitudes to gender and sexuality within a commodity culture that encourages consumption as a means of defining the self. But, as Suzanne Moore notes, it is also a continuation of the troubling of heterosexual norms that began with the women's movement in the 1970s (Moore 2015). Resisting straight sex has always been part of feminism's agenda. Contemporary women's freedom to be 'out' points to the impact of decades of feminist sexual politicking. It also becomes part of this politicking, helping reinforce the importance of women taking control of alternative expressions of sexual identity.

Case study 4.2 **Trans identities**

The exploration of trans identities has emerged throughout feminism's various waves, consistent with the feminist attempt to destabilise and dismantle the gender binary. Gender ambiguity has long been figured as desirable, with Virginia Woolf espousing early on (in 1928, in *A Room of One's Own*) her belief in an androgynous ideal, before second-wave feminists set out to first theorise, and then deconstruct, binary ideas of masculine/feminine (see Chapter 2). Within and alongside this, there have also been attempts to articulate a range of trans identities, including transvestite, transsexual and transgender narratives, that communicate a further destabilising of gender and, by implication, sexual norms. However, as noted in the introduction to this chapter, trans identities are not innately and automatically radical: 'sex change' is sometimes desired precisely so that the subject can enjoy a normative heterosexual rather than a marginalised gay lifestyle.

The relationship between feminism and these trans identities is troubled, however, with some women insisting on the authenticity of their 'cis' female identity, in opposition to trans women. Problematising the unifying figure 'woman' began with the identity politics debates of the 1980s (see earlier in this chapter), where women with different ethnic, socio-economic, sexual and religious positions debated the relative authenticity of their own subjecthood as their gender intersected with these other aspects of identity. The rise of queer further destabilised the concept of a female figure that could represent all women, since gender was fluid, shifting and performative. And contemporary explorations of trans identities encompass a broad spectrum, from drag and disguise to transgressive gender enactments and surgical interventions on the body.

In literary terms, one of the earliest trans narratives is contained in Radclyffe Hall's *The Well of Loneliness*. Hall depicts her character Stephen Gordon as 'trapped' in the wrong body, a situation familiar to trans people, who often describe a similar disjunction between their physiology and psychology, and one which allows us to read Hall's text as a trans rather than a lesbian narrative. Gordon's identity can be read as a desire for a life of heteronormative conservatism, as s/he seeks the validation inherent in marrying a woman while coded as a man. Alternatively, we can read Gordon's story as the wish to construct a more radical, trans identity which defies categorisation as either male or female. Hall's text does not offer a resolution to Gordon's unhappiness and apparent gender dysphoria, but it does constitute an attempt to situate trans identity, as well as interrogate alternative gender constructs, and new sexual identities arising from them.

Following these early examples, further literary exploration of trans identity began during the third wave, taking hold in the 1990s, and spearheaded by trans activists and authors such as Judith/Jack Halberstam and Kate Bornstein. Bornstein argued that the existence of intersex bodies proves that there are more than two bodily identities, and that we have falsely categorised the body as existing only within the parameters of male/female: 'there are, in addition to the XX and XY pairs, some other commonly-occurring sets of gender chromosomes, including XXY, XXX, YYY, XYY and XO. Does this mean there are more than two genders?' (Bornstein 1994: 56). In her account of a life spent 'trying on' different bodies in order to arrive at one which felt authentic, Bornstein argues that all aspects of the sexed body – penis size, menstruation, fertility – alter from person to person, and describes her trans sexuality as part of a rainbow of possible embodiments, in contrast to the black and white of cisgendered bodies. She and other trans theorists, including Pat Califia, brought attention to and understanding of trans lifestyles so that feminism, and culture more broadly, began to incorporate sexualities that were enacted by and on bodies coded neither male or female.

Alongside this critical writing, there has been an exploration of trans lives and trans sexualities in fiction and memoir. Indeed, Jay Prosser argues that transsexuality is 'symptomised in narrative' since transsexuals must write their own story of transition in order to satisfy clinical standards in the UK for transition surgery (Prosser 1998: 103). In 1998 Diane Wood Middlebrook's biography of Billy Tipton, a female-bodied jazz musician who lived and performed as a man, was published at the same time as Jackie Kay's fictionalised version of the same story, *Trumpet*. Kay explores the ways in which the protagonist's body defies categorisation as male or female, inhabiting instead a liminal space within which it still exists as a sexed object. This radical formulation of sex and sexuality has powerful repercussions both for individuals who feel themselves to be not-female or not-male, and for culture itself, which is so structured on the existence of only two body types – for proof of this we need look no further than the way we organise toilet facilities, or the first question that is asked of new parents on the birth of their baby. Bodies that are sexed as neither male nor female have the potential to destabilise our understanding of sex as well as gender. The transgressive body, one that is in progress from male to female, or vice versa, as well as the hermaphroditic body or body in drag, has profound consequences for our understanding and formulation of sexuality. It is this potential that makes trans bodies and trans sexuality so vital from a feminist perspective, since the subjugation of female sexuality has historically been contingent on a binary concept of the sexed body.

However, as noted above, there has long been criticism of trans narratives and the emergence of trans identity, even from within feminism. Quite apart from the fact that the desire of some trans subjects to live normative heterosexual lives may be seen as politically conservative, in 1999 Germaine Greer controversially dismissed the claim of people with androgen insensitivity syndrome (AIS) or intersex people to identify as women. In so doing, Greer made explicit her belief in an essential 'female' body, which must, by her definition, possess a womb. She also argued that 'castrated men' cannot be women, enraging the trans community with statements like 'no so called sex-change has ever begged for a uterus-and-ovaries transplant' (Greer 1999: 64). It is a position she continues to restate. More recently, Ariel Levy's exploration of 'raunch' culture problematised the phenomenon of lesbian 'bois', who, she argues, want to be *like a man*. Their strong identification with historically 'masculine' – and often misogynist – behaviours, she argued, does not signal a queering of the gender binary but rather a restatement of it: 'the confusing thing, of course, is why somebody would need serious surgery [bois often elect to undergo double mastectomies] and testosterone to modify their gender if gender is supposed to be so fluid in the first place' (Levy 2006: 127). Certainly, it is troubling that the surgical industry now in place 'creating' trans bodies is dominated by male clinicians. Equally, there must be further analysis of why so many people find their bodies uninhabitable in their natural form, since this dis-ease must surely arise, at least in part, because of perceived cultural constructions of what our bodies must look like, and must do for us and for others.

Yet in spite of dissenting voices, there has been a distinct move towards greater inclusion of trans identity in culture as feminism has moved into its fourth wave. Celebrities like Caitlyn Jenner, Alexis Arquette and Laverne Cox are now familiar to a global audience via TV, the web and other media. In the UK, the trans body is no longer unfamiliar, dangerous or ridiculous, but part of everyday discourse. For feminism, and for women in general, this acceptance can only be a good thing, since it is part of a dismantling of the patriarchal structures that have long served to police the female body and female sexuality. Telling trans stories and portraying trans sexuality clearly has liberatory potential, but trans identity will also be seen by some to reinforce existing gender binaries and bolster the growing normalisation of the surgical modification of the body. As we saw in the last chapter, the notion of bodily ideals (however conceived) has long been the target of feminist critique and many commentators will be disappointed to see them reproduced in this new arena. The issue of trans identity is therefore set to be one of the key debating points within feminism for some time to come.

Bibliography

Bornstein, Kate. 1994. *Gender Outlaw: On Men, Women and the Rest of Us*. London: Routledge.
Brown, Rita Mae. 1973. *Rubyfruit Jungle*. Vermont: Daughters, Inc.
Butler, Judith. 1990. *Gender Trouble*. London: Routledge.
Califia, Pat. 1997. *Sex Changes: The Politics of Transgenderism*. San Francisco: Cleis Press.
Carter, Angela. 1982. *The Passion of New Eve*. London: Virago.
Duncker, Patricia. 1992. *Sisters and Strangers: An Introduction to Contemporary Feminist Fiction*. Oxford: Blackwell.
Dworkin, Andrea. 1990. *Pornography: Men Possessing Women*. London: The Women's Press.
Eisenstein, Hester. 1983. *Contemporary Feminist Thought*. Boston: GK Hall and Co.
Faderman, Lillian. 1981. *Surpassing the Love of Men: Romantic Friendship and Love Between Women from the Renaissance to the Present*. New York: Morrow.

Greer, Germaine. 1999. *The Whole Woman*. London: Transworld

Halberstam, Judith. 2005. *In a Queer Time and Place: Transgender Bodies, Subcultural Lives*. New York: New York University Press.

Hall, Radclyffe. 1982. *The Well of Loneliness*. London: Virago. (1928)

Hutton, Elaine (ed.). 1998. *Beyond Sex and Romance? The Politics of Contemporary Lesbian Fiction*. London: The Women's Press.

Irigaray, Luce. 1985. *This Sex Which Is Not One*. Translated by Catherine Porter. Ithaca: Cornell University Press.

Koedt, Anne. 1968. *The Myth of the Vaginal Orgasm*. Boston: New England Free Press.

Kristeva, Julia. 1977. *About Chinese Women*. London: Boyars.

Kristeva, Julia. 1984. *Revolution in Poetic Language*. Translated by Margaret Waller. New York: Columbia University Press.

Levy, Ariel. 2006. *Female Chauvinist Pigs: Women and the Rise of Raunch Culture*. London: Pocket Books.

MacKinnon, Catharine. 1989. *Toward a Feminist Theory of State*. London: Harvard University Press.

Marks, Elaine and Isabelle de Courtivron (eds). 1981. *New French Feminisms: An Anthology*. Hemel Hempstead: Harvester-Wheatsheaf.

Marks, Elaine and Sara Mills. 1996. 'French feminism'. In *Feminists Reading/Feminists Reading*. Brighton: Harvester-Wheatsheaf.

McDermid, Val. 2010. 'Niche Off the Leash: Val McDermid on Progress in Lesbian Fiction'. In *The Independent on Sunday*, 12 September.

Merritt, Stephanie. 2000. 'Go On. Name Three Gay Women Writers'. In *The Guardian*, 30 January.

Middlebrook, Diane Wood. 1998. *Suits Me: The Double Life of Billy Tipton*. London: Virago.

Miller, Jacques-Alain (ed.) 1992. *The Ethics of Psychoanalysis 1959–1960: The Seminar of Jacques Lacan*. London: Tavistock/Routledge.

Millett, Kate. 1976. *Sita*. London: Virago.

Mills, Sara and Pearce, Lynne. 1996. *Feminist Readings: Feminists Reading*. Hemel Hempstead: Prentice Hall.

Moi, Toril. 1981. *Sexual/Textual Politics*. London: Methuen.

Moi, Toril (ed.). 1986. *The Kristeva Reader*. Oxford: Basil Blackwell.

Moore, Suzanne. 2015. 'It's Good to be Genderqueer But Don't Forget the Sexual Radicals Who Paved the Way'. In *The Guardian*, 4 November.

Parkinson, Hannah Jane. 2015. 'At Last, Celebrity Women in Lesbian Relationships Are No Big Deal'. In *The Guardian*, 23 September.

Pearce, Lynne. 1994. *Reading Dialogics*. London: Edward Arnold.

Prosser, Jay. 1998. *Second Skins: The Body Narrative of Transsexuality*. New York: Columbia University Press.

Rich, Adrienne. 1981. *Compulsory Heterosexuality and Lesbian Existence*. London: Onlywomen.

Rolfe, Lionel. 2004. *The Uncommon Friendship of Yaltah Menuhin & Willa Cather*. California: California Classics Books.

Rule, Jane. 1964. *Desert of the Heart*. Florida: Naiad Press.

Rye, Gill. 2001. *Reading for Change: Interactions Between Text and Identity in Contemporary French Women's Writing (Baroche, Cixous, Constant)*. Oxford: Peter Lang.

Segal, Lynne. 1990. *Slow Motion: Changing Masculinities, Changing Men*. London: Virago.

Sharistanian, Janet (ed.). 2006. *My Ántonia/Willa Cather*. Oxford: Oxford University Press.

Smith, Ali. 2014. *How To Be Both*. London: Hamish Hamilton.

Thompson, Jessie. 2015. Sarah Waters, Author of 'The Paying Guests', on Why She Invokes the 'Lesbian Writer' Label. At <http://www.huffingtonpost.co.uk/2015/05/01/sarah-waters-baileys-prize-the-paying-guest_n_7187642.html> (accessed 22 November 2015).

Waters, Sarah. 1998. *Tipping the Velvet*. London: Virago.

Wilkinson, Helen. 1994. *No Turning Back: Generations and the Genderquake*. London: Demos.

Winterson, Jeanette. 1985. *Oranges Are Not The Only Fruit*. London: Pandora.

Winterson, Jeanette. 1987. *The Passion*. London: Penguin.

Winterson, Jeanette. 1989. *Sexing the Cherry*. London: Bloomsbury.

Winterson, Jeanette. 1993. *Written on the Body*. London: Vintage.

5 Ethnicity

Ethnicity emerged as a hugely important issue for feminism in the 1980s, as the 'identity politics' of this period led to a theorising of difference rather than sameness under the unifying symbol 'woman'. This insistence on ensuring that the subject was defined according to the specificities of skin colour, class, sexuality and other aspects of identity besides gender in some ways stymied the feminist movement. As Heidi Mirza has critically reflected:

> Identity politics, a political ideology that consumed the 1980s, was based on the premise that the more marginal the group the more complete the knowledge. In a literal appropriation of standpoint theory, the claim to authenticity through oppressive subjecthood produced a simplistic hierarchy of oppression. The outcome was the cliché-ridden discourse which embodied the holy trinity of 'race, class, and gender', within which black women, being the victims of 'triple oppression', were keepers of the holy grail. (Mirza 1997: 9)

In spite of the fractures that the identity politics debates caused, it was essential to formulate a feminism that included Asian, black and minority ethnic (often abbreviated as BME) women's perspectives. This intersection of ethnicity and feminism challenged not only white patriarchy, but also white women's racism, black men's sexism and the privileged site of literature itself. The first section of this chapter traces the emergence of this new perspective and lists its key writers, before Case study 5.1 examines the crucial role the second-wave feminist publishing houses played in enabling BME women to engage in women's politics: as readers, writers and as publishers (an action that provoked a great deal of discussion at the time).

Arising from, and giving rise to, theoretical explorations of BME women's position in feminism and in culture more broadly was a great deal of female fiction that foregrounded ethnicity. During the 1980s and 1990s American writers such as Alice Walker, Maya Angelou and Toni Morrison were published in the UK by feminist presses, alongside British authors such as Joan Riley and Jackie Kay. Following them, the development of postcolonial literary studies meant that there was a further turn reflecting on how Britain's colonial past has impacted on the writing produced by British BME authors. The chapter accordingly goes on to consider the reflection of these issues in women's fiction, focusing on the work of Nadine Gordimer, Andrea Levy and Monica Ali.

Finally, this chapter will explore the contemporary situation of BME women's writing, reflecting on how ethnicity is lived out in British culture and, in particular, how BME British women writers present themselves through their literature. In Case study 5.2 I will foreground the work of Zadie Smith, about whom a huge amount of comment and analysis has been written since she published her debut novel in 2000. The extent to which the UK can be described as truly multicultural and inclusive, as well as the ways in which feminism has embraced different ethnicities, and vice versa, can be discovered in both the fiction and non-fiction writing of BME women in the past decade.

Identity politics and ethnicity – first and second waves

In the 1970s the burgeoning feminist movement in both Britain and the USA was dominated by white, middle-class women; indeed, it is an aspect of contemporary feminism's origins that continues to dog the movement to this day, as much of what feminists bring up for debate is still dismissed as the 'naggings' of a white liberal left. However, as the feminist movement solidified into a coherent political force through the 1980s, early second-wave formulations of female identity were problematised for their oversimplification of women's histories and experiences. BME women (as well as working-class, lesbian and disabled women, among other groupings) started to give voice to their feelings of disenfranchisement, arguing that early figurings of female experience within the women's liberation movement had failed to address the specificity of their experiences. The end of the 1970s saw the first instances of specifically BME feminist solidarity. The Organisation of Women of Asian and African Descent (OWAAD) was established in 1978, the same year that the Brixton Black Women's Group was set up. A year later, Southall Black Sisters was established to meet the needs of Asian and African-Caribbean women in west London, in particular those suffering from domestic violence and abuse. It remains the longest-standing secular organisation supporting the human rights of BME women in the UK.

Critical formulations of the problems with the wider feminist movement for BME women had begun in the US, where a larger proportion of the population was non-white, and where the nation's too recent history of slavery and racist oppression was still very much on the agenda (which is not to say the UK does not possess its own shameful cultural history). American writer bell hooks (elective lower-case spelling) was an early instigator of a black feminist perspective, arguing at the start of the 1980s that contemporary black women could not join together to fight for women's rights because:

[We] did not see 'womanhood' as an important aspect of our identity. Racist, sexist socialisation had conditioned us to devalue our femaleness and to regard race as the only relevant label of identification. In other words, we were asked to deny a part of ourselves – and we did. (hooks 1982: 1)

Second-wave feminism was figured by hooks and other BME feminist writers as dominated by white, middle-class women:

> when black people are talked about the focus tends to be on black *men*; and when women are talked about the focus tends to be on *white* women. Nowhere is this more evident than in the vast body of feminist literature. (hooks 1982: 7)

BME feminists argued that the women's movement had privileged (because it was driven by) the needs of middle- and upper-class university-educated white women. The three stereotypes which second-wave feminist politics set out to deconstruct – the housewife, the mother and the sex object (see Chapter 2) – were formulated in the context of white, Western lifestyles and did not take into account the qualitative difference of BME communities. In Asian communities, by contrast, respect for family meant that problematising the figure of the mother would inevitably alienate Asian women. Similarly, the sexualisation of black women by white men, and their sexual othering through racialised and racist discourse, meant that BME women had specific and different priorities in formulating the ways their sexuality was constructed under patriarchy. Further, the typically lower employment status of BME women in the UK – especially during the years of the second wave – were also not factored into early feminist formulations of work as a route to female emancipation.

Second-wave feminism was forced to realise that, as Virago writer Anne Phillips put it, 'feminists have proved no more immune to racism than the society they inhabit, and as they have documented this, black women have challenged many of the preoccupations of the contemporary women's movement' (Phillips 1987: 6). The formulation of an ethnically diverse perspective within feminist politics was therefore essential in order that all women were represented, and their needs considered. Ethnicity was an issue that feminism simply had to confront.

In literary terms, the challenge to white feminism as well as sexist and racist culture in general came through both fiction and non-fiction writing by BME women. In great part, this literature was enabled by the growing number of feminist presses that were established during the second wave (see Chapter 1) and I will examine their influence later in this chapter (see Case study 5.1, 'Feminist publishing's role in BME women's writing'). The intersections of racism and sexism were explored in novels by Alice Walker, Maya Angelou and Toni Morrison, all of them American but all published in the UK by feminist presses. Black British novelists such as Joan Riley (published by The Women's Press) began, through ground-breaking texts such as *The Belonging* (1985), to describe the specificity of BME women's experience of UK culture. The emergence of the specific genre of black British women's writing was thus instituted during the years of the second wave.

Alongside this fiction, a new form of critical writing emerged which inserted BME experience into literary analysis. The second-wave feminist project of excavating historical writing by female authors (see Chapter 1), for example,

was challenged for its colour-blindness as BME feminist critics set out to redress
the lack of consideration of their history and experience. Prominent second-
wave critic Elaine Showalter was taken to task for her oversight in excluding
ethnicity (and class and sexuality) in her influential theory of gynocritics, for
instance, which set out a new way to study women *as writers* (Showalter 1985).
Showalter's approach, which made women's writing primary, combined biological, linguistic, psychoanalytic and cultural models of critical analysis in order to
categorise women's historical writing and to formulate a theory of how women
write. What it did not include was any mention of the specifics of ethnicity.

Barbara Christian's work was some of the first to challenge this colour-blindness, undertaking the first black 'gynocritical' project in 1979. Her text *Black
Women Novelists* (1980) set out to recover the writing of *black* female authors
who had been left out of literary history: 'there did not exist, in 1979, [. . .] a
single definitive volume of criticism that made available both traditional and
non-traditional analyses and examinations of the works of a representative and
significant segment of skilful Black women writers' (Evans 1985: xvii). Mary
Helen Washington took up Christian's challenge to trace back the history of
black women's writing with her non-fiction work *Invented Lives: Narratives of
Black Women 1860–1960*. This was an attempt to 'piece together those "broken
and sporadic" continuities that constitute black women's literary tradition'
(Washington 1989: xx). Important historical fiction by writers such as Zora
Neale Hurston, credited by critic Gina Wisker (1993) as being the literary fore-
mother of Alice Walker, were unearthed and reissued as part of this campaign
to include BME women in feminism's rewriting of the canon. Although hooks
continued to argue at the end of the 1980s that 'it is profoundly disturbing to
see how little feminist theory is being written by black women and women
of other colour', there was more and more evidence of the emergence of this
critical writing by BME women (hooks 1989: 38).

As black and Asian women's critical writing explicated the failures of 'white'
feminism, these feminist critics instituted both the study and the teaching of
BME women's writing. Fiction and memoirs by BME women giving voice to
their different stories began to be included on course syllabuses in universities,
and BME women themselves moved into the academy to take up teaching positions. All this served to legitimise the critical examination of BME women's
place in UK feminism, as well as their experience as non-white women in sexist
culture more broadly. By the time the second wave moved into the third, with
its changed considerations of sex positivity and the ideas of queer, a distinct,
ethnically diverse perspective had been established within feminism, if not
entirely assimilated into mainstream discussions. I will look at the effect of the
third wave on issues of ethnicity later in this chapter (see 'Postcolonialism and
the new wave of BME British writers') and consider the extent to which the
issue was explored and prioritised in the 1990s and 2000s, and what difference
this has made to BME writers and to women in UK culture within feminism's
current, fourth wave.

Case study 5.1 Feminist publishing's role in BME women's writing

The UK publisher for bell hooks's influential early writing on ethnicity and feminism was Sheba, one of the feminist publishing houses established in the UK during the second wave (for more on the second-wave feminist publishing phenomenon, see Chapter 1). Many of the most important texts by and about BME women writers were published by these feminist presses in the 1970s and 1980s – without them, the discourse around BME women's inclusion in feminism would not have been articulated. BME feminist perspectives fed into, and were fed by, the feminist publishing houses during the second wave.

Sheba was established in 1980 to 'give priority to the work of women writers who continue to be marginalized'.* Sheba boasted important BME authors such as hooks, Audre Lorde and Barbara Burford, and its output included writing describing a wide range of BME communities. Alongside Sheba, The Women's Press became very much associated with BME women writers during the 1980s, thanks not in small part to its publication of Alice Walker's smash hit *The Color Purple* (1983). Indeed, the success of Walker's novel enabled the publication of a raft of other BME writing by The Women's Press. Sales of *The Color Purple*, particularly after the release of Steven Spielberg's film version of the book, secured The Women's Press's financial health throughout the 1980s, helping it increase its visibility and securing both its financial future and greater exposure for future titles.

The Women's Press, and its publisher Ros de Lanerolle in particular, became increasingly identified with a commitment to BME women writers. As Angela Neustatter reported in 1988:

> The collection now includes such impressive black British writers as Joan Riley and Merle Collins, and Ros de Lanerolle is publishing the first novel by a Zimbabwean woman for the [Press's tenth] anniversary. There are writings from India, Iran, Algeria, Central America, Canada and China. She says: 'I believe we now have one of the most international lists in publishing. Now it is important to hear what women with different experiences and from different cultures have to say.' (Neustatter 1988)

Yet in spite of The Women's Press's reputation as a champion of BME women's writing, it was in fact Virago that published the greatest number of texts exploring the issue of ethnicity in feminism and in wider culture.

---

* 'About Sheba Feminist Press', Maryland Institute for Technology in the Humanities <http://www.mith2.umd.edu/WomensStudies/ReferenceRoom/Publications/about-sheba-press.html> (accessed 14 July 2005) (para. 4 of 10).

Its lists during the 1980s show that Virago 'sustained a commitment to publishing Black and Asian women's writing, both fiction and non-fiction' (Scanlon and Swindells 1994: 43). Virago published Maya Angelou's *I Know Why the Caged Bird Sings* (1984) a year after Walker's novel, and reprinted Angelou's text five times in its first year. This text helped secure Virago's fortunes in the same way as *The Color Purple* had for The Women's Press. In 1988, as Virago celebrated its fifteenth birthday, it was its all-time bestselling book. And as with The Women's Press, Virago also published fiction and poetry from a range of BME women, including Paule Marshall, Grace Paley, Grace Nichols, Rosa Guy and Bharati Mukherjee.

There was a concerted effort by the feminist publishers through the 1980s to broaden their output to include a range of BME voices. Alongside novels, memoirs and non-fiction titles proliferated, helping establish an ethnically diverse feminist perspective. It was not until The Women's Press, Sheba, Virago and the rest had proved there was an eager market for BME women's writing that the mainstream publishing houses followed suit. (The only surviving feminist press from this period, Virago, has sustained this effort. It has continued to expand its lists of BME writing, so that it published twice as many books by BME women during the 2010s than in the previous decade.) Virago publisher Lennie Goodings recalled in interview the challenges posed by this issue: 'We were trying to sell Maya Angelou to some bookshops in Belfast and they said they didn't have any black readers. Now that was a shock [. . .] that sense that only black people will read black writing' (8 November 2004). Her anecdote points to the economics of ethnicity in the book industry: BME women (as writers and readers) were not considered a profitable 'market' until the feminist publishing houses had proven otherwise. The profits generated by Angelou's book for Virago, as well as Walker's for The Women's Press, stood as evidence that in spite of Goodings' experiences in Belfast, BME women's writing had huge appeal.

So the feminist presses helped redress the white bias of the early women's movement, and the double prejudice that BME women faced in the attempt to get their writing published. Virago's co-founder Ursula Owen concedes that feminism was culpable for not addressing the issue of ethnicity head-on earlier in its history: 'we concentrated too heavily on the experience of white women [. . .] black women have felt excluded from the account, [but we're] conscious too of the difficulties for a largely white women's press in getting such publishing right' (Owen in Owen 1988: 94). This admission points to another important obstacle for BME women writers: most of the women employed in publishing – feminist or otherwise – were white. With the exception of Sheba, a dedicated BME press, the business of producing books was one dominated by white men and women, as US feminist theorist and publisher Barbara Smith pointed out: 'too often we were required to fight with the white women, who had begun and/or controlled these publications, in order to get what we believed into print' (Smith in Rush and Allen 1989: 203). There was therefore a need for BME women to enter the industry itself in order to mark out their different perspectives.

Again, the second-wave UK feminist publishing houses played a central role in redressing the absence of BME women from their industry. Lennie Goodings and Ros de Lanerolle, along with writer/publisher Margaret Busby, founded Greater Access to Publishing, a group that campaigned for greater diversity across the industry, in an attempt to accelerate this inclusion of BME women. Virago pushed a BME woman through its own ranks – 'Melanie Silgardo at Virago is a one-up on The Women's Press' (Ahmad 1991: 11) – and it was agreed that, by the end of the 1980s, 'feminist writing and publishing, though still overwhelmingly weighted in favour of more privileged groups, is coming to reflect a wider view' (Chester and Nielsen 1987: 15). The result of feminist publishing's engagement with ethnicity was that 'black women made increasing inroads into the world of publishing. While still forming a miniscule minority, individual black women began to acquire positions of political influence' (Lovenduski and Randall 1993: 104). The second-wave feminist publishing phenomenon was key to the institution of a BME perspective in feminism, as well as in publishing itself.

Postcolonialism and the new wave of BME British writers

As feminism moved out of its second wave and into its third, there was a renewed engagement with issues of ethnicity and a growing sense that UK feminism must include not only the perspectives of BME writers in the UK but also a more global view. As Western women in the 1990s increasingly came to reject the label 'feminist' (even while espousing feminist ideas and beliefs), UK feminists pointed out the contrast with women in developing nations, who remained systematically disadvantaged in terms of their education, health, safety, and social and sexual freedoms. In the academy there emerged new 'postcolonial' theoretical positions, arising from critic Edward Said's observation that developing nations and former colonies of Empire were represented as 'other', as different-to-Western culture (Said 1978, 1993). There was a new interest in and focus on representing different national and cultural contexts, particularly through literature, although also in music, art and drama. As these postcolonial theories and postcolonial art forms were explored in the academy and beyond, feminism was required to think about whom it spoke for when it spoke of 'woman' or 'women', and to figure ethnicity not just in terms of BME women's position in the Western world, but also in terms of the status of non-white, non-Western women globally.

Thus, as with second-wave debates about heterosexual middle-class white women dominating feminism and edging out women of different ethnicities, class or sexualities, the 1990s and 2000s saw a similar troubling of a unifying figure around which feminism could organise. Postcolonial feminist critics pointed out that the privilege of a First World perspective and Western women's apathy about feminism was in fact partly predicated on a system that served to maintain the poverty and inequality of women in the developing world. Gayatri Spivak's 1985 essay 'Can the Subaltern Speak?' arguably led the charge against a feminist (literary) politics that had been blind to issues around ethnicity, and which failed to check the privilege of its heroines whose freedoms were predicated on imperialist power imbalances (Spivak in Lewis and Mills 2003). Spivak defined the 'subaltern' in feminist terms: those populations of women who are socially, politically and geographically outside the hegemonic colonial power structures, and are thus always disempowered, always othered and always spoken *for*. She thus helped institute a postcolonial feminist politics that sought to give such women their voices back and their power to write their own stories. A more global feminism, and a global literary feminism, which paid attention to the history, politics and cultures of the developing world, emerged as the 1990s went on.

Sara Mills was one of small group of British feminists who, from the 1980s, championed a new feminist engagement with postcolonial studies. In her book, *Gender and Colonial Space* (1996), she urged feminists to move further away from the binary construct of 'other' that defined colonial discourse, advocating instead a multilayered approach to ethnic and gendered identity as well as articulating the excessive sexualisation of colonial space relations: white men's power over BME women was complicated by white women's simultaneous power and powerlessness, and the exoticised threat of BME men's sexuality. Later articulations of a postcolonial feminist perspective took on the material inequalities between Western and non-Western women, with critics such as Natasha Walter (1999) describing the need to institute a global feminist perspective that incorporated the different, and urgent, needs of women in the developing world. This global feminism incorporated and, to some extent, prioritised a non-Western perspective while acknowledging that women in developed countries still faced inequalities in their everyday lives. As left-wing politician Oona King described in a collection of feminist essays published at the end of the millennium:

women today make up half the world's population, yet do two thirds of its work, receive only one tenth of its income, and own less than one per cent of world property. To say that women have achieved equality, even on paper, is to dabble in fiction. (King in Walter 1999: 41)

Postcolonial feminism reflected on Western cultures' engagement with global issues such as poverty, religion, ethnicity and belonging: 'it has brought about a "worlding" of mainstream feminist theory; feminist theory has moved from a rather parochial concern with white, middle-class English-speaking women, to a focus on women in different national and cultural contexts' (Mills in Mills and Jones 1998: 98). Anglophone feminism developed into a more global politics of women's rights, one that was complicated by the uncomfortable reality that Western women's freedoms were in part predicated on (post)colonial exploitation of the developing world: 'This is a question that feminism must face: if individual rights come at the price of the negative aspects of globalisation, to what extent should that concept of rights define feminist praxis?' (Heywood and Drake in Gillis et al. 2004: 18).

African author Chimamanda Ngozi Adichie reflected on these ideas in her 2012 TedX talk, later published as a book, entitled *We Should All Be Feminists* (2014). This talk/book has become a phenomenon – partly due it being sampled by Beyonce in her song 'Flawless' – with the TedX talk itself being viewed more than three and a half million times, and the print version becoming a bestseller (in 2015 it was distributed to every sixteen-year-old in Sweden) (Flood 2015). Nigerian-born Adichie articulates the complexities of today's global feminism as well as the continuities of oppressions facing women, no matter where they are in the world. She links together the histories, politics and cultures of Western and developing countries within a narrative that tells of her own coming-to-consciousness as a feminist. Her story is not only an effective illustration of the need for a global feminism, as well as a feminist globalism, it is also a call to arms. We should, indeed, all be feminists.

The articulation of global/postcolonial perspectives in feminism was also reflected in fiction written by women, including Adichie herself, as well as others, such as Andrea Levy and Monica Ali. Ali, a Bangladeshi-born British writer and novelist, published her first novel, *Brick Lane*, in 2003, depicting life in Tower Hamlets, east London, as it is experienced by eighteen-year-old Bangladeshi, Nazneen. She arrives in the UK to marry Chanu, a man twice her age, and the novel explores the ways she adapts to life both as part of the Bangladeshi community and as part of the wider London community. The book became somewhat notorious upon publication as the Bengali community in the real Brick Lane objected to their perceived caricaturing within the story, and organised protests which even went as far as burning copies of the novel. This episode articulates succinctly the range of issues brought up by the intersections of postcolonialism and feminism: Ali was attacked by the BME community of which she is a part for presenting a women's perspective of its sexist, patriarchal limiting of women. In seeking to expose the female experience of being a 'Western' Bengali, she is simultaneously silenced by her own community and exoticised by her white middle-class audience, even while being canonised by them. Ali's experience shows that the status of BME British women writers within both popular and literary cultures is a unique and extremely challenging one.

In contrast to Ali, Andrea Levy was born in the UK to first-generation immigrant parents who had sailed to England on the *Empire Windrush* in 1948. Levy's *Small Island* (2004) fictionalises this experience, telling it from the perspective of a group of Jamaican characters that includes Queenie and Hortense, two women she uses to illustrate the particular problems – and prejudices – black women faced in 1940s England. Not only were they subject to the controlling paradigm of patriarchal power, but they were also further disempowered by powerful racist discourses. The intersection of their gender and their ethnicity has a devastating impact on their own autonomy, and through them Levy shows the different needs and priorities of these women, imposed by their status as poor, black and female. It is inevitable that their relationship to feminism will, too, be different.

Literature such as Levy's and Ali's reflects the shift in the UK towards a more multicultural population. As individuals and communities from Britain's former colonies in Africa and Asia established themselves in London, Manchester, Birmingham and other (mainly urban) areas of the UK, culture changed – including literary culture. First- and second-generation immigrants into the UK articulated their experiences through both fiction and critical writing that explored themes of difference, belonging and, for women writers, gender and sexuality in particular. There was a shift in UK feminism towards greater inclusivity of global and postcolonial perspectives, alongside a mushrooming of novels that told the stories of those who had moved to a new life in Britain, as well as those who stayed behind. However, as noted in the Introduction, there has also been a problematic privileging of certain writers (by both publishers and educators) who are seen to fit an idealising 'multicultural' agenda, and less interest in texts that are less obviously written (and marketed) for white audiences.

A global perspective of ethnicity, alongside poverty and religion, has continued to define contemporary feminism as well as influence the work of contemporary female fiction writers. The seismic effect of the 'Arab spring' demonstrations and protests of 2010–12, in first Tunisia, then Egypt, Libya and many other countries of the Arab League, initially inspired hope among Western feminists that women's rights in these countries might, at last, rise higher up the agenda. But it was to be a short-lived optimism:

> a revolution has come and gone, but done little for Arab women. There are only eight women in Egypt's new 500-seat parliament – and not one female presidential candidate. Domestic violence, forced marriage and female genital mutilation

are still part of the status quo across a region covering more than 20 countries and 350 million people. (Chulov and Hussein 2012)

Consequently, there has been a renewal of engagement by UK feminists with non-Western women's rights, and a more global configuring of the battles that twenty-first-century feminism must fight. Use of online social networks underpins the new global protest movement that has emerged this millennium. Feminism in the UK is now looking outward, incorporating the issues facing women in different countries and cultures into its agenda for change and, as more women from non-Western countries benefit from higher education and come to publish their own books (for example, Kanwal 2015), a more complex understanding of cultural and religious difference is, at last, beginning to emerge. Fourth-wave feminist politics is now a truly global movement, and it can only be a good – as well as a strengthening – thing that women in the UK are fighting not only for their own freedoms, but for the freedoms of women right across the world.

Case study 5.2 Zadie Smith

Zadie Smith burst onto the literary – and cultural – scene in 2000, the perfect product of and for a book marketplace dominated by what Joe Moran has since termed 'star authors' (Moran 2000; see also Fowler 2008). Smith and other young millennial authors (such as Alex Garland and Donna Tartt) were totemic of a new 'cool' literary scene. Smith was young, black and very beautiful, and her writing was bold: it chimed perfectly with the climate of 'girl power' and consumerism that marked the start of the millennium, and that conspired to make her extraordinarily sellable: indeed, a sensation. Smith herself was quick to realise the extent to which her literary success was predicated on the selling of her image, as reported in this interview:

> She tells me about the time she went to do a photo shoot for a magazine and found herself lost in a sprawl of make-up artists, dressers and little Prada dresses that could never have fitted her. 'I wouldn't mind it if I saw five-hour photo shoots for Martin Amis, but that doesn't happen. If you're a woman it's as if they want to reduce everything to the same denominator.' Which is? 'That you must present yourself as an attractive woman even if you're a rocket scientist. It's total arse isn't it?' (Hattenstone 2000)

But in spite of the exploitation of Smith's looks, she has established herself as an important literary voice, distinct from the vagaries of cultural zeitgeists. Following her debut novel, Smith has gone on to create

a body of writing that has explored the themes of ethnicity, multiculturalism, femininity and feminism, making her a significant and influential
writer for the twenty-first century.

Her first novel, *White Teeth* (2000), chronicles the lives of two friends,
Archie Jones and Samad Iqbal, their families, and their wider community
in a suburb of north-west London. Smith uses the characters of English-
man Archie and Bengali Samad, a first-generation immigrant to the UK,
to explore themes of race, belonging and tradition. Both men are married
to much younger women: Archie to second-generation Jamaican Clara,
and Samad to the formidable Alsana in an arrangement made for her,
not by her. These characters, along with the Chalfens – a married Jewish/
Catholic couple – are used to show the blurring of lines between ethnic,
religious and cultural boundaries in the 'melting pot' of London life and
culture.

Smith portrays (or imagines) a multiculturalism that is emblematic of
a new style of BME writing – indeed, it is one that would reject the very
label. Rather than addressing racism or sexism overtly, the text instead
describes a moment in UK culture in which ethnicity is simultaneously a
problem and an irrelevance. In an interview she gave on the novel's publication, Smith describes this vacillation:

> 'I think the relationships in the book are something to be wished for, but
> I think they might exist now, and certainly in the future, with the amount
> of mixing up that has gone on. My generation, and my younger brother's
> generation even more, don't carry the same kind of baggage.' But racial
> prejudice is still a part of daily life, especially in London. She tells me how
> her 16-year-old brother was stopped by the police only two days before.
> (Merritt 2000)

While ethnicity doubtless defines identity, the mixing of cultures, customs
and religions that occurs in a diverse city like London offers the possibility
of blurring – even eroding – these boundaries.

White Teeth is thus 'an epochal novel celebrating the heterogeneity
of British urban society around the millennium' (Tancke in Tew
2013: 28). Smith is simultaneously critical of, and celebratory about,
multiculturalism: on the one hand, her story cheers diversity and the
opportunity London offers for a future free from historical prejudices,
while, on the other it, laments the irretrievable loss of cultural and
national identity. Ultimately, however, *White Teeth* is about the wholeness
of humanity, its title referring to a universal human characteristic that
unites Smith's diverse cast of characters, and which contrasts with the
variegations of their skin colour. The concept of 'white teeth' is also suggestive of wealth and a peculiarly Western signification of success – the

'movie-star smile' – and Smith's book accordingly evidences a preoccupation with appearance. In particular, since it is the appearance of women
that is most often, and most closely, scrutinised in our culture, her novel
contains an analysis of sex and gender alongside that of ethnicity.

Smith uses her female characters to show the ways that ethnicity and
gender intersect. Irie, for example, wishes to 'Westernise' her body – to
attain the culturally imposed ideal of slim and smooth corporeality –
but, in spite of her best efforts, her body shows itself to be irrepressibly
Jamaican (Smith 2000: 265). Conversely, Alsana grows fat precisely to
show Samad that he has no control over her body, and in defiance of both
his individual power and the power of men in general in a patriarchal
society. A preoccupation with (changing) the body runs throughout the
text, and points to the influence of feminist ideas on Smith's writing – the
book was written at the tipping point of what Ariel Levy called 'raunch
culture' (Chapter 3), and Smith was part and product of a culture in which
women's bodies were increasingly becoming objectified and commodified.
Her work, inevitably, reflects this and *White Teeth* can thus be read as
being part of the third-wave critique of sexist culture.

In her second novel, *The Autograph Man* (2002), Smith continues to
interrogate the themes of gender, ethnicity, consumer culture and celebrity: 'Smith's engagement with popular culture reveals much about the
highly mediated identities of contemporary individuals and how they
are shaped and defined in the postmodern era' (Parker in Tew 2013: 69).
The character of Alex-Li mediates his life through popular culture, and
is irresistibly drawn to celebrity (indeed, he makes a living from trading
celebrities' signatures), finding it easier to live out imagined intimacies
with famous people than commit to a real one. His fascination with Kitty,
a Russian-American actress who has made her name acting as a Chinese
character, is hugely disruptive of assumptions around ethnicity and authenticity, and Smith also uses Kitty to explore the sexualised 'othering'
of different ethnic identities. *The Autograph Man* thus contrasts ideas of
cultural authenticity and celebrity fakery. Through the character of Honey,
Smith contests Alex-Li's idolatry of celebrity. Honey points out the reality
of movie-making, describing the degrading and disconnecting aspects of
fame in her depictions of the bit-part players who 'sell out' to make it in
Hollywood. Honey is, tellingly, the most 'real' person in *The Autograph
Man*, whose feminist critique of consumerism, self-presentation and the
quest for fame interrogates the foundations of legitimacies of all kinds.

On Beauty (2005) is set between a US academic town and London
(again), thus allowing Smith to unpick some of the different issues around
ethnicity in the UK and the US. The book is focused, too, on the construction and imposition of female beauty ideals, with the three women with

whom the main character, Howard, has sexual relationships embodying different stereotypes of the feminine ideal. Kiki, Howard's wife, is full-bodied and maternal, while Claire, with whom he commits his first act of infidelity, is white and slim. It is this aspect of her physicality that Kiki finds so distressing on discovering Howard's affair. Smith uses this to show us that the cultural imposition of a thin ideal transcends discourses around skin colour – all women are subject to the fat-shaming that is so much part of the twenty-first-century policing of women's bodies. Victoria, who seduces Howard later in the story, is young and curvy and beautiful and black; she is depicted as the ultimate siren, Smith's ironic taking-down of the colonial construction of the dangerous, exotic Jezebel. The book also mocks the world of academics and intellectuals – surely a rebuke against the snobbery with which Smith's writing was greeted within the academy, and with which her work has been often dismissed. Smith uses Kiki's view of her husband's pomposity and infidelity to deride academic posturing, continuing a noble tradition of feminist attack against the male 'gate-keepers' who would strive to exclude women's writing from serious – and canonical – consideration.

Finally, in her 2012 novel NW, Smith destabilises and disrupts a range of ethnic and sexual stereotypes. Her story, once again located in London, depicts successful lawyer Natalie, a black wife and mother who has all the trappings of middle-class suburban success – and is accordingly accused in the narrative of being a 'coconut': brown on the outside but white inside. Yet Natalie is also a sexual predator, meeting strangers for sex using her 'black' name and birthplace as part of this clandestine identity. Natalie's friend Leah, in contrast, is white, somewhat feckless and smokes marijuana – she embodies all the characteristics, in short, of the clichéd young black man. She, too, harbours a secret, deliberately preventing any chance of an apparently longed-for pregnancy. Both Leah and Natalie are trapped by the social structures allotted them by their gender. Neither wants to play the role of devoted sexual partner, and both have troubled relationships with the institutions of marriage and motherhood. Through them, Smith explores the ways in which women struggle with construct-ing their own identities in the face of powerful discourses around ethnic and sexual stereotypes. In NW, as in all her fiction, her female characters show the artificiality of the social and psychological constructs of wife/mother/sex object as discussed in Chapter 2, and the ways that the ethnic and sexual aspects of women's identities are used to contain them.

Bibliography

Ahmad, Rukhsana. 1991. 'What's Happening to the Women's Presses?' In *Spare Rib*, issue 223, May.

Chester, Gail and Sigrid Neilsen (eds). 1987. *In Other Words: Writing as a Feminist*. London: Hutchinson.

Christian, Barbara. 1980. *Black Women Novelists: The Development of a Tradition 1892–1976*. Westport: Greenwood Press.

Chulov, Martin and Rahman Hussein. 2012. 'After the Arab Spring, the Sexual Revolution?' In *The Guardian*, 27 April.

Collins, Patricia Hill. 1990. *Black Feminist Thought: Knowledge, Consciousness and the Politics of Empowerment*. New York: Routledge.

Coote, Anna and Beatrix Campbell. 1987. *Sweet Freedom: The Struggle for Women's Liberation*. Oxford: Basil Blackwell.

Evans, Mari (ed.). 1985. *Black Women Writers: Arguments and Interviews*. London: Pluto Press.

Flood, Alison. 2015. 'Every 16-Year-Old in Sweden to Receive a Copy of *We Should All Be Feminists*'. In *The Guardian*, 4 December.

Fowler, Corinne. 2008. 'A Tale of Two Novels: Developing a Devolved Approach to Black British Writing'. In *Journal of Commonwealth Literature*, 43:3, pp. 75–84.

Gillis, Stacey, Gillian Howe and Rebecca Munford (eds). 2004. *Third Wave Feminism: A Critical Exploration*. New York: Palgrave MacMillan.

Hattenstone, Simon. 2000. 'White Knuckle Ride'. In *The Guardian*, 11 December.

hooks, bell. 1982. *Ain't I a Woman? Black Women and Feminism*. London: Pluto Press.

hooks, bell. 1989. *Talking Back: Thinking Feminist – Thinking Black*. Boston: Sheba.

Jackson, Stevi and Jackie Jones (eds). 1998. *Contemporary Feminist Theories*. Edinburgh: Edinburgh University Press.

Kanwal, Aroosa. 2015. *Rethinking Identities in Contemporary Pakistani Fiction: Beyond 9/11*. Basingstoke: Palgrave Macmillan.

Levy, Andrea. 2004. *Small Island*. London: Headline.

Lewis, Reina and Sara Mills (eds). 2003. *Feminist Postcolonial Theory: A Reader*. London: Routledge.

Lovenduski, Joni and Vicky Randall. 1993. *Contemporary Feminist Politics: Women and Power in Britain*. Oxford: Oxford University Press.

Merritt, Stephanie. 2000. 'She's Young, Black, British – and the First Publishing Sensation of the Millennium'. In *The Guardian*, 16 January.

Mills. Sara. 1996. *Gender and Colonial Space*. Manchester: Manchester University Press.

Mills, Sara and Jackie Jones (eds). 1998. *Contemporary Feminist Theories*. Edinburgh: Edinburgh University Press.

Mirza, Heidi Safia (ed.) 1997. *Black British Feminism: A Reader*. London: Routledge.

Moran, Joe. 2000. *Star Authors: Literary Celebrity in America*. London: Pluto Press.

Neustatter, Angela. 1988. 'A Cause for Celebration'. In *The Guardian*, 13 April.

Owen, Peter (ed.). 1988. *Publishing – The Future*. London: Peter Owen Publishers.

Phillips, Anne. 1987. *Divided Loyalties: Dilemmas of Sex and Class*. London: Virago.

Riley, Joan. 1985. *The Belonging*. London: The Women's Press.

Rush, Ramona and Donna Allen (eds). 1989. *Communications At the Crossroads: The Gender Gap Connection*. Norwood: Ablex Publishing.

Said, Edward. 1978. *Orientalism*. London: Penguin. (1973)

Said, Edward. 1993. *Culture and Imperialism*. London: Vintage.

Scanlon, Jean and Julia Swindells. 1994. 'Bad Apple'. In *Trouble and Strife*, 28 (spring).

Showalter, Elaine. 1985. *The Female Malady*. London: Virago.

Smith, Zadie. 2000. *White Teeth*. London: Hamish Hamilton.

Smith, Zadie. 2002. *The Autograph Man*. London: Hamish Hamilton.

Smith, Zadie. 2012. *NW*. London: Hamish Hamilton.

Tew, Philip. 2010. *New British Fiction: Zadie Smith*. Basingstoke: Palgrave Macmillan.

Tew, Philip. 2013. *Reading Zadie Smith: The First Decade and Beyond*. London: Bloomsbury.

Walker, Alice. 1983. *The Color Purple*. London: The Women's Press.

Walter, Natasha (ed.). 1999. *On the Move: Feminism for a New Generation*. London: Virago.

Washington, Mary Helen. 1989. *Invented Lives: Narratives of Black Women 1860–1960*. London: Virago.

Wisker, Gina. 1993. *Black Women's Writing*. Basingstoke: Macmillan.

Part II. Genres

6 Romance

Part II of the book explores the effect of feminism on the *form* of women's literature, beginning with romance in this chapter. Feminist investigation into, and employment of, different literary modes, genres and narrative styles has created a rich library of fiction and criticism that has expanded the boundaries of the English canon. The derogation of certain genres of writing as 'low' literary forms – including romance writing – has historically been used as a way of disregarding women's writing. Indeed, the sexism endemic in the review tradition (see Chapter 1) meant critics once categorised *all* women's writing as 'romance', and therefore as inferior in literary terms. Prior to feminism's first wave, many great female novelists – the Brontë sisters and George Eliot among them – adopted male pseudonyms in order to have their work taken seriously, rather than dismissed as mere romantic entertainment, and therefore frivolous. Jane Austen, now regarded as one of the greatest English novelists, was derided by US poet and essayist Ralph Waldo Emerson. In a journal entry for 1861 he bemoaned the fact that all anyone in her books cared about was money and marriage:

> I am at a loss to understand why people hold Miss Austen's novels at so high a rate, which seems to me vulgar in tone, sterile in artistic invention, imprisoned in their wretched conventions of English society, without genius, wit or knowledge of the world. Never was life so pinched and so narrow [. . .] Suicide is more respectable. (Porte 1982: 495)

I will look in this chapter at the lasting influence this pigeonholing of women's writing as second-rate 'romance' has had, focusing in particular on recent feminist theorising of women readers' consumption of popular romance fiction (especially under the Mills and Boon and Harlequin imprints, or what's now commonly referred to as 'chick lit'), as well as the recent feminist re-scriptings of romantic love.

In the early twentieth century, the modernist movement featured the first literary interrogation of the genre as well as of the concept of romantic love itself. Women writers such as Virginia Woolf and Dorothy Richardson developed new literary experiments – 'stream of consciousness' techniques, for example – to capture the subjective and emotional lives of their characters. Alongside this, there was a freeing up of the structures informing romantic love, as Woolf and the other writers that made up 'Bloomsbury set' to which she belonged imagined – and lived out – new romantic practices, including lesbian and bisexual relationships and what we would now refer to as 'polyamory' (relationships involving more than two people).

Later in the century, second-wave feminism brought a new, hard-nosed scrutiny to romantic love (and, indeed, the family structures associated with it), with commentators like Germaine Greer (1970) and Shulamith Firestone (1976) determined to expose romantic love as a pernicious 'ideology' that should be resisted at all costs. Within literary studies, the feminist re-appraisal of romance writing was spearheaded by the American critics Janice Radway (1984) and Tania Modleski (1982), and developed into more complex/pluralised discussions by critics such as Catherine Belsey (2003), Lynne Pearce (1994, 1997, 2007) and Pamela Regis (2003) over the next two decades. These critics reinvested romantic fiction (and its readers) with interest and value, while female novelists took on the conventions of the romance narrative to write new, feminist versions of the love story.

The publication of texts that took on narratological and other conventions of the form and destabilised them was a notable aspect of this effort to reclaim the romance – and, indeed, *all* genre fiction – from its classification as 'low-brow' or at best 'middle-brow' literature. As Anne Cranny-Francis observed in her ground-breaking survey of feminist genre fiction in 1990:

> Generic fiction, characterised as feminine by a masculinist (political, psychological, artistic) establishment, is now being transformed by feminist ideology. Rather than rejecting the mass culture to which they were relegated (and which, as female, was relegated to them), feminist writers have embraced it, seeing its characteristic popularity as a powerful tool for their own propagandist purposes. (Cranny-Francis 1990: 5)

Women writers thus self-consciously appropriated the formal properties and styles of romantic genre fiction in order to recast the traditional love story as one with literary value as well as feminist potential. Alongside critical (re) formulations, women writers began to use the conventions of the romance genre to portray strong, independent images of women and new conceptions of romantic unions. This is evidenced in the fiction of Margaret Atwood, Angela Carter, Michèle Roberts, Alice Walker, Janet Frame, Jeanette Winterson and many other important female writers of the 1980s and 1990s. There was also a growing recognition that, no matter how problematic, 'falling in love' was a life event that few of us would escape. As feminist publisher Ursula Owen argued: 'if love, friendship, birth, death, work, travel, affection comprise a limited world, it is a ghetto many of us would choose to live in' (Owen in Owen 1988: 92). Consequently, concerted efforts were made by both authors and critics to revision the 'boy (or girl) meets girl (or boy)' story as feminist ideology intersected with the oldest story ever told: the love story.

Reinventing the generic romance

There is, for most of us, pleasure in reading a love story. Yet the correlation of *women readers* with romantic narratives – one traditionally employed by hostile critics in order to denigrate *women writers* – is firmly established in literary culture. However, while this stereotyping is regrettable, it does contain a kernel of truth: women readers *do* consume romance stories in much greater numbers than men, with mass-consumption series such as the Harlequin and Mills and Boon franchises, and the more recent 'chick-lit' genre, evidencing a hunger among women for stories about love. Understanding the reasons for this appetite, and analysing women readers' relationships with the romance genre, thus constituted an important political undertaking as second-wave feminism threw a spotlight on the problematic aspects of women's actual, 'real life' love stories and their representation in fiction.

Rachel Brownstein theorised the ways that women readers have historically been encouraged to identify with the romantic narratives of female literary characters, arguing that 'the idea of becoming a heroine marries the female protagonist to the marriage plot, and it marries the woman who reads to fiction' (Brownstein 1984: xvi). She argues that the marriage plot in romance fiction makes explicit the coexistence of sexuality and morality within patriarchal discourse – the two are inextricably bound together. Brownstein also argues, however, that women can escape this limited and limiting destiny *through* literature, both by theorising escape through feminist literary criticism and by imagining new freedoms in reading, writing and *living* different romance stories.

During the 1980s, feminist critics Tania Modleski and Janice Radway undertook a radical reassessment of the worth and significance of the popular romance genre from the perspective of women readers. Modleski proposed that formulaic romance fiction offered women an escape into a fantasy world where they are not restricted by the gendered inequalities they experience in real life. Moreover, when reading romance, women readers proactively impose their own agendas and desires on the characters in the texts, and are therefore able to assume a position of superiority over both the 'hero' and 'heroine' and the outcome of the story: 'since she knows the formula, she is superior in wisdom to the heroine and thus detached from her' (Modleski 1982: 41). Modleski further argued that women's satisfaction in romance reading is often predicated upon a revenge fantasy: the woman reader shares the satisfaction enjoyed by the woman in the text as she brings the man to his knees – a process she provocatively named 'taming the beast' (Modleski 1982). This satisfaction is heightened by the reader's command of a narrative that, in contrast to the female character in the book, she *does* have the authority to direct and control.

Nevertheless, the popularity of 'bonkbuster' novels (by the likes of Jilly Cooper, Shirley Conran and Jackie Collins), as well as the mass-produced Mills and Boon/Harlequin fantasies that Modleski and Radway interrogated, remained troubling for feminism as a political movement, since the texts' storylines were so at odds with the quest to break down traditional, and limiting, (hetero)sexual roles. Even allowing for an increasingly complex theorisation of the role of the woman reader's empowerment when consuming such texts, it is hard not to regard it as an essentially 'escapist' pleasure:

> There's a large middle market to be tapped of intelligent, broadly feminist women who resent having to suspend their political views for the sake of a rollicking read, yet who are addicted to the traditional blockbuster. Who has not, be they the staunchest hardliner, plunged into a sex and shopping saga between chapters of *Sexual Politics*, says Alexandra Pringle [then managing director of Bloomsbury Press], 'I've always enjoyed reading Celia Brayfield, Shirley Conran, Jilly Cooper and so on, and there are a lot of intelligent women in demanding jobs who go home at night and watch *Dallas* or read something completely relaxing. It's like an anaesthetic. (Briscoe 1990)

What such 'confessions' seem to confirm is that the romance novel has long been a panacea to women's real-life struggles.

Janice Radway, meanwhile, argued that romance fiction acts as a means by which women are able to fulfil their psychic and emotional needs – needs that are not met in their everyday lives: 'romance reading, it appeared, addressed needs, desires, and wishes that a male partner could not' (Radway 1984: 13). Radway regarded the consumption of generic romances as a means of private, self-focused pleasure for women, 'the opportunity to experience the kind of care and attention they commonly give to others' (Radway 1984: 100). She also observed that romance reading is a way of women seeking – and finding – solidarity with one another in ways that may be thought of as feminist. She did not, however, deny that fantasy was central to this communal pleasure:

> all romantic fiction originates in the failure of patriarchal culture to satisfy its female members. Consequently, the romance functions always as a utopian wish-fulfilment fantasy through which women try to imagine themselves as they often are not in day-to-day existence, that is, as happy and content. (Radway 1984: 151)

Working closely with a focus group of female popular romance readers in the US, Radway was also able to discover which aspects of the typical popular romance novel gave most pleasure, and she came to the fascinating – if disturbing – conclusion that the readers discovered in the 'explanations' for the hero's initial emotional coldness and 'bad' (sometimes violent) behaviour a means of exonerating their own flawed husbands and partners (Radway 1984).

As feminism entered its third wave, British and American feminists argued even more strongly for the romance text being a site of proactive exploration and resistance as well as the locus of a discourse that none of us can escape. Stevi Jackson, for example, employed psychoanalytic theory to demonstrate the way in which romance narratives determine our understanding of 'love' and are integral to the way in which we experience our 'real life' relationships (Jackson 1999). However, while such constructions of romantic love may be problematic in that they make women complicit in patriarchal power dynamics, knowledge of the way in which the discourse functions (through literary and media representations, for example) facilitates a re-scripting of how we might prefer to conduct our intimate relationships (Pearce and Wisker 1997). Thus, through their engagement with romance as *readers*, women may be seen to proactively generate new ways of 'doing romance' (Pearce 2007: 1) in 'real life'.

One of the main issues with (hetero-normative) romance for feminists has, of course, been the way in which it naturalises male conquest and female submission. However, as noted above, Radway observed a very different gender dynamic at work in the consumption of the texts: namely, that women readers formed particular identifications or relationships with the female protagonists in the texts and also felt supported by the community of female romance readers of which they were a part. In the 1990s, Lynne Pearce theorised the reading process in general in a similar way by suggesting that the relationship between the reader and the text may be thought of as a kind of love story. Looking at the special relationships that can develop between women readers and female-authored texts (including romances), in particular, she drew upon Mikhail Bakhtin's work to argue that such reading can (on occasion) take the form of a 'conspiratorial dialogue' between women. Following Bakhtin's work on intonation, she demonstrates how intimate communication between individuals always depends upon the existence of an addressee capable of decoding not simply the verbal component of the speech act but also the speaker's tone of voice and various other contextual factors that both parties are familiar with (possibly to the exclusion of others).

Pearce identified a conspiratorial tone – 'gender-specific subtleties of intonation and extra-verbal context' – in spoken communications between women (Pearce 1997: 74) and proposed that a similar dynamic may exist between women readers and certain texts. Elsewhere, Pearce also distinguished between reader activity and reader *inter*activity and argued that it is the latter that is required for a fully emotional engagement with the text, and grants women's writing its galvanising, even revolutionising potential for women readers. The exclusivity of address from woman writer to woman reader thus becomes a potent symbol of female bonding:

> this, I suggest, is why many of us choose to read women-authored texts for our pleasure: it is not simply that they focus on themes and issues that relate to our 'experience' as women but that they address themselves to us (either literally or analogously, through the surrogate presence of a female interlocutor in the text). (Pearce 1994: 106)

Pearce's theory, like Modleski's and Radway's, foregrounds the role of the female reader in actively constructing a text's meaning – and doing so in ways that can be empowering. Such reframing of the text–reader relationship is essential if we are to fully understand the enduring appeal of the romance genre and rescue it from its traditional figuring as a 'low' art form and as demeaning to women. Further, the focus on text–reader interactivity helps us appreciate the extent to which the fantasies that fuel romance are effectively *co-authored* – and hence subject to a radical revisioning on the reader's part. Such revisioning of both the romance genre and romantic love itself is found across a wide spectrum of contemporary women's writing. Some of these texts may present themselves as love stories; others – like Toni Morrison's *Beloved*, to which I now turn – are rarely thought of in those terms, but engage with romantic discourse in powerful and thought-provoking ways.

Case study 6.1 Changing the romantic narrative – *Beloved*

Toni Morrison's Pulitzer Prize-winning novel *Beloved* (1987) exemplifies the feminist project of restaging the romance narrative in ways that illuminate women's experiences and seek to empower them to live differently. Her novel contains a powerful retelling of multiple love stories: the love between a woman and a man, a woman and her children, and a woman and herself. Morrison uses her narrative to explore the meaning of these love bonds as they are experienced by her character Sethe, whose gender, race and poverty intersect in specific and, for her, catastrophic ways. Through Sethe, Morrison evokes the motif of 'love conquers all' that is familiar from romance novels, but subverts this narrative by showing, through Sethe's relationships, that love can be a prison, as well as an escape. Although Sethe's relationship with Paul D, which I will explore shortly, is shown to survive in spite of a series of terrible and troubling events – a classic romantic narrative – it is not only this love story that makes Morrison's novel such a rich restaging. Her book also evokes the trope of a doomed romantic fable, as Sethe and Beloved seek to escape from the bonds of the 'mother love' that serves only to deny them their freedom.

Beloved is set in the 1860s and begins in Sethe's home in Cincinnati, Ohio, a place filled with 'a baby's venom' (Morrison 1987: 3). We learn that Sethe, a former slave, is living with the ghost of her infant daughter, whose life she took when she was recaptured by the slave owners from whom she had temporarily fled seventeen years previously. In desperation, Sethe had cut her daughter's throat, preferring to have her die than to return her to the brutality of her imprisoners: '"I stopped him," she said, staring at the place where the fence used to be. "I took and put my babies where they'd be safe"' (Morrison 1987: 164). The 'ghost' of her daughter is enraged by Paul D's arrival in Sethe's life, as a jealous lover would be, and seeks to drive him away: the first indication of her displeasure comes with her rocking the house's very foundations. This sets the dynamic between Sethe's daughter and Paul D, as rivals for Sethe's love – a rivalry that can be ended only by death. In all these ways, *Beloved* takes on the classic narratives of the questing romance novel, but with a cast of very different characters.

Evoking these romantic narratives gives Morrison's novel a strange familiarity, even as it tells a horrific tale of barbarity, racism and enslavement. Morrison successfully uses a formal structure commonly employed to explore the 'highest' human emotions – love, passion, desire – and also to depict the very worst of human nature. She situates her portrayal of Sethe's love for her daughter, and for Paul D, within a broader portrayal of America's history of slavery and racism, using the dynamism and familiarity of the love story to drive her messages about the multiple oppressions faced by poor black women, historically and in the present.

The cast of characters in *Beloved* is thus simultaneously unique and universal. Sethe is in many ways the 'everywoman' of black slave narratives, the brutalised and downtrodden object put to economic and sexual use by men. But Morrison uses the formula of the slave narrative, along with the conventions of the romance genre and even the ghost story, to tell a remarkable new tale. Sethe's eventual redemption, following Beloved's physical incarnation and return, is arrived at through a kind of reliving of the moment of her daughter's death: this time, however, Sethe tries to kill the white man and not her daughter. It is the intervention of the community of black women that saves her from living another terrible fate, Morrison thus intimating that the real 'hero' in her story is not Paul D, not even an individual, but all the brave, unbending women who collectively survive, together.

Feminist literary critics have explored Morrison's presentation of women's cooperation and mutual support in her novel. *Beloved* is part of the feminist project of foregrounding women's experiences of historical events, a counterpoint to the chronicling of men's experiences that is offered as 'history'. *Beloved* also addresses the themes of vengeance and the psychology of loss. Sethe's grief for her daughter is so powerful that it shuts out life, her other children living in the shadow of this terrible loss. The past is continually present, and the climactic exorcism of Beloved comes when Paul D's arrival signals hope of moving on to a new present. Sethe must make peace with her past in order to move into this new life, and through this Morrison's narrative takes on the history of black women's oppression in North American history and posits forgiveness, not vengeance, as the route to a better future.

Paul D's return to Sethe at the novel's end does, however, fulfil the conventions of the love story's happy ending. Throughout the novel, Paul D's gentleness is emphasised, although his seduction by Beloved temporarily reduces him to the role of weak, lustful man. It is also the moment when he relives the horrors of his own past, Morrison thereby showing that black men's sexuality, too, was limited and limiting under the terrible strictures of slavery. Paul D's masculinity is analogous to that of the thrusting romantic hero, but Morrison shows that his 'manliness' and inscrutability are in reality the manifestation of a life ruled by others. Paul D's sense of identity is always at odds with his past as someone else's property. His feelings for Sethe are always intersected with their shared past as slaves, their bodies as well as their minds scarred by this mutual history. Love really does conquer all in Paul D's return to Sethe, which marks an overcoming of not only the obstacles between them as individuals, but also the obstacles they share as part of black America's oppressed history.

Ultimately, however, it is not Paul D's love for Sethe, but rather his teaching her to love herself, that is the real happy ending of the story: '"You your best thing, Sethe. You are"' (Morrison 1987: 273). Morrison's reuniting of these two lovers fulfils the formula of the romance narrative – as readers we experience the vicarious pleasure of Sethe and Paul D being reunited, following Radway's and Modleski's theories of the romance genre's appeal – but it is not quite the end of the story. In the final chapter, the author reveals that Sethe has taken control of her own narrative, and that her love for her daughter endures. Sethe's life moves forward, and independently of her lover she has made peace with her past, and been empowered. This is the radical restaging that Morrison achieves in the telling of Sethe's love stories, and *Beloved* succeeds in showing the complex, multiple layers of a woman's experience of love, in all its forms.

The rise of 'chick lit'

Following the feminist critical reformulation of the romance narrative as potentially liberating for women readers, the 1990s saw the rise of a new phenomenon – 'chick lit' – which has since become embedded in literary culture. Arising in part from a new emphasis in publishing on both the look of a book and the (sex) appeal of its author, chick lit also benefited from the theoretical reassessment of romantic narratives by Modleski, Radway, Pearce et al., which had given women readers 'permission' to indulge their enjoyment of this kind of storytelling.

Chick lit came to exist, and proliferate, as publishers saw the commercial potential of repackaging the romance genre and marketing it to a new readership of urban, employed, successful and independent women. Powerful marketing and publicity combined to drive demand for these female-authored romance narratives that nodded to contemporary concerns – workplace stress, balancing public and private life – while allowing women to indulge in the old-fashioned escapism of a classic romance novel. Through the 1980s and 1990s distinct visual shorthands emerged for this kind of literature, evidenced in the conformity of its appearance – the thick, glossy metallic colours that had defined 1980s design were replaced with 'sweetie-coloured' covers in pastel shades which identified a book as a woman's text (Colgan 2001). The packaging of women's writing in such 'feminine' tones – pink having become *the* shorthand for femininity in the last twenty years – is now firmly established: 'there are gazillions of books available and something has to help you decide. Loud shades of pink seem to help and increasingly chick-lit books sparkle with sequins and gemstones on the cover' (Groskop 2011). The chick lit 'look' has even spread to a rebranding of canonical classics, now assimilable under this new shorthand: 'earlier this year Penguin brought forward the publication of its Red Classics editions of Jane Austen to get ahead of Headline, which has since given *Pride and Prejudice* a horrible chick-lit-style cover in pretty pastels' (Cooke 2006).

Chick lit writer Jenny Colgan attributes the rise of chick lit directly to feminism, and in particular the impact of feminism's discourses around sex and empowerment:

> We really are the first generation who grew up with education as a right; with financial independence; with living on our own and having far too many choices about getting married (while watching our baby boomer parents fall apart), having children (while watching our elder sisters run themselves ragged trying to do everything) and hauling ourselves up through the glass ceiling. (Colgan 2001)

She argues that chick lit satisfies a desire in younger women to see themselves authentically represented in fiction, rather than a reinstatement of patriarchal ideas of appropriate femininity. She also points out that the tag 'chick lit' is often used as a catch-all moniker for (young) women's writing, a sexist dismissal that continues the long tradition of women's writing being labelled as romance and thus disregarded.

The Ur-text of the chick lit genre is Helen Fielding's 1996 novel *Bridget Jones's Diary*, one of the 1990s' bestsellers, with eight million copies sold worldwide in its first decade, and the book translated into thirty-three languages (Ferris and Young 2006). The novel's very success troubled the boundaries between literary and popular fiction, with some critics dismissing it as low-brow 'chick lit' but others arguing that its very popularity required it to be examined as a culturally important novel. In addition, it became central to discussions of third-wave and post-feminism, and the end-of-the-millennium questioning of what empowered womanhood looked like. Bridget Jones represented the growing number of young women who refused to compromise in their search for a partner:

a woman who chooses to be single and live without a man is making a political decision, consciously or unconsciously, because it's saying that she won't share her life with a man unless he's good enough, or unless, on some level, he accepts her as she is. (Viner in Walter 1999: 25)

Sales figures and film franchise aside, the novel is many things: a classic romance narrative, a none-too-subtle reworking of Jane Austen's *Pride and Prejudice*, a confessional novel for the postmodern age, and also a chronicle of one woman's obsession with her physical appearance and search for Mr Right. These two aspirations – to be thin and to be in a relationship – seem uncomplicatedly 'not-feminist', and *Bridget Jones's Diary* has duly been critiqued for simplistically reinforcing such narratives of what successful femininity looks like. Yet Bridget and her friends are all career women, living independent and ostensibly fulfilling lives. *Bridget Jones's Diary* was written in, and came out of, a commodity-obsessed culture of consumption, and it is its ironic treatment of life-as-consumption that complicates any classification of the text as non-feminist. The pervasiveness of consumer culture's messages, and the discourse of spurious 'empowerment' that underlies many of these messages, means that Bridget's quest for a thinner body and a handsome man must also be interpreted as a send-up of culturally sanctioned self-improvement.

The popularity of the novel indicates Fielding's success in chiming with a specific demographic of British white, working women in their thirties – the 'third wave' generation – who felt that feminism did not speak to their needs, did not reflect their realities and did not allow them to enact the freedoms they felt they had. This muddled understanding of 'feminism' through the 1990s and 2000s is reflected in many women's fiction texts of this period – indeed, it perhaps defines the 'chick lit' genre itself – in which female characters are portrayed as emancipated yet vulnerable. It is no coincidence that the women writing these books, and being depicted within them, constitute the demographic most prized by marketers and advertisers. In a culture that sells women the idea of happiness-through-consumption (or lack of), literary manifestations of these issues are inevitable as well as illuminating.

Fielding's conclusion to the novel, in which her protagonist records a final diary entry without logging calorie/alcohol/cigarette intake or her weight now that she is happily coupled off, can be read as both interrogating and capitulating to these ideals of consumer culture. Bridget is happy, and feeling confident enough to shrug off the demand that she police her body – yet that very happiness is predicated on her having 'achieved' the goal of being in a relationship. *Bridget Jones's Diary* thus reflects many of the ambivalences of third-wave feminism itself, both incorporating and denying feminism's impact. The text not only instituted the chick lit genre, it also exemplified the contradictions inherent within it. Fielding's rewriting of the romance narrative – including her use of the confessional form of diary writing, long associated as one of the fripperies of women's romantic literature – is thus simultaneously an interrogation of the narrative form of generic romance and a restatement of it.

Imelda Whelehan has written at length about Fielding's novel and has turned critical attention to the origins of the chick lit genre itself. She draws a line of inheritance from 1970s bestselling feminist fiction through to chick lit, arguing that both genres seek to address women's attempts to resolve the tension between female empowerment and (hetero)sexual desire, drawing on a form of realism that encourages close identification with the central character(s) by the reader (Whelehan 2005). Both genres also instigated media storms and instituted new lexical terms: the 'zipless fuck' of Erica Jong's *Fear of Flying* (1973), for example, is comparable to the 'singletons' and 'smug marrieds' of *Bridget Jones's Diary* (1996). Whelehan argues that the consciousness-raising dimension of 1970s feminist fiction is identifiable, too, in chick lit, but is changed in emphasis to accommodate the 1990s (and beyond) 'post-feminist' distancing from the f-word. This ambivalence about identifying as a feminist, she argues, means that chick lit has a role to play in engaging young women in political debates around sex and gender:

> fiction, more freely than political writings, can take opposing sides and study conflicted opinions and ambiguity, and is therefore far more likely to chime with the uncertainties of women attracted to feminism but confused by the mess of emotions generated by their own personal lives. (Whelehan 2005: 12)

I am convinced by Whelehan's argument that without second-wave feminism, chick lit would not exist. Chick lit writing, while centred on the romance narrative, also incorporates discussion of various aspects of women's gendered identities, as well as the theories posited by Radway, Modleski et al. of the potential for empowerment romance writing offers women readers. Other feminist critics have traced its origins back beyond the second wave, with Stephanie Harzewski, for example, finding connections with the traditional prose romances of the fifteenth and sixteenth centuries, the seventeenth-century 'novel of manners' and serialised sensation novels of the nineteenth and twentieth centuries (in Ferris and Young 2006). And there has also been a renewed effort to invest romance writing with literary worth, counteracting the derogatory connotations of the chick lit moniker as 'low' literature and highlighting the persistence of men's domination of literary culture:

> When was the last time anyone saw Marian Keyes or Elizabeth Buchan on *Newsnight Review*? Yet both are excellent storytellers who are unafraid of dealing with the darker side of life [. . .] Women writing for women about issues other women are interested in are not taken seriously by the male-dominated cabal that rules lit crit. (Kean 2005)

Since its inception in the 1990s, the chick lit genre has spawned a variety of subgenres – mum lit and sistah lit, for example – which also bear the mark of second-wave feminist concerns, albeit in somewhat 'pop' packaging. During its third wave and into the fourth, feminism has moved to incorporate the intersections of gender with age, race, class, sexual identity and so on, and all these subject positions are now being reflected in chick lit's expanding subcategories. This allows a wider demographic of reader to enjoy the escapism of its romantic narratives, without being compromised by its myopic view of how women in contemporary culture experience sex and relationships. Therefore, although chick lit, in its various guises, may not appear especially 'feminist', it succeeds in tapping into issues that affect real women's lives, and offers them narratives to help them understand their relationships, and perhaps to change them – just as earlier classic and popular romances have been seen to do. The romance stories they offer might not contain a greatly revised cast of characters with respect to the 'love interest', but they undeniably reflect changed priorities and concerns. Their continuing popularity – and profitability – pays testament to the power of the love story to move its reader, and to offer both escapism and, potentially, empowerment.

Case study 6.2 A postmodern restaging of romance – *A Girl Is a Half-Formed Thing*

Eimear McBride's deeply affecting debut novel *A Girl Is a Half-Formed Thing* (2013) centres on a love story: the love between a girl and her older brother. This story is told as an 'against all the odds' narrative, familiar to anyone who has ever read a romantic novel, as the two siblings endure brutality at home and at school but survive, and find (fleeting) solace and happiness with one another's support. Both the hero and heroine of McBride's story are damaged: the narrator by a sexually predatory older man, the brother by the effects of a tumour that leave him cognitively impaired and profoundly unwell. The narrator's sororal love for her brother matches the intensity of the romantic narrative but remains rooted in familial affection and sisterly protectiveness. In McBride's story, the only love that endures is that between the siblings. Indeed, the novel works by showing that this 'love story' sustains the narrator in ways that romantic love has traditionally been shown to do. The author uses the siblings' relationship to posit an alternative and beautifully innocent bond of love that is every bit as powerful as a sexual romance, and further destabilises the form of the romance genre by telling her story through a radical new linguistic style.

   A Girl Is a Half-Formed Thing builds on the modernist legacy of experimenting with language and the formal structure of the novel. McBride takes us beyond the 'stream of consciousness' experiment of writers such as Richardson and Woolf, utilising instead what has been described as a 'stream of cognition' style. In her writing, she attempts to convey experience at the point at which it is perceived, before that perception is turned into language: 'McBride [. . .] has created a new form of prose which deploys a spartan lexicon in fragmentary vernacular syncopations to represent the form of thought at the point before it becomes articulate speech' (Collard 2014). This makes her novel a sometimes dizzying read, but it allows her to show us that meaning is always in flux, always just-becoming, and it heightens the readers' sense that they are 'experiencing' what the narrator experiences.

In telling the narrator's story, McBride not only portrays the love story of brother and sister, but also allows this to form the backdrop of her exposition of the themes of female sexuality, youth and (loss of) innocence. McBride has been explicit about her intention to write about female sexuality in a different way in her novel, and her depiction of complicated, vulnerable, damaged and defiant female youth institutes a new presentation of the heroine figure. The narrator reveals the cultural lie of the traditional romantic narrative, showing that the cliché of finding 'completion' with a man is a long way from the reality of the exploitative and abusive sexual encounters she experiences, in all their rawness and viscerality.

McBride's story is a chronicle of abusive and unloving sexual encounters. The author shows, repeatedly, the damage wrought on the narrator's psyche, as well as her body, by the many and different men with whom she has sex. Most devastating of all is the older man who rapes her as a thirteen-year-old, then returns in adulthood to further conflict her sense of her own sexuality. McBride uses all these male characters to expose the ways that women's bodies are culturally figured and sexually objectified. The narrator ultimately experiences sex as a way of disassociating from her body, and a means of taking power from those who take it from her. There is no love in these sexual encounters. In an interview with David Collard, McBride explains:

> Her sexual behaviour is not that of someone at peace with their sexuality and she generally utilises it for every reason but the two basics: physical pleasure and/or closeness to another person [. . .] There isn't a single description of her deriving either from any of her encounters [. . .] She is not someone enjoying the hard won fruits of sexual liberation, she is almost the opposite. The product of a system that could offer nothing to women but sexual shame, ignorance and servitude. (Collard 2014)

McBride contrasts the purity of the narrator's love for her brother with the squalidness of her experiences with other men. She is driven to ever-riskier sexual behaviours as she attempts to think, and act, a way through the experience of sexual abuse in her childhood; and as her brother becomes gravely ill her psychological disintegration is mirrored by the fragmentation of words on the page:

> Silent.
> Breath.
> Lungs go out. See the world out.
> You finish that breath. Song breath.
> You are gone out tide. And you close. Drift. Silent eyes. Goodbye.
> My. lllllllllllllllll. Love my. Brother no.
> Silent.
> He's gone. He's gone. Goodbye.
> No. Oh please. My.
> Done. And quiet.
> And.
> Gone.
> (McBride 2013: 188)

Her brother's death marks the end of their love story, the point at which the narrative shifts into a different, but still familiar, 'romantic' trope: that of the broken-hearted, tragic heroine. But in McBride's story, the heroine seeks respite from her grief in damaged, frantic sexual encounters with abusive men. With her brother gone, all the love in her life is also gone. The narrator's tragedy does not end with his loss, but plays out to the devastating denouement of her own (presumed) death, punctuated by acts of vicious sexual brutality.

The bleakness of McBride's ending is a radical departure from the romance narrative. Her restaging of the love story, then, locates it in a relationship between siblings, showing how protective and empowering the shared bond is for each of them. Yet McBride's depiction of sexual relationships in general is unremittingly bleak, the author exposing through the narrator's experiences the falsity of the happily-ever-after romance formula. Instead, her story chronicles a young woman's quest to become whole, no longer 'a half-formed thing', in the face of her continual objectification by men. The narrator is striving to *become*, and it is this desire – one which is ultimately unrequited – which drives McBride's novel to its unique and heart-breaking conclusion.

Bibliography

Belsey, Catherine. 2003. *Critical Practice*. London: Routledge.

Briscoe, Joanna. 1990. 'Feminist Fatales'. *The Guardian*, 1 February.

Brownstein, Rachel M. 1984. *Becoming a Heroine: Reading About Women in Novels*. Harmondsworth: Penguin.

Colgan, Jenny. 2001. 'We Know the Difference Between Foie Gras and Hula Hoops, Beryl, But Sometimes We Just Want Hula Hoops'. *The Guardian*, 24 August.

Collard, David. 2014. 'Interview with Eimear McBride'. *The White Review* (May). Available at <http://www.thewhitereview.org/interviews/interview-with-eimear-mcbride> (accessed October 2017).

Cooke, Rachel. 2006. 'Warning! These Pretty Packages May Contain a Lot of Long Words'. *The Guardian*, 23 July.

Cranny-Francis, Anne. 1990. *Feminist Fiction: Feminist Uses of Generic Fiction*. New York: St Martin's Press.

Ferris, Suzanne and Mallory Young (eds.). 2006. *Chick Lit. The New Woman's Fiction*. New York: Routledge.

Fielding, Helen. 1996. *Bridget Jones's Diary*. London: Picador.

Firestone, Shulamith. 1970. *The Dialectic of Sex*. London: Paladin.

Greer, Germaine. 1970. *The Female Eunuch*. London: MacGibbon and Kee.

Groskop, Viv. 2011. 'There's Nothing Wrong With Judging a Book by Its Cover'. *The Guardian*, 4 September.

Jackson, Stevi. 1999. *Heterosexuality in Question*. London: Sage.

Jong, Erica. 1973. *Fear of Flying*. London: Vintage.

Kean, Danuta. 2005. 'Let's Hear It For Romance'. *The Guardian*, 14 April.

McBride, Eimear. 2013. *A Girl Is a Half-Formed Thing*. London: Faber and Faber.

Miles, Rosalind. 1990. *The Female Form: Women Writers and the Conquest of the Novel*. London: Routledge.

Modleski, Tania. 1982. *Loving with a Vengeance: Mass-Produced Fantasies for Women*. London: Routledge.

Morrison, Toni. 1987. *Beloved*. London: Chatto and Windus.

Owen, Peter (ed.). 1988. *Publishing – The Future*. London: Peter Owen Publishers.

Pearce, Lynne. 1994. *Reading Dialogics*. London: Edward Arnold.

Pearce, Lynne. 1997. *Feminism and the Politics of Reading*. London: Edward Arnold.

Pearce, Lynne. 2007. *Romance Writing*. Cambridge: Polity.

Pearce, Lynne and Jackie Stacey (eds). 2005. *Romance Revisited*. London: Lawrence and Wishart.

Pearce, Lynne and Gina Wisker (eds). 1997. *Fatal Attractions: Re-scripting Romance in Literature and Film*. London: Pluto Press.

Porte, Joel (ed.). 1982. *Emerson in His Journals*. London: Harvard University Press.

Radway, Janice A. 1984. *Reading the Romance: Women, Patriarchy and Popular Literature*. London: Verso (1994).

Regis, Pamela. 2003. *A Natural History of the Romance Novel*. Philadelphia: University of Pennsylvania Press.

Walter, Natasha (ed.). 1999. *On the Move: Feminism for a New Generation*. London: Virago.

Whelehan, Imelda. 2005. *The Feminist Bestseller: From 'Sex and the Single Girl' to 'Sex and the City'*. Basingstoke: Palgrave Macmillan.

7 Crime

The genre of crime writing is one that has long been associated with women, such has been the success of authors such as Agatha Christie, Ruth Rendell and Val McDermid. In this chapter I will look at the genesis of the crime genre in the gothic and sensation novels of the mid-nineteenth century, and women's role in both situating this tradition and contributing to the genre itself.

During the 1980s and 1990s there arose a new determination to locate women's contributions to crime writing. Feminist literary critics began to investigate the origins of the crime novel, and found that women writers had always been part of the evolution of the genre – indeed, that it was a woman who had authored the first 'proper' crime novel. This excavation of women's contributions to crime writing helped establish a strong female tradition of such writing, and challenged the accepted notion that it was writers such as Arthur Conan Doyle – with his famous Sherlock Holmes character – who had 'invented' the crime genre.

The chapter then moves to consider the second-wave reappropriation of the crime genre. During the 1970s, 1980s and early 1990s there was a blossoming of 'feminist' crime writing that took on its generic conventions and reimagined them in ways that were empowering for women. For example, there emerged a new female hard-boiled private investigator character, one who assumed all the characteristics of a man – tough-talking, independent, unafraid – but recoded them as female. There was thus a critical reformulation of what crime writer Barbara Wilson identified as the archetypes and narrative conventions of crime writing, as feminist literary critics found in them ways that women writers could tell new kinds of crime stories.

This feminist engagement with the crime genre was taken on by the feminist publishing houses that, by the 1980s, had become established in significant numbers in the UK's literary scene. Many of them launched dedicated crime series, reflecting the demand for women's writing that featured this new style of female sleuth, and which provided vicarious pleasure for the reader in seeing justice done for women. This chapter goes on to look in detail in Case study 7.1 at one of the writers of this new kind of female crime writing, Val McDermid, whose Lindsay Gordon character was perhaps the first 'lesbian sleuth' and helped generate – particularly as a result of McDermid's impressive sales figures – a new subgenre within crime writing. The lesbian sleuth novel proliferated through the early 1990s, coinciding with the emergence of queer theory and the impact of queer ideas of 'gender-identity-as-performance' on literary culture. Such crime writing took on the queer project of representing sexual identity and gender in terms of performance and masquerade, as the lesbian sleuth enacted her gender and her sexuality in ways that destabilised traditional constructions of male/female, masculine/feminine. This new breed of private investigator (PI) was feminist in politics, fluid in gender identity and often lesbian in sexual orientation, although McDermid's own Kate Brannigan series is focused on a heterosexual PI; I will look at her in more detail later in this chapter.

Finally, the chapter turns in Case study 7.2 to look at the evolution of female crime writing from 'whodunits' to 'whydunits', examining the writing of one of Britain's most prolific authors, Ruth Rendell. Writing as both Rendell and her pseudonymous alter-ego Barbara Vine, she helped oversee the transition of the detective novel from golden age-style investigative fiction to today's psychologically driven crime narratives. Rendell/Vine's texts evidence the shift in both literary and popular culture to foreground aspects of psychology in the everyday, and have established in the contemporary a literary style that incorporates cultural critique and exposition of feminist ideology within the conventions of the crime novel.

Establishing a female crime writing tradition

There is a long and noble tradition of women writing crime fiction, dating back through feminism's many different 'waves'. As critic Maureen Reddy explains, late-twentieth-century women writers of crime fiction 'belong on a continuum that begins with the writers of female gothic and that occasionally intersects with the continuum that includes Edgar Allan Poe and Conan Doyle. A feminist tracing of the history of crime fiction would acknowledge literary foremothers as well as forefathers' (Reddy 1988: 9). Reddy herself traces the emergence of the female crime writing tradition back to the gothic and sensation novels of the Victorian era, noting the parallels between these earlier literary genres. Sensation fiction, which featured highly dramatic stories centred on criminal conspiracies, secret contracts and hidden illegitimacies, was hugely popular in the mid to late nineteenth century, alongside gothic storytelling, which had been popularised by such texts as Mary Shelley's *Frankenstein* (1818) and the contributions of the romantic poets Percy Bysshe Shelley and Lord Byron. Crime writing very much carried on in the traditions of these two genres of literature.

Susan Rowland (2001) similarly traces a line of inheritance in women's crime writing from gothic and sensation novels, going on to examine in depth the evidence for this in the writing of the 'golden age' crime novelists Agatha Christie, Dorothy Sayers et al. – whom I will shortly turn to examine. Rowland argues that the recurrence in gothic/sensation novels of spiritualism, the 'uncanny' and a reliance on the senses carries through to crime fiction – in both genres, women are shown to have control, even mastery, over their environment and over others. The female medium is equivalent to the female detective, and both are counterpoints to the patriarchal structuring of law and order as male. As Elaine Showalter points out, the sensation novels expressed female anger, frustration and sexual energy in a way that was entirely new for a Victorian readership: 'readers were introduced to a new kind of heroine, one who could put her hostility toward men into violent action' (Showalter 1977: 160). In the 1970s and 1980s there was a distinct turn in feminist literary criticism to examine the relationships between the crime text, its writer and its readers, with Showalter's idea that fiction provided vicarious satisfaction being central to much of the theory produced through these debates (see 'Crime writing in the contemporary' later in this chapter). As Reddy put it in her linking of the sensation and crime writing genres: 'feminist crime writers, like sensation novelists before them, frequently locate the source of crime in attitudes that underpin the patriarchy, with their female murderers generally male-identified women acting in desperation' (Reddy 1988: 148).

The crossover from sensation to crime writing occurred during the latter half of the nineteenth century, although texts such as Wilkie Collins's *The Woman in White* (1859) arguably straddled the two genres. The very first crime novel 'proper' was written by a woman: *East Lynne* by Mrs Henry Wood (1861). It was followed the next year by Mary Braddon's *Lady Audley's Secret* (1862). Feminist critics Linda Semple and Ros Coward rediscovered both these texts in the 1980s – and Virago reprinted Braddon's novel as one of its Modern Classics – since they had long gone out of print. Semple and Coward went on to work for the feminist publishing house Pandora, on its Women Crime Writers series, which reissued some of the texts by women crime novelists that had, like Braddon's, been allowed to go out of print in the UK. By the time Semple and Coward were researching the history of women's crime writing, the literary tradition had succeeded in suppressing women's contribution to the genre – as indeed so much women's writing had been historically suppressed (see Chapter 1). Semple had earlier brought another female proponent of the crime genre to the attention of the literary world: 'Linda Semple, speaking at the ICA in 1988, identified the first female crime novel as being *The Dead Letter* by Seeley Regester (1866), and reported that she has discovered a further 400 writers between then and 1950' (Munt 1994: 5). Semple's efforts, alongside those of other feminist literary critics investigating the crime genre, overturned the generally accepted view that it had been writers such as Conan Doyle who had 'invented' the crime genre. The first Sherlock Holmes story was in fact published in 1886, more than a quarter of a century after Wood and Braddon had created their detective stories and characters.

Jessica Mann argues that 'the crime novel reflects – rather than tries to alter – the society in which and for which it is written' (Mann 1981: 59). Perhaps for this reason, then, the 1920s and 1930s have come to be known as the 'golden age' for women's crime writing; they are the decades that follow women's final enfranchisement to vote, so it is logical that the crime fiction written during this period might reflect a rather freer cultural paradigm. The golden age writers were not all women, although a considerable proportion were and four of them in particular have come to be remembered as the 'queens of crime' for their extraordinary output during this period: Margery Allingham, Ngaio Marsh, Dorothy L. Sayers and Agatha Christie. They created characters that remain familiar today. Allingham's Albert Campion, Marsh's Roderick Alleyn, Sayers' Lord Peter Wimsey and Christie's Hercule Poirot captivated audiences and helped propel their inventors into bestselling authors. Arguably, it is also the escapism offered by their descriptions of good-looking, well-heeled characters unravelling their mysteries in beautiful country estates and other idyllic settings that helped make these novelists so successful. Their books were published during the years of the Great Depression, and golden age novels' descriptions of the trappings of upper-class comfort were surely as much part of their readerly appeal as the challenge of calculating whodunit.

Mann also observes that in spite of the gender of these 'queens of crime', the detective characters they portrayed tended to be men: 'even in the Golden Age of detective fiction when women had the vote, entered professions and expected equality, a properly investigating woman was still apparently implausible' (Mann 1981: 94). This points to the cultural paradigm in which these female writers were working: although, as Mann notes, women did have the vote by the 1930s, the years of the golden age cannot truly be described as ones in which women 'expected equality' – or if they did, they would be bound for disappointment. The prevalence of male detectives, even in the work of extremely successful female crime writers, points to the way culture was constructed during this time: men were leaders, executors and organisers, and hence within this discourse of patriarchy even a writer with feminist sensibilities tended to gender her sleuth male in order for her characters to make sense to her audience. Christie does give us one notable exception: her character Jane Marple remains one of the great female investigators, and stands as a radical early example of the kind of self-sufficient, empowered female detective who would become commonplace in crime novels by later women writers (see 'Crime writing in the contemporary' later in this chapter). Christie herself is remarkable: the bestselling novelist of all time, she has amassed sales in excess of two billion since publication of her first novel in 1919.

The Second World War brought an end to the 'golden age' of crime writing, and it was not until after the second wave of feminism had gathered momentum that a new appropriation of the crime genre began, which proliferated through the 1980s and beyond. There were some successful and stand-out female crime writers to emerge in the years between the war and the women's movement, with authors such as P. D. James holding her own against male writers Len Deighton and John Le Carré on the bestseller lists. But it was the intersection of feminist politics with crime writing in the 1970s and 1980s that was to revitalise the genre, creating for women writers and readers new ways to explore empowerment, retribution and restitution. The huge popularity of Val McDermid and Barbara Wilson, for example, points to crime's continuing appeal in the contemporary, and the transition that has taken place between generic crime fiction merely 'reflecting' society and it actually seeking to change it.

Crime writing in the contemporary

At the start of the second wave, there was no discernible fashion for female crime writers, although there were one or two authors (such as the aforementioned P. D. James and the similarly commercially successful Ruth Rendell) who had become big names within the genre. In literary terms there was a sense that crime writing, like other generic forms such as romance or science fiction, was not 'proper' literature, and so in the same way that feminists sought to reinvest these other genres with literary authority, a similar attempt was made with crime writing. American writer and feminist literary critic Carolyn Heilbrun, who had pseudonymously written a successful series of crime stories featuring Kate Fansler (the first of which was published in 1964), 'came out' as the real person behind her Amanda Cross pen-name in 1972. She argued that she had kept her identity secret because the profile of 'crime writer' would hamper her academic career, indicating the problematic formulation of high-brow and low-brow fiction that had historically been used to derogate women's writing (Cooper-Clark 1983). Heilbrun began her literary experiment before the second wave of feminism had started to make its impact on the themes and forms of women's writing, so she could be less sure that her work would be understood in the context of the discussions that were to follow on readerly empowerment and writerly subversions.

As with romance writing (see Chapter 6), there was a determined feminist effort during the second wave to theorise the crime genre and to position women's writing as important within it. Maureen Reddy links this to women's embracing of the sensation novel 100 years earlier:

> Sensation fiction arose at a time when women were attempting to destroy the male publishing monopoly, founding presses and feminist journals, editing magazines, and reviewing manuscripts for mainstream publishers. Feminist crime fiction is emerging at a similar time in history, as the past twenty years has seen the rise of numerous feminist journals, newspapers, and presses, and the growing influence of feminist thought on culture and society. (Reddy 1988: 149)

The crime genre, with its motifs of power and retribution, was thus perfectly poised for a renaissance under the auspices of a newly established feminist movement.

Crime writer Barbara Wilson argued that the genre's 'low-brow', formulaic characteristics were in fact part of its very appeal in this feminist re-appropriation. She describes how she and other crime writers used the distinct set of icons and patterns contained within the genre for their own purposes: 'precisely because of the set structure, women writers were able to move into and utilise the same icons and patterns that made the genre familiar and at the same time change some of the expectations' (Wilson in Gibbs 1994: 219). Wilson is clear that her intent was to use the generic conventions of the crime novel to explore feminist ideas:

> the appeal of the investigator novel to women writers and readers would seem obvious. For to be a woman is to have been silenced and socialised into passivity. To be a woman is to have been the victim or bystander of many nameless and hidden crimes: battery, rape, sexual abuse, harassment. (Wilson in Gibbs 1994: 222)

In crime stories with a female investigator, the passivity and victimhood are overturned, and the power of being in charge, and in control, is handed to a woman. Echoing Mann's statement that crime novels reflect the society in which they are written, Wilson continues: 'crime novels are about society and power. What changed when women began to write crime novels in the 1980s was that traditional notions of authority and justice were called into question' (Wilson in Gibbs 1994: 222). That the motive for crime can lie in social injustice was explored in the work of writers such as Stella Duffy, who explains: 'the contemporary detective or amateur PI is more often than not interested as much in what makes people bad as in investigating the actual crime. Certainly the reasons behind the crimes are where my own interests lie' (Duffy in Windrath 1999: 88).

In this way, then, the crime genre was refigured for women readers, with books by Wilson, Duffy, McDermid, Heilbrun/Cross and Spark generating huge sales among an audience who vicariously enjoyed their representations of female empowerment. Feminist crime fiction allowed both writer and reader to see justice done for women, as women crime writers exploited readerly familiarity with the genre's forms to put across feminist meaning: 'because many people are used to reading mysteries for the plot, I assumed that the audience wouldn't put the thriller down even if it came across new and unusual political perspectives' (Wilson in Gibbs 1994: 223). Another crime writer, Val McDermid, concurs: 'whenever they [crime fiction readers] encounter a writer they enjoy, they immediately rush out and grab everything else that person has ever written, regardless of whether it's the kind of mystery they normally buy' (McDermid in Windrath 1999: 20–1). For her, this had the result that 'people who would never have considered buying a lesbian thriller have become avid fans of Lindsay [Gordon, her lesbian sleuth]' (McDermid in Windrath 1999: 21).

Given this, it is perhaps not surprising that the feminist publishing houses which, by the 1980s, had sprung up across the UK (see Chapter 1) began to give crime writing greater profile on their lists. Feminist engagement with the crime genre was a marked development of the 1980s and 1990s.

> From modest beginnings when The Women's Press brought out their first titles in
> 1982, crime fiction has stealthily nosed its way to bill-topping status, outstripping
> all other categories of feminist publishing, with hefty promotional backing from
> the major women's publishers and a host of new titles. (Briscoe 1989)

The Women's Press, Virago, Onlywomen and Pandora launched their own
crime series during the 1980s and 1990s as the feminist appropriation of the
genre generated a strong demand: 'in July [1989] Virago will rejacket its individual titles, including the popular Kate Fansler mysteries, in a flurry of ads
and dump bins and launch its first cohesive crime list. For women, crime is
starting to pay' (Briscoe 1989). The emergence of crime fiction as a growth area
in women's writing points to two things: the increasing power of the feminist
publishers to direct and respond to literary trends, and the continued attempt
by women writers to use crime's generic conventions to communicate feminist
messages. As critic Joanna Briscoe put it, 'as feminist publishing gains an increasingly secure foothold, it can afford to explore a less palatable underside'
(Briscoe 1989). As well as introducing the crime genre to a wider audience in
this way – and, as with women's writing generally, the feminist publishers'
experiment paved the way for mainstream publishers to expand their crime
sections, once the market had been proven – the feminist publishing houses also
helped establish new traditions within the genre itself.

As noted earlier, the feminist take on crime fiction saw the introduction
of a new type of character to the genre: the 'hard-boiled' female private investigator (PI). The first such character was Marcia Muller's heroine Sharon
McCone, introduced (to a US audience) in 1978 in *Edwin of the Iron Shoes* and
to a UK readership with its reprinting by The Women's Press in 1993. McCone
troubled and expanded traditional notions of femininity, exploiting the conventions of crime fiction's traditional 'PI' persona to interrogate women's
traditional figuring within cultural constructions of gender: 'her tough-talking,
wise-cracking approach is thus both familiar and new – a female appropriation of "masculine" discourse' (Plain 2001: 93). The 'feminist' PI was used to
interrogate traditional gender roles, coding as female the attributes of control,
agency and power typical of this kind of literary character. The eagerness with
which readers engaged with this female 'tough guy' was evidenced in sales: 'the
gradual acceptance of hard-boiled female investigators is supported by the
bestseller status of the works of Grafton, Muller and others' (Betz 2006: 5).

For female fans of the crime genre, the construction of a hard-boiled *female*
PI was exhilarating:

> you can get completely wrapped up in the excitement and pace, yet you're not
> being thrown these very male Raymond Chandlerisms. I actually like Chandler
> but I find his sexual politics offensive, whereas with feminist crime fiction I don't
> feel torn. (Briscoe 1989)

Briscoe observes that crime fiction's greatest pull is that 'it provides the sleuth
or narrator with an automatic pretext for examining society' (Briscoe 1989).

The character of the female PI is a challenge to the stereotype of the rational, logical male detective. Feminist crime fiction thus set up new models for female behaviour by allocating control and command to a woman, a usurpation of the genre's usual structuring of male agency. Hence, as Reddy puts it, 'feminist crime novels, far from being mere escapist literature or isolated, peculiar experiments in an essentially masculine preserve, participate in the larger feminist project of redefining and redistributing power, joining a long and valuable tradition of women's fiction' (Reddy 1988: 149).

Female writers of female detectives thus violated gender boundaries, and in doing so became part of the feminist challenge to dismantle traditional formulations of masculinity and femininity. But as the genre of feminist crime writing became established, it also came to reflect some of the problems within feminism itself as it moved from its second to third wave. Heilbrun's Kate Fansler character, for example, was taken to task for embodying a certain kind of female privilege: 'white, professional, and middle-class, often holding a PhD from a well-known university, this intellectual has integrated liberal feminism into her texts as political discourse' (Munt 1994: 33). As feminism was fractured by the emergence of the competing demands of ethnicity, class and sexuality during the identity politics debates of the 1980s and 1990s, Heilbrun's academic sleuth represented the problems the second wave had thrown up in terms of its biases and privileging of certain subject positions.

In her 1994 review of female crime writing, Sally Munt identifies the absence of black writers from the genre as part of the long history of Western racism:

> orientalist discourse locates the Other as criminal, and a threat. This discursive construction of Black identity and criminality is so powerful that even feminist writers trying to write against it largely fail to deliver an alternative because the White discourse and the crime form itself are so resistant to change in this aspect. (Munt 1994: 85)

Munt does, however, explore the ways that women writers have attempted to write against the racist paradigm that she argues has informed the crime genre.

These debates reflect the complexity of feminism in the third wave, and mirror the wider arguments being made about the need for the women's movement to be more diverse and less exclusive. As awareness of these issues increased, there was a growing realisation that 'the world of crime fiction is almost exclusively white, with some representation of ethnic and working-class people' and that this limited the extent to which the genre was empowering for those belonging to minority groups (Reddy 1988: 16). Looking back on this period now, however, we see that some of these academic observations were overstated, since, during the period 1990–2000, British crime fiction saw the emergence of a significant number of black authors and the establishment of a press – the X Press – that promoted a distinctive and, indeed, controversial brand of text which was dedicated to exposing, and taking revenge upon, white racism. Although the majority of the X Press authors were male, some women, like Karline Smith – author of *Moss Side Massive* (2000) – rose to prominence. Although the crime genre, as discussed earlier in this chapter, has always been one with which women have been closely associated – as writers and as readers – there was a more nuanced critique of its reach to different subject groupings of women as feminism moved from its second to its third wave.

Third-wave feminist crime fiction consequently incorporated this new political awareness into its own publications. Texts such as Claire Macquet's *Looking for Ammu* (1992), for example, explored the construction of race through the narrative structure of a detective story. Gillian Slovo's socialist feminist sleuth Kate Baeier can similarly be read as an attempt to bring class politics into crime writing. And even though the PIs themselves remained predominately white, authors like Cath Staincliffe have ensured that her Mancunian PI Sal Kilkenny deals with racism and the particular crimes that face black and Asian communities (while not shying away from the fact that some criminals might also come from these communities). Feminist crime fiction thus expanded its reach, in accordance with the third wave's more inclusive formulation of identity and subjectivity, and its incorporation of both a critique and a continuation of second-wave ideology. As Barbara Wilson put it: 'the crimes focus on injustice towards women and explore family secrets and institutionalised oppression. They also call into question some of the hypocrisy and rhetoric of the feminist movement' (Wilson in Gibbs 1994: 224).

The feminist appropriation of crime writing has, since the 1990s, lost some of its impetus, but its legacy remains. Crime writer Lesley Grant-Adamson noted in 1996 that 'successful feminist writers are producing fine novels that show strong-minded modern women working as detectives or active in other kinds of crime or suspense novel' (Grant-Adamson 1996: 48). From today's perspective, in popular culture the figure of the female investigator is firmly established, with TV series including *Prime Suspect* in the 1990s and 2000s, and *The Bridge*, *The Killing* and *The Fall* in the 2010s, all featuring independent, intelligent women in the lead role. In literary terms, the mainstream market for women's crime writing has grown, arguably because of the work of the feminist publishing houses in the 1980s and 1990s to popularise it. Along with commercial big-hitters such as Ruth Rendell (until her death in 2015), Marina Cole, Sheila Quigley and Gillian Flynn, women writers such as Stella Duffy, Kate Atkinson and Val McDermid have continued to write crime novels that contain nuanced gender role modelling and non-traditional portrayals of both individual identity and relationships. These books are the legacy of feminism's assimilation of the generic conventions of crime to tell new kinds of stories. Contemporary crime writing by women has been directed and indelibly reshaped by the feminist incursion into the genre.

Case study 7.1 **Val McDermid and lesbian crime writing**

One marked outcome of the feminist appropriation of the crime genre was the emergence of the lesbian sleuth character. Lindsay Gordon, created by Val McDermid and mentioned earlier in this chapter, was perhaps the original of this literary 'type'. The Women's Press published three novels featuring this character during the 1980s, before the success of McDermid's writing saw her 'poached' by a mainstream publisher (HarperCollins). The Women's Press and the other feminist presses, as with crime fiction generally, had a pivotal role in publishing writing such as McDermid's: the lesbian themes and content of her novels meant that a readership had to be established before mainstream publishers would take a chance on them. We can see this, for example, in the trajectory of McDermid's publishing career. McDermid introduced a heterosexual character, Kate Brannigan, in order to broaden the appeal of her novels beyond the lesbian, or simply female, readership guaranteed by publication with The Women's Press. Following this, the bulk of her work was published in the UK by HarperCollins. McDermid says this was a deliberate move to mainstream Gordon, and thus mainstream lesbian characters in crime writing. 'If I was ever going to make a living from writing, I was going to have to break into the mainstream. I also knew that breaking out with Brannigan was a way of giving Lindsay Gordon a wider audience' (McDermid in Windrath 1999: 20–1). The calculation certainly paid off. McDermid is now one of Britain's bestselling novelists, with sales of more than ten million books under her belt.

McDermid, who identifies as a lesbian, says she created Gordon because 'I just wanted to write about a world I understood' (McDermid in Windrath 1999: 18). Her Lindsay Gordon novels (e.g., *Report for Murder* (1987), *Common Murder* (1989), *Final Edition* (1991)) are important for their role in situating this 'world' in the mainstream, at a time when lesbian lives and identities were anything but. She also realised that the crime genre would help in this effort to encompass alternative lifestyles and subject positions, in particular because of the shift in crime writing – thanks in no small part to the UK's feminist publishing scene – to include a broader range of characters and themes. As Betty Kirkpatrick observed after interviewing McDermid in 1993:

> Val McDermid is of the opinion that the whole genre of crime fiction has widened out recently. Indeed she feels that in many ways it imposes no more constraints as to subject matter and situation than do other mainstream forms of literature. She contends that 'you can now cover just about every aspect of life within the format of the crime novel. All manner of people from the highest echelons of society to the lowest can be introduced within the context of its plot'. (Kirkpatrick 1993: 10)

This makes the crime genre a perfect vehicle, then, for conveying lesbian storylines.

The six novels in McDermid's Lindsay Gordon series are focused on their lead character's lifestyle and love interests as much as the crimes she investigates. In this, as journalist Nicholas Wroe notes, they marked out a distinctly new staging for crime writing, totally at odds with the quintessentially provincial settings of, for example, Agatha Christie's Miss Marple novels: 'McDermid's contribution to breaking that mould came via her cynical, socialist, lesbian journalist, Lindsay Gordon' (Wroe 2011). Gordon's sleuthing is conducted in the settings of newspaper offices, publishing houses and even peace protests – places very familiar to her readers that allow a particular kind of identification with her heroine. It is not until her later work that the themes and storylines become much darker – these early novels are very much about establishing a readerly identification with a heroine they can relate to. In addition, they may be seen to be part of a wider 'Scottish literary renaissance' that was starting to emerge at the time that Lindsay Gordon was invented; Glasgow, and Glasweigan humour, are a crucial ingredient in these early novels, and it is important to note that McDermid's career developed parallel to that of other notable Scottish women poets and novelists such as Liz Lochhead, Janice Galloway and A. L. Kennedy, as well as inspiring more recent authors like Ali Smith.

As the second wave gave way to the third, Lindsay Gordon was followed by a growing number of lesbian detectives: 'in the last fifteen years the number of professional lesbian detectives on the literary marketplace has more than tripled from fourteen in 1986 to forty-three in 1995' (Plain 2001: 201). Much of this fiction foregrounded lesbian lifestyles, politics and relationships over the detective plot, using the conventions of the genre to introduce lesbian thematics: 'solving the crime is only part of the attraction; situated within the dominant narrative of detection a second story is being told. This is the everyday life of its lesbian characters' (Betz 2006: 12). The formula of generic fiction is thus once again used 'politically' in order to transmit subversive or simply alternative messages; the familiarity of the crime genre helps normalise the lesbian stories that also form these texts.

The emergence of what is typically referred to as lesbian crime writing (on account of the PI's own sexual preference), coinciding as it did with the theoretical move to figure gender identity 'as performance' (Judith Butler's *Gender Trouble* was published in 1990), was quickly recognised by critics as a decidedly 'queer' moment in the evolution of contemporary fiction. Paulina Palmer has argued that lesbian detective novels did much more than simply offer readers positive and 'normalised' representations of lesbian lifestyles; more subversively (and in line with the 'queer paradigm' discussed in Chapter 2), they troubled traditional constructions of cultural authority and sexual orthodoxy. Citing Barbara Wilson's *Gaudí Afternoon* (1991) as one such example, Palmer writes:

> Postmodern motifs which find expression in the lesbian thriller include the representation of the individual as the product of cultural and psychic drives, the portrayal of sexuality and subjectivity as produced through fantasy, and the representation of sexual identity and gender in terms of performance and masquerade. Ideas relating to the performative nature of gender lend themselves particularly well to fictional treatment. (Palmer in Messent 1997: 96)

The lesbian detective novel thus contains both alternative sexual personae and 'queer' gender performances – its female sleuths act out 'male' roles, as Plain also contends:

> although, as Judith Butler has observed, the concept of queer is itself a 'site of collective contestation', queer notions of performativity, displacement and the disruption to the heterosexual matrix undoubtedly suit the lesbian detective novel. (Plain 2001: 203)

Twenty-first-century manifestations of the lesbian detective novel still include elements of this self-conscious interrogation of gender roles and their performance, but the reception of McDermid's work today also evidences something even more radical: the mainstreaming of lesbian existence to a much greater degree than ever before, reflecting a cultural shift in Britain towards embracing greater diversity (see Chapter 4). As McDermid continues to produce lesbian characters and narratives within the crime genre, there has been a shift in the way that her lesbian storylines are both perceived and received. In an interview she gave to *The Independent* in 2010, she explained this change:

> I think there's been an opening up of British culture and a relaxing of British society. [Lesbian] novels have done well at the same time as we've made legal gains; civil partnerships have come along. There's been a bit of a sea change that would have been unimaginable even 10 years ago. (McDermid 2010)

She notes the contrast with her earlier experiences of publishing novels featuring 'the UK's first openly lesbian detective, Lindsay Gordon', arguing that these novels were only considered publishable by a feminist press at first:

> Something has changed in the past seven years. My latest novel, *Trick of the Dark*, is probably the most lesbian book I've ever written in terms of the number of its gay female characters. And not an eyebrow has been raised at my publisher, Little, Brown. The sales and marketing effort that has been

put into this book is, as far as I can gauge, exactly the same as any other
book with my name on it would have received. (McDermid 2010)

The lesbian detective novel may therefore be seen to have lost its counter-
cultural styling thanks to the success feminism has had in mainstreaming
alternative gender enactments and sexual identities.

Case study 7.2 Ruth Rendell and the invention of the 'whydunit'

The popularity of feminist crime writing peaked in the 1980s and early
1990s, as women readers consumed in numbers the new character type
of the empowered, independent female detective. Arguably, as feminism
moved from its second to third wave, the female sleuth story lost of some
the appeal it had held through its portrayals of non-traditional gender
roles and behaviour, as ideas around gender construction, sexuality and
identity became more complex and nuanced. During the 1990s, a growing
interest in all manner of cultural constructions of the self took hold in
both popular culture and literary theory, so in crime fiction – as across
many other genres – there emerged a new focus both on the individual
and on psychologically and culturally constructed motives for behaviour.

This meant that all novels preoccupied with crime and misdemean-
our increasingly came to foreground the transgressor as much as the
redeemer, a trend that has continued into the twenty-first century. Lee
Horsley identifies a 'literary noir' genre – an exploration of the condition
of powerlessness in which the reader's own sense of empowerment might
derive from identification with the victim or the transgressor rather than
the detective hero (Horsley 2005: 281). The feminist crime novel per se
might have fallen out of fashion – although more recent writers like Cath
Staincliffe evidence a continued interest in such new manifestations of the
genre – but the psychologically focused *thriller* rides high at the top of bestseller lists each year, and women writers are among the big-name authors
of this category: Donna Tartt, Lionel Shriver, Stella Duffy, Gillian Slovo
and even Sarah Waters have all gravitated towards this kind of fiction.

The transition from crime writing's formula of identifying the culprit
to, instead, chronicling *why* events happened emerged in the 1980s as psychology and, in particular, psychoanalysis was becoming firmly embedded
in the academy. Spearheading this new mode of writing was a female
author, Ruth Rendell, who had already established her reputation as a
contemporary 'queen of crime' with the Inspector Wexford mystery series
that had made her name in the 1960s and 1970s. In 1986 she published

the novel *A Dark-Adapted Eye* under the pseudonym Barbara Vine, and established a new kind of crime writing, one which was infused with a compulsion to understand the motives behind her characters' actions – the 'whydunit'.

Barbara Vine's first novel actually came with an explanation of the author's intent. In the Preface she wrote:

> I have wanted Barbara to have a voice as well as Ruth. It would be a softer voice speaking at a slower pace, more sensitive perhaps and more intuitive [. . .] there would be nothing surprising to a psychologist in Barbara's choosing, as she asserts herself, to address readers in the first person. (Vine 1986: xx)

This shift in address marks the evolution from simply plotting out and solving mysteries to directly invoking the psychology of the protagonists – as well as that of the reader. Rendell/Vine's direct address to the reader in this first novel explains the duality of her writing persona, and her need to express herself in new ways. It is a fascinating conceit, helping establish intimacy and consequently the loyalty that Val McDermid describes as being central to the crime reader's contract with the genre (see Case study 7.1).

The introduction of a new alter-ego – Barbara Vine – also indicates Rendell's development as a woman writer from the one who penned the Wexford mysteries, books that reflect her generation's being 'caught up in the web that one writes about men because men are the people and we are the others' (Cooper-Clarke 1983: 139). Born in 1930, Rendell had lived through the patriarchal culture of the post-war era that had given rise to the second wave, and in spite of her critical portrayal of militant feminism in the 1985 Wexford novel *An Unkindness of Ravens*, she was certainly a feminist herself by the time she came to write under her *nom de plume* (she campaigned on a range of women's issues and was instrumental in introducing the legislation that would become the Female Genital Mutilation Act 2003).

As with her Wexford books, Vine did not take on the female PI persona in the same way other feminist crime writers did. Instead, she evidenced her feminist sensibility by bringing attention to a range of gender issues in her storytelling, including domestic violence, transvestism and female sexuality. As she told a journalist in 2002: 'I think that all women, unless they are absolutely asleep, must be feminists up to a point' (Brooks 2002). Rendell, who died in 2015, wrote more than sixty books, and oversaw the evolution of a new kind of crime writing, incorporating feminist ideology as well as social commentary into her storylines. Literary critic and author Joan Smith argues that her books use crime as a vehicle to explore how people live, including shining a light on the intersections of class and gender with criminality: 'if someone from another planet were to ask how the UK has changed over the last 40 years you could do a lot worse than tell them to read the novels of Ruth Rendell' (quoted in Brooks 2002).

Rendell's relationship with the title of 'crime writer' was always ambivalent. She vehemently repudiated the title of 'queen of crime' and argued throughout her career that her writing was not 'generic', contesting the connotations of inferiority that came with that label: 'it's pure sexism – everyone knows that women can write detective fiction, so they're allowed to succeed at it,' says [fellow writer] Smith (quoted in Brooks 2002). Her refusal of the moniker 'crime writer' points, then, to the devaluing of the crime genre as a literary category. As fan and fellow crime writer Val McDermid told Libby Brooks:

> Anyone writing within genre fiction is not seen as writing within the literary establishment. There's even [a sense of] being too prolific. Had she [Rendell] not had bodies in her books she would have been seen as one of the premier writers of the day, but she has a huge readership who appreciate her. (Brooks 2002)

Rendell/Vine thus exemplifies the complexity of women writers' relationship with genre fiction: they are 'permitted' to excel in writing crime, romance and science fiction while at the same time their work is devalued as generic.

In spite of this contradiction, or perhaps because of it, Ruth Rendell was instrumental in developing the crime genre into the 'whydunit' format now familiar to contemporary readers, incorporating both feminist and psychological perspectives into her work. With *A Dark-Adapted Eye* Rendell dramatically departed from the formula of previous crime novels. The central criminal act – the murder of one sister by another – is described early on, and factually. It is not the unravelling of who committed this crime that is central to the novel, but *why*. As McDermid writes in the introduction to the 2016 edition of the novel: 'It's hard to remember how strikingly ground-breaking *A Dark-Adapted Eye* was. No other crime writer was producing anything so emotionally and psychologically complex at the time' (Vine 2016: viii).

In these books, the 'investigator' (who is also the narrator) is an ordinary woman, niece to both the murdered woman and her murderer, and it is her piecing together of her own family history that 'solves' the mystery of the deaths of her aunts thirty years earlier. McDermid concludes: '*A Dark-Adapted Eye* was one of the crucial landmarks in the landscape of crime fiction for writers and readers alike' (Vine 2016: x).

Rendell's literary legacy is, therefore, surely assured.

Bibliography

Betz, Phyllis M. 2006. *Lesbian Detective Fiction: Woman as Author, Subject and Reader*. Jefferson: MacFarland and Company.

Briscoe, Joanna. 1989. 'Femme Fatalities'. In *The Guardian*, 26 April.

Brooks, Libby. 2002. 'Dark Lady of Whodunnits'. In *The Guardian*, 3 August.

Cooper-Clark, Diana. 1983. *Designs of Darkness: Interviews with Detective Novelists*. Bowling Green: Bowling Green State University Popular Press.

Gibbs, Liz (ed.). 1994. *Daring to Dissent: Lesbian Culture from Margin to Mainstream*. London: Cassell.

Grant-Adamson, Lesley. 1996. *Writing Crime and Suspense Fiction and Getting Published*. London: Hodder and Stoughton.

Horsley, Lee. 2005. *Twentieth-Century Crime Fiction*. Oxford: Oxford University Press.

Kirkpatrick, Betty. 1993. 'The Feminist Plot Thickens'. In *The Herald (Glasgow)*, 19 October.

Mann, Jessica. 1981. *Deadlier Than the Male: An Investigation into Feminine Crime Writing*. Newton Abbott: David and Charles.

McDermid, Val. 1987. *Report for Murder*. London: The Women's Press.

McDermid, Val. 1989. *Common Murder*. London: The Women's Press.

McDermid, Val. 1991. *Final Edition*. London: The Women's Press.

McDermid, Val. 2010. 'Niche Off the Leash: Val McDermid on Progress in Lesbian Fiction'. In *The Independent*, 11 September.

Messent, Peter (ed.). 1997. *Criminal Proceedings: The Contemporary American Crime Novel*. London: Pluto Press.

Munt, Sally R. 1994. *Murder By the Book? Feminism and the Crime Novel*. London: Routledge.

Plain, Gill. 2001. *Twentieth Century Crime Fiction: Gender, Sexuality and the Body*. Edinburgh: Edinburgh University Press.

Reddy, Maureen T. 1988. *Sisters in Crime: Feminism and the Crime Novel*. New York: Continuum.

Rowland, Susan. 2001. *From Agatha Christie to Ruth Rendell: British Women Writers in Detective and Crime Fiction*. Basingstoke: Palgrave Macmillan.

Russett, Margaret. 2002. 'Three Faces of Ruth Rendell: Feminism, Popular Fiction and the Question of Genre'. In *Genre*, 35:1, pp. 143–66.

Showalter, Elaine. 1977. *A Literature of Their Own: British Women Novelists from Brontë to Lessing*. London: Virago.

Smith, Karline. 2000. *Moss Side Massive*. London: The X-Press.

Vine, Barbara. 1986. *A Dark-Adapted Eye*. London: Penguin (2016).

Windrath, Helen (ed.). 1999. *A Career in Crime: Inside Information from Leading Women Writers*. London: The Women's Press.

Wroe, Nicholas. 2011. 'Val McDermid: A Life In Writing'. In *The Guardian*, 12 August.

8 Science fiction

Women writers took science fiction writing out of male hands and made it their own during feminism's second wave. As with the crime and romance genres, women writers took on the generic conventions of science fiction to tell new kinds of stories. These conventions – extra-terrestrial life, space and time travel, cyborgs and robotics – were utilised by women writers politicised by the feminist movement to offer new explorations of gender and sexual identity. Through their employment of sci fi's techniques of exploring the extraordinary, these writers of a new type of science fiction writing – feminist sci fi – were able to obliquely reveal the way ordinary and everyday identities are constructed. As this new subgenre of sci fi emerged, there simultaneously arose a literary critical assessment of the oeuvre whose proponents argued: 'at its best science fiction must shake us from our complacencies. For women this is no luxury' (Armitt 1991: 136).

Feminist science fiction writers sought to expand the remit of 'women's writing', attempting to counter the historical dismissal of their work as formulaic by subverting and usurping the very structures of such formulae: 'the postmodern canon has systematically excluded a wide range of important feminist writing by dismissing it as genre fiction' (Barr 1992: xiii). As with women's crime writing, feminist sci fi texts were hugely popular (a popularity again initiated and enabled by the UK's second-wave feminist publishing houses) and this popularity helped reposition science fiction as culturally and canonically valuable. The feminist publishing houses were able to achieve this for feminist sci fi writing by exploiting established readerships already committed to its ideology – feminism – while also reaching out to fans of the genre to further disseminate its political messages. In so doing, they helped reshape the literary landscape of the 1980s and early 1990s, and instituted authors such as Ursula Le Guin, Margaret Atwood and Marge Piercy as important and influential science fiction writers.

The British writer Jane Palmer was part of this second-wave literary scene, writing a series of sci fi stories in the 1980s that were published by The Women's Press. In Case study 8.1 I examine her second novel, *The Watcher* (1986), to show the ways it typifies the feminist sci fi genre, utilising the motifs of time travel and extra-terrestrial life in order to make the everyday seem alien, and thus to convey messages about women's unequal status in the contemporary world. This exploration of gender was central to the feminist science fiction that emerged in the second wave. As the problematisation of masculinity and femininity was set up in feminist theory, feminist sci fi writers used the genre's stylistic and formal elements to explore the ways in which gender was constructed and perpetuated culturally and politically. The use of futuristic settings, alien landscapes and the figure of the cyborg – what Anne Cranny-Francis (1990) refers to as 'secondary world fantasy' – enabled the writers of these texts to present gender in ways that made the ordinary strange: and thus illustrated the arbitrariness of rigid gender roles and the limitations imposed upon both sexes by the stereotyped binaries of masculine/feminine.

The first, hugely influential, examples of this kind of text were written in the US, but due to the overlapping of the UK and US feminist and literary scenes at the start of the second wave they quickly traversed to a British audience, and had a major influence on UK writers and readers. American writers Ursula Le Guin, Joanna Russ and Marge Piercy initiated the raft of feminist sci fi writing that emerged in the 1970s and 1980s, alongside the work of cyberpunk author Pat Cadigan, all of it focused on exposing and challenging naturalised assumptions around gender and sexual identity. I will look at their trend-setting examples before examining in greater detail the explorations of gender made by British writers using the conventions of the science fiction genre.

The chapter then ends with a study of recent writing by Margaret Atwood, whose 1985 novel *The Handmaid's Tale* is perhaps the best-known and most widely cited feminist work of science fiction. In spite of this, Atwood prefers her writing to be described as 'speculative fiction' and in Case study 8.2 I will look at the reasons for this, as well as the messages and motifs contained in her MaddAddam trilogy, published between 2003 and 2013. In this series of novels Atwood imagines a dystopian future created out of corporate greed and mis-governance, genetic modification of the natural world, and ingrained misogyny and hetero-normativity. As with *The Handmaid's Tale*, she examines human relationships and the false imposition of specially gendered identities onto both men and women, alongside a devastating depiction of a future world in which human life itself has been all but wiped out by the quest to design the 'perfect' human form. In its focus on what some might describe as a 'worst-case scenario' for the future, Atwood's text belongs to a long and critically revered tradition of dystopian science fiction in Western literature (see also George Orwell's *Nineteen Eighty-Four*, Aldous Huxley's *Brave New World* and Cormac McCarthy's *The Road*), which, in feminist futures-fiction, is balanced against a great many utopian fantasies, such as Charlotte Perkins Gilman's *Herland* (1915) and Sally Miller Gearhart's *The Wanderground* (1979). The MaddAddam trilogy is one of contemporary fiction's most creative and comprehensive explorations of the preoccupations of twenty-first-century feminism, with its interwoven interests in the environment, ecology, corporatism, technology and virtual environments. It has become, like Atwood's earlier texts, a classic of the science/speculative fiction genre.

The emergence of female science fiction writing

Women's contributions to the genre of science fiction writing were on the whole overlooked until the women's liberation movement began to gather pace at the end of the 1960s. Sci fi was held to be a masculine realm, with fictional explorations of space and time travel, robotics and extra-terrestrial life emerging from the rapidity of technological and scientific change during the Victorian era – change associated with male scientists, explorers, mathematicians and astronomers, since employment in these fields, and indeed access to education, was largely denied to women. Early sci fi novelists such as H. G. Wells and Jules Verne established the motifs and themes of the genre for a British readership, but it was in fact a woman who is now widely regarded to have written the *first* science fiction novel. Mary Shelley's *Frankenstein* (1818) was written two centuries before the works of Wells and Verne, incorporating a feminist critique of motherhood, gender and the advances of science into a revolutionary new kind of novel. Feminist literary critic Anne Cranny-Francis (1990) helped establish Shelley's *Frankenstein* as the originator of the sci fi genre, but, as with so much other literature by women writers, it was not until her intervention – and that of other feminist literary critics – in the 1980s and 1990s that women writers' contributions to the genre(s) were recognised.

The onset of feminism's second wave in the 1960s generated a new kind of sci fi writing, one that incorporated both the motifs and themes of the genre as well as a new focus on issues around femininity, sexuality and identity. Sci fi's generic conventions were utilised by an influx of women writers, including Ursula Le Guin, Pat Cadigan, Joanna Russ and Marge Piercy, to foreground and explore the issues at the heart of second-wave feminist politics. In this, they followed in the footsteps of Shelley, using the structures and stories of sci fi to create an estrangement from the everyday in order to highlight social and political injustices, as Cranny-Francis describes: 'science fiction offers the feminist writer a number of conventions which can be used to construct a story in which the writer denaturalises institutionalised modes of behaviour, of representation and self-representation, in contemporary Western society' (Cranny-Francis 1990: 74).

So 'the emergence of a distinctive female voice [in science fiction writing] coincided with the resurgence of the women's movement in the sixties and seventies, after a period when women were almost in hiding' (Holliday 1990). The first female sci fi texts were published in the US, where the genre was arguably a bigger part of the literary scene than in the UK, with American authors Alice Sheldon (who wrote pseudonymously as James Tiptree Jr), Ursula Le Guin, Joanna Russ and Octavia Butler publishing their 'feminist' sci fi texts in the 1960s and 1970s. But as with so many other texts and trends within the second wave of feminism, there was a marked overlap between the US and the UK literary scenes, and these US texts were consumed in great numbers by British readers eager to engage with this new exploration of gender and genre. The result was the institution of a new subgenre – feminist science fiction:

> feminist theory and the experiential knowledge of women went into the making of feminist SF and the result was the remaking of a literary genre, a fundamental investigation of the conventions of that genre, both for their literary or narrative implications and for the embedded ideological significance(s). (Cranny-Francis 1990: 43)

Following these American foremothers, British authors such as Doris Lessing and Angela Carter helped institute the genre within the UK literary scene. It soon proliferated to encompass fantasy, horror, supernatural and other types of sci fi, all of which subgenres were explored and expanded by women writers.

This is not to say that women writers did not experience resistance and even outright hostility from within the literary sci fi scene. Cranny-Francis describes how Alice Sheldon's work was lauded by the masculinist review press in the US because its reviewers believed it to be the work of a male writer. Even her feminist short story 'The Women Don't See' was credited by her editor as exhibiting strong 'male' language, as Cranny-Francis recounts:

> Tiptree [Sheldon's pseudonym] simulates an 'entirely masculine manner' in the story by constructing a narrative voice from a number of sexist discourses which are so effectively naturalised that even the editor, Silverberg, did not suspect that the narrative voice was part of, not simply the authoritative medium for, the 'feminist story'. (Cranny-Francis 1990: 31)

Thus, women writers of sci fi 'brought the politics of feminism into a genre with a solid tradition of ignoring or excluding women writers, and in so doing [. . .] politicised our understanding of the fantasies of science fiction' (Wolmark 1993: 2). Their exploration of sci fi and the opportunities it provides for explicating feminist messages left an indelible mark on the genre.

In the UK, the feminist appropriation of sci fi was a marked characteristic of the literary scene during the second wave, incorporating a number of different varieties of fantasy writing, from horror to fairy-tale to what are typically referred to as 'secondary world fantasies' (i.e. storylines located in or on an alternative time, space or planet). In both her short-story writing and her novels, Angela Carter used the genre's motifs of time travel, technology and extra-terrestrialism to expose the ways that women and men are culturally constructed, and thus constrained. Carter has been credited by Roz Kavaney and others, including her biographer Lorna Sage, with renewing the genre by defamiliarising the everyday in order to make visible injustices in the historical present and to suggest alternatives. However, given the sophistication and complexity of Carter's writing, there are other readers and critics who would not immediately regard her texts as belonging to the sci fi, or even fantasy, genre (especially given the fact that, in recent times, the concept of 'magic realism' has provided us with another means of labelling and understanding fiction which moves between realistic and surrealist depictions of the material world). Carter's novels are nevertheless rich with fantastical creations that defy reality, playing with causality and presenting non-unified identities and blurred moralities: 'Carter was keen on expressing the mutability of individuality' (Kaveney in Sage 1994b: 172). *The Passion of New Eve* (1977), for example, is a dazzling and dizzying example of her exploitation of some of the generic conventions of sci fi (in particular, the 'Frankenstein' myth) in order to show the arbitrariness of gender constructs (for more on this theme, see 'Gender explorations in science fiction' later in this chapter). Its legacy was to make Carter 'one of the critical influences on a whole generation of British SF writers' (Kaveney quoted in Sage 1994b: 171).

Alongside Carter, other British women writers, including Josephine Saxton, Margaret Elphinstone and Jane Palmer, were experimenting with the science fiction genre (for more on Jane Palmer see Case study 8.1) and by the mid-1980s feminist sci fi was a burgeoning market. As critic Dale Spender noted at the time:

> Whether strong women come first and are called science fiction, or vice-versa (and we could do with some order here), there can be no doubt that there is some exciting women's fiction being written. And there's a growing demand for it, which is why The Women's Press launches its new (cheap) science fiction list this year. Women want strong, independent characters they can identify with – and creative solutions for world problems – and if this is labelled science fiction, so be it. (Spender 1985)

As with the romance and crime genres, the feminist publishing houses played their part in establishing a home for sci fi writing, with The Women's Press and Virago both publishing sci fi series alongside reprints of historical works by women writers such as Naomi Mitchison which had been allowed to fall out of print, and reprinting seminal US texts by Ursula Le Guin, Joanna Russ and Octavia Butler for a UK audience.

Spender wrote her assessment of the feminist sci fi scene in 1985, the year in which Margaret Atwood's *The Handmaid's Tale* – which would go on to become perhaps the best-known twentieth-century novel of this genre – was published (for analysis of Atwood's more recent sci fi see Case study 8.2). In her story, Atwood usurps traditional science fiction narratives to present a distinctly *feminist* dystopian vision of the future. She employs the conventional imagery and structure of sci fi storytelling to put across her feminist intent, presenting her protagonist, Offred, as 'otherworldly' – a classic science fiction motif – to show that 'women are aliens in a world in which humanity is described as masculinity' (Cranny-Francis 1990: 194). The estrangement created by the sci fi motifs in *The Handmaid's Tale* provides a vantage point from which Atwood can highlight social and political injustices, revealing the double standards enforced by gender conditioning and the imprisonment of women (and men) within binary sexual and gender roles. While we initially perceive Offred's position as one of classical 'feminine' passivity and subservience, we learn over the course of the novel that some of the male characters in the text are similarly disempowered, their identities imposed upon them. Offred's fertility and sexuality are assets to be bargained with under the brutal regime of the Republic of Gilead – yet she is aware, too, that men in this schema are just as oppressed:

> I know they're watching, these two men who aren't yet permitted to touch women. They touch with their eyes instead and I move my hips a little, feeling the full red skirt sway around me. It's like thumbing your nose from behind a fence or teasing a dog with a bone held out of reach, and I'm ashamed of myself for doing it, because none of this is the fault of these men, they're too young.
>
> Then I find I'm not ashamed after all. I enjoy the power; power of a dog bone, passive but there. (Atwood 1985: 32)

Atwood's story continually reveals the ways in which both sexes are brutalised under a system that allows them no freedom of expression, either sexually or in other aspects of their identity. Her narrative switches from Offred's present – Gilead – to her past, allowing us to appreciate the rapidity of the transition from free society to repressive regime and the terrifying way in which ideologies can take hold of an individual and destroy memory. It is a stark warning, with Atwood using her sci fi setting to put into dramatic relief the effect of curtailing the kinds of freedoms that second-wave feminists were fighting for. She shows through the character of the Commander how easily and ruthlessly such freedoms can be rolled back: 'the problem wasn't only with the women, he says. The main problem was with the men. There was nothing for them any more' (Atwood 1985: 221). Her text, like much feminist sci fi, thus comments directly on the historical period in which it was written, characterised as it was by the Christian fundamentalism of Ronald Reagan's United States and the Muslim fundamentalism taking hold in the Middle East. In interviews, Atwood has reinforced this messaging about the ease with which liberal ideas can be rolled back or reversed.

Atwood has always challenged the categorisation of her work as pure science fiction, arguing rather that it is 'speculative' fiction:

> [it] conned some people into believing it is science fiction, which, to my mind, it is not. I define science fiction as fiction in which things happen that are not possible today [. . .] but in *The Handmaid's Tale*, nothing happens which the human race has not already done at some time in the past, or which it is not doing now, perhaps in other countries, or for which it has not yet developed the technology. (Atwood 2005: 85)

Atwood's text was written at a time when the second-wave feminist movement was beginning to infiltrate the mainstream and, in so doing, provoking a backlash. Her novel consequently dramatises this dangerous scenario and points to the fragility of women's hard-won civil rights and equality. Indeed, the figure of Offred's mother may be seen as a stark reminder of what is at stake in this respect, since she represents the feminists of Atwood's own generation who, in Gilead, have been declared 'unwomen' and whose 'radical' stance on women's liberation Offred and her contemporaries have rejected to their cost.

As feminist critic Jenny Wolmark argues 'what the narratives of feminist science fiction can do is to test the limits of the dominant ideology of gender by proposing alternative possibilities for social and sexual relations which conflict with the dominant representations' (Wolmark 1993: 35). Atwood's text does just that, imagining a future patriarchal culture in which the erosion of women's rights – the 'freedom' that had been so hard-won in the 1960s, 1970s and 1980s – has been taken to an extreme conclusion. In so doing, it illustrates the destructiveness, and also the arbitrariness, of the ways in which nations and societies can very easily revert to highly conservative norms of gender and sexuality (as is evidenced in so many parts of the world at the present time). Sarah Lefanu, one of the genre's most important commentators, posited science fiction as intrinsically radical *and* feminist, a place where the writer can weave between modernity and futurity in order to imagine new outcomes and convey subversive messages (Lefanu 1988).

The celebrated American science and technology studies (STS) scholar Donna Haraway similarly looked at the potential of (feminist) science fiction to destabilise normative categories, invoking the figure of the cyborg to interrogate gender, sexuality, feminism, politics and ethnicity. Her influential *Cyborg Manifesto* (1985) (which I will look at later in this chapter) was crucial to the development of feminist science fiction, establishing both a critical framework for the genre and a futuristic 'body' against which women writers could compare the human form. This blurring of the boundary between human and machine has been further explored by writers such as Jenny Wolmark and, more recently, Katharine Hayles, whose work on the 'post-human' continues to explore the ways that sci fi bodies evoke 'the exhilarating prospect of getting out of some of the old boxes and opening up new ways of thinking about what being human means' (Hayles 1999: 285). Along with romance and crime writing, as discussed in Chapters 6 and 7, science fiction has thus been embraced by women writers wishing to make visible the 'alien' nature of socially constructed sex, gender, sexuality and other markers of identity. I will now turn to look in detail at the way that gender has been problematised by this genre of writing, and the lasting impact that feminist sci fi has had on both literary and popular culture.

Case study 8.1 Jane Palmer's *The Watcher*

Jane Palmer's feminist sci fi novels were published by The Women's Press during the second wave, part of a series that also featured writers such as Joanna Russ, Naomi Mitchison, Sarah Lefanu and Rhoda Lerman. Palmer's first novel, *The Planet Dweller* (1985), was followed by a sequel, *Moving Moosevan* (1990), but I am focusing here on her second work of fiction, *The Watcher* (1986). This text contains classic elements of the science fiction genre – time travel, extra-terrestrial life and androids – as well as the feminist sci fi inclusion of a gendered perspective in the story. Palmer's (anti)heroine, the Star Dancer, is shown to inhabit the body of a teenage girl, while the alien beings that oversee the smooth running of the universe are hermaphroditic single-parent aliens (the Ojalie). The overall message the text conveys is that 'men' – of the human kind – are largely absent from all the important work.

After various planet-threatening moments are survived, the character of Gabrielle is ultimately revealed to be a Watcher, the most powerful force in the universe. Palmer playfully sets up an interchange between Gabrielle and Wendle, a man from the eighteenth century who, because of alien intervention, is still alive in the 1980s. He observes of her: 'you'd never make a good wife. You've too much mind of your own', to which Gabrielle replies, 'I can't have children anyway' (Palmer 1986: 74). Palmer thus presents the contemporary attitudes of patriarchal culture, in which a 'good wife' is meek, subservient . . . and fertile. She also makes clear the historical lineage of this construction of gender by voicing these sexist ideas through a man who has lived for hundreds of years. It is, of course, also hugely ironic that the character who in fact turns out to be the most powerful entity in the universe is chastised for not being 'good wife' material.

The story is ultimately one of love conquering all, as an android develops the ability to feel emotion and falls in love with a middle-aged woman, Penny. Palmer deliberately constructs the romantic heroine as a somewhat unlikely one – neither young nor very beautiful, and the former partner of a violent and abusive man who continues to threaten her throughout the narrative. She gives Penny the adventure of a lifetime, and leaves her at the end of the story with a protective and loving – albeit non-human – partner. In turn, Weatherby – the 'Kybion' android whom she marries at the end of the novel – is shown to develop a sense of humanity, and it is this that saves him from 'dismantling' as he delivers himself into Penny's arms: 'you were not spared because you developed a human biology, but because you somehow acquired a spirit along the way' (Palmer 1986: 177).

Palmer thus uses the character of Weatherby to provide a commentary on inequalities arising from ethnicity as well as gender. Indeed, she shows through her black-skinned android that it is his 'ethnicity' rather than his cybernetics that makes him an outsider. The novel also contains a critique of corporate greed, as the various characters who seek to exploit the universe's dwindling power source are each dispatched in spectacular style. The text's predominant preoccupation, however, is with what it means to be male, female and human, with Palmer showing us that, inasmuch as all human behaviours and systems are 'learnt', all can be *re*-learnt in different ways. In her descriptions of the 'advanced' alien species, the Ojalie – whose sophistication is emphasised throughout the narrative, along with their ability to reproduce parthenogenetically – Palmer presents us with an alternative to our own restrictively gendered world on Earth. As the Watcher, Vian Solran, explains to his protégé Gabrielle: 'thought has no gender' (Palmer 1986: 112). Palmer's story, then, is a bold attempt to imagine a world where gender difference has disappeared entirely – one that she locates very, very far away from Earth.

Gender explorations in science fiction

Revealing the social and political construction of gender roles was a fundamental goal of second-wave feminist politics. Accordingly, it was central to the feminist sci fi experiment that emerged in the 1970s and 1980s, with women writers using the generic conventions of traditional science fiction to explore and disrupt dominant notions of subjectivity. As Wolmark explains, feminist sci fi's representations of alien beings, times and places had the effect of foregrounding the strangeness of 'reality': 'the unfixing of the seemingly stable categories of identity constructed around gender, race and class, becomes a means of contesting definitions of otherness, and in so doing, reconstituting subjectivity and identity in a non-totalising way' (Wolmark 1993: 26).

One of the first of these feminist sci fi texts was *The Left Hand of Darkness* (1969), in which author Ursula K. Le Guin explores the nature of gender and its constructedness. Her story is told from the perspective of Genly Ai, a native of the planet Terra, which substitutes for Earth. Ai is dispatched to another planet, Gethen, whose inhabitants are ambisexual, with no fixed gender identity. They can both choose, and change, their gender during a brief period each month in which they are sexually active; however, for the remainder of the time they are androgynous, and there is no demarcation of role, status or behaviour according to sex characteristics. Accordingly, their culture is depicted as hugely different from that of Terra, and Ai's quest to persuade the inhabitants of

Gethen to join the Ekumen confederacy becomes a very different pursuit. His journey becomes one in which he must make sense of his own identity and his ingrained assumptions about what gender means for himself and for those around him: 'in a sense, women are more alien to me than you are. With you I share one sex, anyhow' (Le Guin 1969: 191). Le Guin thus shows, through Ai's incomprehension of Gethen's culture, how arbitrary and often absurd our rules around gender and identity are, and her text is established as foundational of the feminist sci fi genre. Although an American writer, Le Guin's novel was hugely influential within the UK feminist movement and literary scene. It set up a new formula for women writers so that they could employ science fiction to explore feminist ideas, and thus paved the way for the glut of feminist sci fi writing that followed in the next two decades. It was also commercially very successful and is now established as a classic of the genre.

In another founding text of the feminist sci fi oeuvre, Joanna Russ depicts the lives of four women living in parallel worlds, differing in time and place, to similarly explore gender. *The Female Man*, written in 1970 but not published until 1975 in the US, portrays four female protagonists from different times and places crossing over into each other's worlds, and trying to make sense of the very different gender roles assigned to them within their respective cultures. The novel ends with each of its four female characters evaluating their lives and the society in which they live, and analysing what it means for each of them to be a woman: 'we will be ourselves. Until then I am silent; I can do no more. I am God's typewriter and the ribbon is typed out' (Russ 1975: 206). As with Le Guin's 1969 novel, Russ's was hugely influential for both the US and UK feminist and literary scenes, between which there was much crossover, and was published for a UK audience in 1985 by The Women's Press.

Along with these novels, Marge Piercy's 1976 *Woman on the Edge of Time*, helped set up the science fiction genre as one in which women writers could advance a feminist critique of gender difference. Rather like Palmer's novel in Case study 8.1, Piercy's story includes the depiction of an idealised – 'utopian' – world in which biological sex is irrelevant and gender difference, as we know it today, does not exist. Piercy juxtaposes this futuristic vision of harmony and happiness with a grim depiction of America in the 1970s, demonstrating that it is the oppression of women (and minority groups including BME men and women and LGBTI+ communities) in Western cultures that have created our dystopian present. Through her central protagonist, Connie, Piercy shows the development of an understanding of the limitations prescriptive gender identity places on all humanity. Connie is initially uncomprehending of, and revolted by, the genderless society to which she travels, and expresses this on her encounter of a hormonally modified man breastfeeding: 'these women thought they had won, but they had abandoned to men the last refuge of women' (Piercy 1976: 142). By aligning the reader with Connie, Piercy exposes our own expectations and prejudices, including, most notably, a fixed sense of what is 'natural' when it comes to sex and gender. Like the feminist theorist Shulamith Firestone, whose

The Dialectic of Sex was published six years before *Woman on the Edge of Time*, Piercy challenges us to look beyond this normativity and, in particular, our reverence for the 'biological' body. As with Donna Haraway's philosophy, we are challenged to consider the ways in which science and technology – rather than something to be feared – could become the cornerstone of our liberation.

Women have, of course, long been problematically associated with 'nature', which means that those technologies which promise to transcend, or at least question, what has traditionally been seen as women's biological destiny – principally, bearing children – have been of particular interest to feminist sci fi writers and academics. As noted earlier, the figure of the cyborg is especially significant in this regard, and in her immensely influential 'Cyborg Manifesto' (1983), Donna Haraway figured the cyborg as a post-gender being with the potential to defy normalising categories and to posit radically new ways of being: 'the cyborgs populating feminist science fiction make very problematic the statuses of man or woman, human, artefact, member of a race, individual entity, or body' (Haraway in Bell and Kennedy 2000: 314).

Following Haraway, numerous literary critics have explored the way in which cyborg technologies have enabled writers to rethink gender through the lens of the human/non-human. As Jenny Wolmark observes in her essay on the subject, 'the cyborgs in these novels are made but not born, just as they are different but not "other"' (Wolmark in Pearce and Stacey 1995: 167). Wolmark, here, is invoking Simone de Beauvoir's famous assertion that 'one is not born, but rather becomes, a woman' (see Chapter 2) in order to highlight the surprising similarities between women and cyborgs; while, on the surface, a robotic machine might appear to be everything that a 'flesh and blood' woman is not, both have been constructed according to very precise – and precisely gendered – social and cultural expectations. The contradictory identities cyborgs embody – as both human and not-human – thus present an opportunity for sci fi writers and scholars to expose and problematise the foundational assumptions that underpin Western thought.

As the second wave gave way to the third, the feminist imagination – inspired by Judith Butler's own queer vision (see Chapter 2) – was drawn to more fluid formulations of gender and sexuality and the popularity of feminist sci fi began to wane. Newly complex cultural manifestations of gender began to emerge that defied the masculine/feminine dyad – for example the lesbian 'femme' and the metrosexual man (see Chapter 2) – and the feminist sci fi project of dismantling the gender binary lost its impetus. This is not to say that women writers have abandoned the genre altogether, but rather that there has been a move away from deconstructing gender identities and towards the creation of a new kind of 'hero/ine'. In the twenty-first century, the science fiction genre as a whole has been mainstreamed by the huge popularity of book series such as Twilight and the Hunger Games trilogy, both written by women, as well as TV franchises such as *Buffy the Vampire Slayer* and *Xena: Warrior Princess*. What all these contemporary sci fi texts and programmes have in common is the centrality of strong female characters; this is surely a legacy of second-wave feminist sci fi writing, even if the interrogation of gender per se has once more slipped from view. At the same time, influential proponents of feminist sci fi such as Margaret Atwood have expanded upon their early preoccupation with issues of gender and are now writing speculative fiction with an intersectional focus on the many and complex challenges (social, virtual, environmental) facing our twenty-first-century world, as I now go on to discuss.

Case study 8.2 Margaret Atwood's MaddAddam trilogy

Canadian writer Margaret Atwood is one of the great innovators in the realm of 'speculative fiction'. As already noted, she rejects the categorisation of her work as science fiction, arguing that everything that happens in her novels is feasible and may even have already happened; her work is a speculation on the 'already-possible'. Nearly twenty years on from the phenomenal success of her 1985 'sci fi' text *The Handmaid's Tale*, Atwood embarked upon a trilogy of novels – *Oryx and Crake* (2003), *The Year of the Flood* (2009) and *MaddAddam* (2013) – which similarly anticipate and/or describe gendered aspects of the future, as well as speculating upon the impact of virtual reality, changes to female sexuality, the fate of the environment and the impact of global corporations. This said, in many ways Atwood's MaddAddam trilogy continues the project she began in *The Handmaid's Tale* of portraying the ways in which the unequal and unethical appropriation of technology and natural resources in the present has direct and devastating consequences for gender equality in the future. The texts also tackle contemporary concerns about corporate greed and the domination of multinational companies and, in this, may be seen to be responding directly to the vision of academics such as Naomi Klein (2000) who have expressed concerns about the twenty-first century proving a terrifying 'tipping point' in the history of the world.

Even though we are still only in the second decade of the twenty-first century, Atwood's prescience has proven uncanny: the genetic splicing, global pandemics and corporate bullying of government described in the first novel of her MaddAddam trilogy, published in 2003, are already part of our everyday world, suggesting that even the more outrageous details of her dystopian imaginings are just a genetic adaptation, or corporate error, away from reality. *Oryx and Crake* foretells of environmental disaster and the end of humanity, exploring the consequences of a devastating exploitation of nature in the same way as *The Handmaid's Tale* portrayed the consequences of the centralisation of patriarchal power in a profoundly misogynist theocracy: 'just as her most celebrated novel *The Handmaid's Tale* unveiled an apocalyptic vision, so too does *Oryx and*

Crake, but this time it is an ecological rather than a reproductive horror story' (Pepinster 2003). *Oryx and Crake* differs, too, in that it uses a male narrator, emphasising that the effects of the rapacious commodification and corporatisation are fundamentally *human* concerns:

> Atwood has long been known for her accounts of women trapped by circumstance. There was Offred in *The Handmaid's Tale*, Grace Marks in the penitentiary in *Alias Grace* and Elaine, paralysed by childhood bullying, in *Cat's Eye*. Here she turns her attention to a man similarly imprisoned. (Pepinster 2003)

The narrative of *Oryx and Crake* addresses the corrupting power of corporate multinationals and their monopolies on human and natural resources, the mainstreaming of pornography in culture and its effects on human relationships, and the technological development of weapons of mass destruction. Atwood uses the setting of a not-very-distant future to portray one possible outcome of the ways in which these issues are unfolding in the contemporary. Through the character of Crake, she also reveals the destructiveness of the drive to 'control' nature and to dictate human behaviour, showing how Crake's obsession with creating an idealised 'race' – the Crakers – leads him from eugenicist ideas of human perfection to the genocidal extermination of all human life. His genetically engineered Craker people are evocative of Ursula Le Guin's Gethen inhabitants; like them, the Crakers are sexually active only during set times and in prescribed ways, and are thus a tool for Atwood to highlight the constructed nature of human sexual behaviours:

> No more prostitution, no sexual abuse of children, no haggling over the price, no pimps, no sex slaves. No more rape. The five of them [four male and one female Craker according to the routine programmed by Crake] will roister for hours, three of the men standing guard and doing the singing and shouting while the fourth one copulates, turn and turn about. Crake has equipped these women with ultra-strong vulvas – extra skin layers, extra muscles – so they can sustain these marathons. (Atwood 2003: 194–5)

But what Crake conceives of as a perfecting of human sexual impulse inevitably eradicates the pleasures associated with emotional intimacy, and thus Atwood's depiction of Craker sexuality reveals it to be absurd. It is telling, too, that Crake bases his idea of perfect female sexuality on the former porn star, Oryx, with whom he is obsessed. As Pepinster observes:

> unusually in Atwood's fiction, this female character is the book's least compelling creation, and it is strangely hard to care about her fate. Perhaps this blankness and superficiality just at the place where the novel's emotional

centre ought to lie is another way in which Atwood conveys the extent to which humanity has declined. (Pepinster 2003)

Oryx is a bland and disconnected cipher, her vacuity linked to the absence of emotion evident in all products of the sex industry, and my sense is that Atwood uses this female character, and the technologically engineered race named after her, to convey the ways that female sexuality and gender identity continue to be problematic themes for contemporary feminism, as well as ones which can be effectively highlighted through the conventions of speculative fiction writing.

In the second MaddAddam book, *The Year of the Flood*, Atwood switches perspective to chronicle Crake's pandemic from the point of view of two of its survivors, Toby and Ren. Both these women are subject to male sexual brutality, with Toby escaping the sadistic Blanco to find safety in the Gardeners' community, while Ren leaves the Gardeners to work in a sex club – ironically finding protection there from Crake's pandemic by virtue of a bio-containment unit. Atwood continues her interrogation of gender and sex roles amid the chaos of a post-apocalyptic landscape offering, according to Ursula Le Guin, who reviewed the novel for *The Guardian*, a devastating critique of contemporary culture via the device of a futuristic setting:

> Much of the story is violent and cruel. None of the male characters are developed at all; they play their roles, no more. The women are real people, but heartbreaking ones. Ren's chapters are a litany of a gentle soul enduring endless degradation with endless patience. Toby's nature is tougher, but she is tried to the limit and beyond. Perhaps the book is not an affirmation at all, only a lament, a lament for what little was good about human beings – affection, loyalty, patience, courage – ground down into the dust by our overweening stupidity and monkey cleverness and crazy hatefulness. (Le Guin 2009)

In *The Year of the Flood*, the post-pandemic lives of men and women are ruled by violence, sexual exploitation and the proliferation of exploitative corporate greed. The character of Blanco, for example, is used to show the effects of the normalisation of women's sexual objectification and the sexual violence arising from the ways women are portrayed in popular and online cultures:

> He wasn't above a random stomp-and-rape. He'd drag her up that very same alleyway, the one where the pleebrats had gone. Then he'd rip off the cone and see who she was. And that would be the end, but it wouldn't be a quick end. It would be as slow as he could make it. He'd turn her into a flesh billboard – a not-quite-living demonstration of his rank finesse. (Atwood 2009: 121)

Atwood uses Blanco to show the extent to which demeaning and disempowered depictions of women have become part of everyday discourse around sex and female sexuality. *The Year of the Flood* thus evidences contemporary feminism's concern with the role the internet and virtual technology play in actively constructing ideas of appropriate and/or enjoyable sexual behaviours, and shows that Atwood is once again drawing attention to the gross absence of equality and respect for women in much of contemporary culture, as she did in *The Handmaid's Tale*.

In the final book of her trilogy, *MaddAddam*, Atwood concludes her imagining of a future in which the nation state has been entirely displaced by global corporations, so depicting a set of possible outcomes of current political trajectories. She once again describes and situates feminist discussions around women in technology and virtual environments, the commodification of women's bodies in these contexts, gendered aspects of environmental futures and the gendered consequences of the rapacious commodification and corporatisation of our culture. *MaddAddam* reunites the reader with Jimmy from the first novel of the trilogy, and Toby and Ren from the second, as well as the Crakers, with whom the few human survivors of Crake's pandemic are now attempting to rebuild some sort of civilisation.

MaddAddam ultimately shows that salvation – or simply, the reprieve of a possible future – lies in the coming together of disparate communities or 'tribes'. As Michèle Roberts put it in her review of the novel, 'people formerly suspicious of one another have had to join together' (Roberts 2013). In order for a future of any kind to be possible or even imaginable, Atwood's narrative advocates local cooperation as an antidote to corporate takeover, communality over the cult of the individual. She thus utilises the conventions of the sci fi/speculative fiction genre to posit a hypothetical version of the future which calls for action in the present, showing the devastating consequences of continued exploitation of the world's natural and human resources. Indeed, Atwood's MaddAddam trilogy is a powerful, often chilling, exploration of the possible trajectories humanity may take under the seemingly unstoppable non-human forces of capitalism, neo-liberalism, globalisation and the digital revolution. It is therefore fitting that this fiction series ends with the Craker child Blackbeard, symbolic of humankind's hope for the future, learning to write – a statement on the importance of storytelling to human health and happiness. As Michèle Roberts observes:

> This neo-Biblical language underlines how the Fall charted by the trilogy, caused by the would-be godly arrogance and greed characterising late capitalism, became necessary. Paradise Regained embodies the

acknowledgment of failure, of death, which permits re-growth. Babies will be born, both Craker and human. Atwood's story ends intensely movingly, with the damaged world potentially renewed through storytelling, through writing. (Roberts 2013)

This is a powerful message from one of feminism's most powerful story-tellers.

Bibliography

Armitt, Lucie (ed.). 1991. *Where No Man Has Gone Before: Women and Science Fiction*. London: Routledge.

Armitt, Lucie. 1996. *Theorising the Fantastic*. London: Arnold.

Atwood, Margaret. 1985. *The Handmaid's Tale*. London: Virago (1987).

Atwood, Margaret. 2003. *Oryx and Crake*. London: Virago.

Atwood, Margaret. 2005. *Curious Pursuits: Occasional Writing 1970–2005*. London: Virago.

Atwood, Margaret. 2009. *The Year of the Flood*. London: Bloomsbury.

Atwood, Margaret. 2013. *MaddAddamm*. London: Bloomsbury.

Barr, Marleen S. 1992. *Feminist Fabulation: Space/Postmodern Fiction*. Iowa City: University of Iowa Press.

Cranny-Francis, Anne. 1990. *Feminist Fiction: Feminist Uses of Generic Fiction*. New York: St Martin's Press.

Firestone, Shulamith. 1970. *The Dialectic of Sex*. London: Paladin.

Gearhart, Sally Miller. 1979. *The Wanderground*. Boston: Persephone Press.

Haraway, Donna. 1983. 'A Cyborg Manifesto: Science, Technology and Socialist Feminism in the Late Twentieth Century'. In *The Cybercultures Reader*. David Bell and Barbara M. Kennedy (eds). London: Routledge (2000).

Hayles, Katherine. 1999. *How We Became Post-Human: Virtual Bodies in Cybernetics, Literature and Informatics*. Chicago: University of Chicago Press.

Hite, Molly. 1989. *The Other Side of the Story: Structures and Strategies of Contemporary Feminist Narrative*. Ithaca: Cornell University Press.

Holliday, Liz. 1990. 'War of the Words'. In *The Guardian*, 4 October.

Klein, Naomi. 2000. *No Logo*. London: Flamingo.

Le Guin, Ursula. 1969. *The Left Hand of Darkness*. London: Orbit.

Le Guin, Ursula. 2009. '*The Year of the Flood* by Margaret Atwood'. In *The Guardian*, 29 August.

LeFanu, Sarah. 1988. *In the Chinks of the World Machine: Feminism and Science Fiction*. London: The Women's Press.

Palmer, Jane. 1986. *The Watcher*. London: The Women's Press.

Pearce, Lynne and Jackie Stacey (eds). 1995. *Romance Revisited*. London: Lawrence and Wishart.

Pepinster, Catherine. 2003. 'When Pigoons Attack, Readers Run for Cover'. In *The Independent on Sunday*, 1 June.

Piercy, Marge. 1976. *Woman on the Edge of Time*. New York: Ballantyne.

Roberts, Michèle. 2013. 'Book Review: *MaddAddam*, By Margaret Atwood'. In *The Independent*, 16 August.

Russ, Joanna. 1975. *The Female Man*. London: Gollancz.

Sage, Lorna. 1994a. *Angela Carter*. Plymouth: Northcote House Publishers.

Sage, Lorna (ed.). 1994b. *Flesh and the Mirror: Essays on the Art of Angela Carter*. London: Virago.

Spender, Dale. 1985. 'Inner Thoughts From Outer Space'. In *The Guardian*, 10 January.

Wolmark, Jenny. 1993. *Aliens and Others: Science Fiction, Feminism and Postmodernism*. New York: Harvester Wheatsheaf.

9   Life-writing

Because of the popularity of 'authentic realist' feminist reading practices in the 1970s (see Mills and Pearce 1996) – whereby women were inspired to read books by other women in order to validate and/or challenge their life experiences – there is a long tradition of memoir and autobiography in contemporary women's writing. As women learned to re-evaluate their own lives, the first-person narrative accounts of other women played a vital role in raising consciousness and showing alternative ways of living. In this chapter I will look at women's engagement with the various types of what is now known as 'life-writing', encompassing autobiography, epistolary writing, memoir and personal narrative.* Women's engagement with life-writing thus includes private jottings in diaries and letters as well as self-conscious tellings of individual stories.

There has been a complex and rich critical engagement with life-writing, as feminist critics set out to understand and elucidate the genre and to establish the reasons for its strong female tradition. As Sidonie Smith and Julia Watson explain in their contribution to Trev Broughton's exhaustive compendium of critical works on women's life-writing: 'in the multiple plottings, separate voices, divergent memories, and diverse audiences that even apparently uncomplicated life narratives invite, there is a world of identities and stories to emerge' (Smith and Watson in Broughton 2007: 367).

During feminism's first wave, many women wrote their own life stories as a way of transmitting solidarity with other women, as well as claiming their experiences to be worthy of retelling. One of the most famous of these life stories was that of Vera Brittain, comprising three books, the first of which was published in 1933. *Testament of Youth* is a remarkable and important autobiography which describes one woman's experience of the First World War (Case study 9.1). Brittain's text was one of a number of other 'feminist' autobiographies penned in the wake of the first wave which set out the struggles women faced in a culture that was starkly limiting of their freedoms. As her biographer Mark Bostridge explains:

> for an understanding of *Testament of Youth* in a broader context, the book
> needs to be viewed as one of the large number of women's autobiographies and

---

* It is important to register that autobiography and memoir are two distinct forms: autobiographies tell a story of the author's life (often from childhood through to maturity), while memoirs focus on particular episodes and events in a life – often in fragmented and/or non-sequential ways.

biographical histories published in the twenties and thirties, which attempted to
reconstruct and assess the pre-war period and the years between 1914 and 1918.
(Bostridge 2004: xiii)

These first-wave autobiographies helped institute the idea that the personal
was political. Reading women's autobiographical writing was, in the same way,
to form an important aspect of the consciousness-raising that was critical to
early formulations of second-wave feminism. Texts such as Sue Kaufman's
Diary of a Mad Housewife (1967) provided literary examples of the frustrations women felt in their everyday lives, allowing them a focus through which
to express their frustrations. As the second wave progressed, there was also a
critical engagement with women's life-writing, which constituted an important
element of the feminist literary critical project, inserting women's contributions
into analyses of autobiographical writing in general, for example, to show that
it shares 'the distinction of being one of the first literary genres shaped with the
active participation of women' (Pomerleau in Jelinek 1980: 22).

This critical reframing of women's life-writing was intended to rescue the
genre for women since male critical appraisal had served to denigrate it and to
prevent women from imagining themselves as individuals with their own stories
to tell. This was in large part because the most celebrated autobiographies of the
nineteenth and early twentieth centuries focused on the public lives and achievements of great men – such as John Ruskin's *Praeterita* (1885). Second-wave
feminist literary critics argued that mainstream assessment of life-writing continued to relegate women's contributions to the margins, 'uncritically conflating
the dynamics of male and female selfhood and textuality' (Smith 1987: 15). They
countered this false framing of women's life-writing by exploring the way in
which it both distorted facts and evaded 'truths', and they posited new models
for how we should read such writing. Alongside this analysis of women's autobiographical writing, the second-wave feminist publishing houses played a key
role in providing textual examples, thus helping to make newly visible women's
contributions to public and intellectual life. Republishing historical life-writing
texts was a crucial part of early second-wave politicking, reintroducing important autobiographies such as Harriet Martineau's, which had dropped out of
circulation, to a contemporary – and feminist – readership (Martineau 1877).

Arising from this feminist analysis, women writers created some radical reinventions of the life-writing genre, and Case study 9.2 examines in detail one
such example. Jeanette Winterson's *Oranges Are Not The Only Fruit* (1985)
is simultaneously both an autobiography and a contestation of the meaning
of the genre. Winterson's debut novel reveals the fluidity of 'truth'-telling in
all fiction writing, with the author simultaneously denying that the text is a
memoir while also insisting that it tells the 'real' story of her childhood. This
'quasi-autobiography' is thus a textual example of the radical reinvention of the
genre that played out during feminism's second wave, challenging the edifices of
a tradition from which women had historically been excluded.

Following the discussion of Winterson, this chapter turns to look at contemporary feminist engagements with life-writing, from the perspective of both the authors and their women readers. This includes exploration of the collective experience of reading autobiography, by which – as Mary Jacobus (1986) argued – women 'read' themselves into the life stories of other women (and men) in order to generate a sense of solidarity and validate their own experiences. Life-writing thus makes reading into an identificatory exchange, in which the reader sees herself in a text and compares her experiences with the author's and that of other readers. Other critics such as Carolyn Ellis (2004) went on to examine the 'autobiographical turn' in feminist criticism itself, noting how 'autoethnography' has proven an increasingly popular methodology in textual/cultural analyses (see also Jackie Stacey and Janet Wolff's *Writing Otherwise*, 2013).

Post-millennium, the cultural shift towards ever-greater reification of the individual and the explosion of celebrity culture (promoted, in part, by the rise of digital and social media) has seen a trend towards ever more life-writing entering the public domain. In a literary and cultural *zeitgeist* in which the cult of the individual is so pervasive, life-writing nevertheless retains the possibility of communicating political messages through personal storytelling. Indeed, it has enabled many prominent feminist activists to harness the autobiographical genre for explicitly political ends, especially those that depend upon creating female/feminist communities. However, as critics such as Liz Stanley (1992) have pointed out, autobiography per se (i.e. the stories we tell retrospectively about our lives as opposed to diaries and letters which record the historical present) also comes with a warning when engaging with 'real life' and/or political issues, since memory is necessarily selective and limited. Critical appraisal of life-writing in the third and fourth waves has become increasingly aware of the psychological complexities and differences of the types of writing included under its umbrella, and has challenged, in particular, the more naïve assumptions about autobiographies being authentic records of people's lives. This has had repercussions for feminist analyses of both writerly and readerly engagements with the genre.

Case study 9.1 Vera Brittain's *Testament of Youth*

Vera Brittain's *Testament of Youth* was published in 1933, and was an immediate success, selling out its first print run of 3,000 copies on the day of its release. Brittain's literary contemporaries were united in their praise for her memoir, with Rebecca West, Pamela Hinkson and Storm Jameson (other notable first-wave feminists) among those British women writers who gave her glowing reviews. Virginia Woolf later wrote to Brittain to acknowledge the links the book made for her between feminism and pacifism, themes that Woolf would make central to much of her own writing in the years that followed. *Testament of Youth* was published at the same time as autobiographical texts by other feminist writers, such as Beatrice Webb and Sylvia Pankhurst, and was part of a literary 'moment' – for the first time, women took on autobiographical writing to celebrate their lives, and to wrest the genre from men who had made it a 'masculine' mode of expression.

The popular conceptualisation of autobiography as a male form of writing meant that Brittain had, at first, tried to write her story as fiction:

> first she made several attempts at fictionalising her wartime experiences, without much success. It was only when she decided to write as herself that her authorial voice seemed to flow and the events she had endured were given a poignant immediacy to which readers could relate. In *Testament of Youth*, the words seemed to pour out of her, a potent mixture of rage and loss, underpinned by lively intelligence and fervent pacifist beliefs. (Day 2013)

Giving herself the freedom to write in her own voice meant that Brittain was able, finally, to articulate the particular experience of being a woman and living through the war. It is this immediacy that gives her memoir its lasting power.

As well as challenging the historical construction of autobiography as a masculine genre, *Testament of Youth* also challenged the ways in which writing about the war was constituted as male. Until *Testament of Youth*, literary representations of the First World War had been the preserve of male writers such as Wilfred Owen and Siegfried Sassoon. With the immediate sales success of Brittain's text, and its wide readership, she quickly shifted these parameters to include and illuminate women's experiences of war, and to make these as important as the experiences of the men who fought. This was implicitly her intent, as she wrote in the journal *Nation and Athenaeum* in 1931, two years before her memoir was published: 'the woman is still silent who, by presenting the war in its true perspective in her own life, will illuminate its meaning afresh for its own generation' (Brittain 1931).

Brittain's text focuses not only on the heartbreak of the personal losses she experienced – her fiancée Ronald Leighton, brother Edward and two friends Victor Richardson and Geoffrey Thurlow were all killed in the war – but also the horror of her experiences as a Voluntary Aid Detachment (VAD) nurse in Britain and France, tending to wounded soldiers. It institutes these experiences as being of equal importance to those of the men on the front line, and as worthy of retelling. Brittain's account foregrounds the drudging endlessness of the deaths she deals with during the years of the war, of men she loved and men she tended to only briefly. The private losses she endures force her to question public attitudes towards the war, and towards a culture that preached heroism and glorious death on the battlefield for one sex, and dutiful obedience for the other. In this, 'Brittain helped to pioneer the feminist approach that explores how the apparently personal is also deeply political' (Roberts 2014). In telling her story as autobiography, Brittain helped promote the idea that personal experiences are inextricably linked to political positions – the power of her story is in the linking of the two. For writer and feminist Natasha Walter, it is this ability to weave the political into the personal that makes Brittain's memoir so riveting:

> You just feel this journey she's going on. She tells it with incredible immediacy [. . .]. It all comes through in this torrent of force and personal power. You don't have to be at all interested in feminism or pacifism to get it. (Quoted in Day 2013)

Making the personal political was, of course, a central tenet of second-wave feminism, and it was the second-wave feminist publisher Virago that revived *Testament of Youth* for a new generation of readers in 1978. Following the outbreak of the Second World War, Brittain's pacifism fell out of favour and her book out of print, and she died in 1970 believing that she would not be remembered as a writer of any note. In fact, she is now regarded as one of the most important women writers of the twentieth century, and *Testament of Youth* as one of its most important autobiographical texts. This is largely down to the intervention of Virago, and specifically its publisher, Carmen Callil (and a TV series that followed in 1979 brought the work to an even wider audience). Elizabeth Day reported in *The Observer* in 2013 that:

> Carmen Callil [. . .] says it is Brittain's refusal to comply with accepted norms that gives the book its power. 'To some degree I suppose it had the impact it did because of the anguish in it, which so many women must have felt,' says Callil. 'Brittain wasn't going to put up with it. She was saying: "This is awful." Those women who lost their sons, who sent their sons away – it was just accepted. I think that's an outrage, myself. I think you feel the same when you see these people dying in Iraq. Vera Brittain taught millions of people that you didn't have to put up with war if it wasn't a just war'. (Day 2013)

Although Brittain's autobiography is now synonymous with the First World War, it is not only a story of war:

it has sometimes been overlooked that little more than a third of *Testament of Youth* is concerned with Brittain's account of her wartime experiences. Two chapters of almost a hundred pages precede the beginning of her narrative of the war, which describe Brittain's attempts to escape the living death of her provincial young ladyhood and her personal struggles for education. (Bostridge 2004: xii)

Brittain's story chronicles the injustices not only of war but also of a woman's place in a patriarchal culture which limits her ambition, her opportunities and her freedom:

Brittain's feminism courses through her memoir. Growing up in a conservative middle-class family in Buxton, Derbyshire, she writes unapologetically about her own ambitions to better herself, and wins an exhibition to Oxford despite her parents' traditional ideas about a woman's place being in the home. When the war breaks out, she rages against the injustice of it and, frustrated by her own powerlessness, volunteers as a nurse in order to make a difference. (Day 2013)

Testament of Youth is, indeed, an extraordinary chronicle of a young woman defying societal expectations and gender norms. It is as powerful for its feminist politics as its pacifism, as Brittain records her frustrations with the limits her gender places upon her at a time when the suffragette movement was gaining pace:

'It feels sad to be a woman!' I wrote in March 1913 – the very month in which the 'Cat and Mouse' Act was first introduced for the ingenious torment of the militants.* 'Men seem to have so much more choice as to what they are intended for.' (Brittain 1933: 42)

Feminism's influence on Brittain is evident in the choices she makes as a young woman – to pursue her education, to take an active role in the war, as far as her gender allows her – as well as in the way she chooses to tell her own story in later life. Making *Testament of Youth* an autobiography is as powerful a feminist choice as is her decision to take up a place at Oxford, or to leave Oxford to become a VAD nurse during the war. Brittain very deliberately positions her story in a genre that afforded it a different kind of critical view, one that could not be devalued as mere 'fiction' – and in that, it leaves its own very powerful feminist legacy.

---

* The 'Cat and Mouse' Act sought to deal with hunger-striking suffragettes by allowing them an early release from prison, then re-incarcerating them upon their recovering their health, hence avoiding the potential scandal of having them die in prison.

Feminist critical appraisal of autobiographical writing

The arrival of feminism's second wave gave Brittain's text new meaning for a new generation of readers. The feminist publishing house Virago reprinted *Testament of Youth* in 1978 as part of its project to reclaim – and reprint – women's history. Former Virago publisher Carmen Callil believed that historical autobiographies were important for contemporary feminism in shining a light on women's histories and experiences: 'we knew that women had recorded their lives in memoirs and autobiographies, their pasts in biographies and histories – by 1976 most of them unavailable for decades' (Callil 1980: 1001). Virago began the Reprint Library to excavate women's memoirs and autobiographies in order to allow women in the present to trace continuities with writers from the past. Accordingly, Virago published memoirs by Storm Jameson, the diaries of Beatrice Potter Webb, essays by Rebecca West, and memoirs by Mary Stott, Kathleen Dayus and Antonia White, among many others, during its early years.

This effort was part of a growing project within feminism to interrogate and illuminate women's autobiographical writing. Virago also published a significant number of contemporary texts, as did the other UK feminist publishing houses, including The Women's Press, Sheba and Pandora. Ursula Owen, one of these second-wave feminist publishers, recalls:

> Virago's early autobiographies and diaries drew in a wide readership and became essential texts for students in the humanities, arts and social sciences [. . .] all demonstrated the scale of women's contribution to understanding social and political life, war and peace, poverty and education [. . .] While speaking in the first-person singular, they brought to light experience of whole social groups and classes. The autobiographical element brought new dimensions of experience – accounts of friendship, birth and death, children, work, abortion, loving wrong men and right men (these women were particularly good at examining love). The personal in their hands informed the political culture – one of the most important ideas of the second-wave women's movement. (Owen 2009)

As Owen argues, women's life-writing helped establish the idea that middle-class women had always contributed to public life and academic pursuit. Publishing contemporary memoirs and autobiographies that demonstrated women's ongoing cultural and intellectual contributions, alongside the earlier, historical works, was thus a crucial part of early second-wave politicking (indeed, during its first decade of publishing, life-writing of various kinds made up around 10 per cent of Virago's total published output). This was also enabled, and was enabled by, the emergence of a feminist critical appraisal of the genre during this period, as discussed above. Just as the genres of crime, romance and science fiction were refigured as being of literary significance by feminist critics, so too was life-writing.

In her iconic critical study *The Female Imagination* (1976), Patricia Meyer Spacks examined women's life-writing in order to reveal its liberatory potential. She sees evidence in the writing of nineteenth-century women, for example, of an obsession with selfhood and identity which evidences their struggle to reconcile their wholly private, protected existence with the writing that took them beyond this domain: 'to write about themselves for the public eye represented significant activity, defying the social expectation of female inertness and invisibility' (Spacks 1976: 72). Spacks reasons that the historical restriction of women's freedoms meant that the antagonistic nature of male–female relations found expression in autobiographical writing, albeit often elliptically. In their self-writing, women's anger 'emerges more unequivocally than anger usually does in novels, where the demands of fictional form urges resolution' (Spacks 1976: 197). She is clear, however, that in spite of there being a 'female imagination' that manifests in women's writing, there is no fundamental difference between the life-writing of men and women: 'all autobiography must rest on a foundation of self-absorption; men as well as women indulge in self-manufacture and self-display' (Spacks 1976: 306).

Spacks does argue, though, that women have a problematic relationship with autobiography because it necessitates a claim of significance, one which is more difficult for women writers to make than men (Spacks 1976: 72). She uses the example of Charlotte Perkins Gilman's text *The Yellow Wallpaper*, first published in 1892 and republished in the UK in 1981 by Virago, to illustrate many of her points about autobiography. Her analysis enables a re-reading of the text that establishes it not simply as a detached study of madness, but rather as an autobiographical account of one woman's psychological breakdown. In reprinting the text, Virago included in its edition Gilman's reflective preface to her work 'Why I Wrote *The Yellow Wallpaper*'. This inclusion of Gilman's own account of how the text came into being means the Virago edition gives the author a critical/analytic voice, allowing her to frame her story as a political autobiography rather than a fanciful fiction. Virago's version thus opens with a feminist discussion of the autobiographical genre, and then in turn becomes part of that very discussion.

In this way, Spacks links the 'private' nature of autobiographical writing with the private, domestic realm to which most middle-class women had historically been limited. 'Women, for obvious social reasons, have traditionally had more difficulty than men about making public claims of their own importance. They have excelled in the writing of diaries and journals, which require no such claims' (Spacks in Jelinek 1980: 122). Other feminist critics of the genre similarly turned their attention to its gendered historical roots, with Estelle Jelinek arguing that women's autobiography (as with so much other women's writing) had been sidelined within the literary tradition:

> [A]s men, these women's experiences would be described in heroic or exceptional terms: alienation, initiation, manhood, apotheosis, transformation, guilt, identity

crises, and symbolic journeys. As women, their experiences are viewed in more conventional terms: heartbreak, anger, loneliness, motherhood, humility, confusion and self-abnegation' (Jelinek 1980: 5)

What emerges, therefore, in these early attempts to capture and evaluate women's intervention in the genre is not only the fact that, historically, middle-class women were living very different lives to men – ones in which the private and the domestic contrasted with a life lived in the public realm – but also that they were positioned very differently in terms of their prospective audience. Whereas male public figures tended to turn their lives into a 'hero-narrative' (and still do, many would argue!), women autobiographers struggled to break free from self-perceptions predicated on popular stereotypes: well into the twentieth century, middle-class women tended to see themselves in passive, supportive and caring roles – not as active agents in the world (even when they were).

Following Spacks and Jelinek, Domna Stanton set about refiguring women's autobiography as worthy of literary merit. She coined the term 'autogynography' to refer specifically to women's autobiography, although she was clear that such writing was not *inherently* different to male autobiography. The distinction enforced by this new term, however, was in the ways women struggled to take on the position of the subjective 'I' in their writing: 'because of women's different status in the symbolic order, autogynography, I concluded, dramatised the fundamental alterity and non-presence of the subject, even as it asserts itself discursively and strives towards an always impossible self-possession' (Stanton 1984: 16). She argued that the scarcity of critical writing on women's autobiography was evidence of the masculinist assumption that *all* women's writing was in fact autobiographical, and she went on to assert that, in fact, women's 'autogynography' is not inherently different to men's, in spite of critical opinion that men write linear, coherent, chronological narratives, and women do not.

Stanton thus contests many of the gendered assumptions inherent in the literary review tradition, arguing that women, too, have written linearly, just as some men write elliptically or discontinuously. The difference, rather, is that a patriarchal culture and elite literary value systems make it much more difficult for women writers to achieve and demonstrate agency through their autobiographical writing, a self-possession that male writers assume unproblematically. This psychic restriction on women's writing is thus intrinsic to a cultural tradition that formulates women (readers and writers) as 'feminine' – a category that is, in their own experience, inferior and unvalued. Hence the critical reformulation of women's life-writing became a crucial feminist endeavour in the second wave, part of the challenge to a masculinist literary tradition that relegated women's contributions to the margins.

Theorising women's life-writing thus became of central significance in feminist literary criticism in general. Alongside this critical appraisal of the genre, feminist writers began to invent new ways of writing their own life stories, with texts such as Jeanette Winterson's *Oranges Are Not The Only Fruit* (1985) radically destabilising the notion of 'authentic' autobiography and memoir writing (for more on this text see Case study 9.2). Further, in her introduction to the 1983 edition of Kathleen Woodward's *Jipping Street* (1928), Carolyn Steedman proposes that female autobiography can be utilised to pose challenges to *cultural assumptions* around identity, as well as how we construct our own sense of self:

> *Jipping Street* is a psychological account of growing up female and working class. It is about a mother who is not the martyred saint of traditional male working-class autobiography, whose child, Kathleen Woodward, is bound to her not by love, nor by gratitude, but by a fierce sense of resentment and debt. (Steedman 1983: vi)

The characters in Woodward's text immediately challenge the historical construction of eternally loving mother and obedient, dependent daughter:

> what results from the relationship between mother and daughter described here seems not to have been the need to mother, but the impossibility of Kathleen Woodward's reproducing herself. On the evidence of *Jipping Street* she knew as a child that she was a burden to her mother, that she need never have been born, that mothers could indeed kill their children. (Steedman 1983: xiii)

Steedman argues that the author of the text is using her autobiography to posit alternatives to cultural norms:

> it becomes clear that, consciously or not, Kathleen Woodward wanted her readers to understand the tricks she played with autobiography and narrative, her reversals of topography, and her ironies of characterisation and literary allusion. (Steedman 1983: xi)

Steedman herself went on to write her own memoir, through which she continued this interrogation of the nature of autobiography – and the cultural myths that have surrounded the mother–daughter relationship. In *Landscape For a Good Woman* (1986), Steedman purports to tell her own life story, yet draws our attention throughout to the fact that it is simultaneously both the story of her relationship with her mother in her childhood, but also just a *story*. The book demonstrates the way autobiography, fiction and cultural analysis can be tangled together in ways that are both distorting and illuminating, and in this regard contributes to the radical re-appraisal of the life-writing genre that feminist critics spear-headed during this period.

Case study 9.2 Jeanette Winterson's *Oranges Are Not The Only Fruit*

Jeanette Winterson's *Oranges Are Not The Only Fruit* (1985) is simultaneously both an autobiography and a refutation of the 'truth' of 'autobiographical' writing. Winterson has always contested the boundaries of the genre, arguing that there is 'vulnerability' in the writing process so that 'truths' can never be absolute. What is important, she reasons, is not the 'truth' of a story but rather its authenticity: 'there is no such thing as autobiography. There is only art and lies' (Winterson 1995: 141). In *Oranges Are Not The Only Fruit* she tells the story of her childhood and early adulthood, but she describes her book as a novel, a work of fiction. This quasi-autobiography, which propelled Winterson to literary stardom, brilliantly exemplifies the radical reinvention of the genre that played out during feminism's second wave. *Oranges* destabilises the notion of a 'true' account of the past, even of our own pasts, and thus stands as a challenge to the literary tradition that historically bestowed value on (men's) self-storying. Instead, Winterson plays with the very concept of autobiography and in so doing challenges the edifices of a tradition from which women were for so long excluded. As she writes in *The Passion*: 'I'm telling you stories. Trust me' (Winterson 1987: 13).

As Sidonie Smith argued, these reinventions of autobiography allowed new possibilities to emerge: 'the woman autobiographer rereads the stories of man and of woman. She greets, identifies with, rebels against, cannibalises, and ultimately transforms public forms of selfhood' (Smith 1987: 175). Winterson herself acknowledged the profound influence of other radical reinventions of the autobiography on her own writing:

> *The Autobiography of Alice B. Toklas* is a delightful book, and a true groundbreaking moment in English literature – in the same way that Virginia Woolf's *Orlando* (1928) is groundbreaking. Woolf called her novel a biography, and Stein wrote somebody else's autobiography. Both women were collapsing the space between fact and fiction – *Orlando* used the real-life Vita Sackville-West as its heroine, and Stein used her lover, Alice B. Toklas [. . .] Woolf and Stein were radical to use real people in their fictions and to muddle their facts – *Orlando*, with its actual photos of Vita Sackville-West, and Alice Toklas, the supposed writer, who is Stein's lover but not the writer [. . .]. For me, fascinated with identity, and how you define yourself, those books were crucial. Reading yourself as a fiction as well as a fact is the only way to keep the narrative open – the only way to stop the story running away under its own momentum, often towards an ending no one wants. (Winterson 2011: 118–19)

Winterson's writing can be read as part of this literary genealogy, similarly playing with fact and fiction in order to keep her 'narrative open'.

In telling her own life story she seeks to demonstrate that 'truth' is never fixed or objective – instead, true art lies in the craft of the storyteller, weaving 'real' and imagined stories together: 'she [. . .] consciously weaves herself and the people she knows into the fabric of her fiction in the belief that identity is in an important sense fictional and that it is through stories that we come to understand ourselves most fully' (Andermahr 2009: 44).

As with the rest of her novels, *Oranges*, her first, demonstrates Winterson's belief in the power of storytelling. Her self-storying is all part of her art, and her art is a deliberate obfuscation of her self-storying:

> Though the novel does tell us of its protagonist's most private life, it is the opposite of confessional. It declines the memoirist's confidence that the past can be 'revealed'. With its short sentences and stripped-down vocabulary, it generally refuses to be eloquent after the event. (Mullan 2007)

The writer's experience and ego will always be a barrier to objectivity in autobiography, hence all 'truths' in such texts are necessarily mediated not only by the writer but also by readers, who will interpret their own meanings of the stories presented. Winterson says of her first novel:

> I think it is an explanation, in code, of myself to myself, but all my books are that, and if they were only that, no one else would want to read them. The trick is, the gift is, the miracle is, that what begins as private notation becomes language other people can use. The books we love speak for us and speak to us. I am always in dialogue with the books that have affected me. Stories start other stories. That's how it is. (Winterson 2007)

Winterson continued her experiment with life-writing by writing a second memoir – one she identified as autobiographical, in the way *Oranges* was not – *Why Be Happy When You Could Be Normal?* (2011). This tells again the story of her childhood and early adulthood, but this time the story is continued to her university experiences, career and later life. It also incorporates Winterson's discovery of her birth mother and learning about her biological family, and in so doing hints at why the 'truth' of autobiography is so complicated for Winterson. Her own 'truth' – who she is – is always contested, always liminal, since she exists as a composite of two lives: the one she led as the adopted daughter of an abusive (female) Evangelical preacher, and the one she could have lived had she stayed in the care of her biological parents.

In her 2011 text, the names of the cast are different – 'Mother' is now Mrs Winterson, Melanie becomes Helen, and Katy is Janey – but the story remains the same. Or almost the same. As Winterson says, there will always be variations in any retellings: 'I have always been interested in stories of disguise and mistaken identity, of naming and knowing. How are you recognised? How do you recognise yourself?' (Winterson 2011: 220). The older Winterson fills in some of the narrative gaps of the earlier 'fictional' text, while also providing an account of her therapeutic journey through mental breakdown and rehabilitation – hinting through this at the reasons for the absences we realise exist in *Oranges*, too painful then to explore.

Winterson's 2011 text may therefore be seen as evidence supporting the author's assertion that autobiography is always fiction, and fiction always autobiographical. It shows, through the retelling of the same life events, how perspectives change and stories differ:

> I have done nothing about finding my past. It isn't 'my past', is it? I have written over it. I have recorded on top of it. I have repainted it. Life is layers, fluid, unfixed, fragments. I could never write a story with a beginning, a middle and an end in the usual way because it felt untrue to me. That is why I write as I do and how I write as I do. It isn't a method: it's me. (Winterson 2011: 156)

Through her writing, then, Winterson is always playing with the limits of identity, selfhood and history – her entire career has been an experiment with the genre of autobiography, and the canon of English literature is much the richer for it.

Bringing women's autobiography into the contemporary

The second-wave interrogation of autobiography continued to grow during the 1980s and 1990s. Estelle Jelinek developed her earlier work on women's autobiographical writing by tracing back their contributions to the genre, beginning with tomb transcriptions in 2450 BC and taking in seventeenth-century spiritual self-storying, eighteenth-century confessionals and modernist retellings such as Gertrude Stein's *Autobiography of Alice B. Toklas* (1933) (Jelinek 1986). Felicity Nussbaum similarly historicised women's contributions to the genre, as the influence of the feminist publishing project of reprinting historical autobiographies had an impact on feminist literary criticism of the genre (Nussbaum 1989).

There was further analysis, too, of the special mechanisms of autobiography – both for the writer and for the reader. Mary Jacobus argued, for instance, that when women read one another's life stories, the reading itself becomes a form of autobiography – it constructs a sense of self in the reader: 'in order to read as women, we have to be positioned as already-read (and hence gendered); by the same token, what reads us is a signifying system that simultaneously produces difference (meaning) and sexual difference (gender)' (Jacobus 1986: 4). As noted earlier, women's life-writing in general – and autobiography in particular – can thus make reading into an identificatory exchange, in which the reader sees herself in a text and links her own experiences to those of its author – as well as other women. This modelling of the woman reader's special relationship with female-authored texts also echoes the 'dialogic' theories of why women are attracted to the romance genre, as discussed in Chapter 6. However, this notion of 'identification' becomes complex once we acknowledge that it often occurs *despite* the existence of significant material differences – historical, national, cultural and ethnic – separating the author and reader.

Angelou's *I Know Why The Caged Bird Sings* was published in the UK in 1984, having been originally published in the US in 1969, and, once again, constituted a challenge to the stability of the traditional 'memoir'. Angelou changes and expands the content of her 'life story' so that her text incorporates a celebratory reflection on black identity and motherhood, as well as a critique of racism, alongside her autobiographical narrative. The extraordinary sales figures for *I Know Why The Caged Bird Sings* suggest that large numbers of women must 'read' their own stories through Angelou's, and identify with the issues that are explored through the telling of her story, notwithstanding the fact that many of them will be white and have no direct experience of the particular challenges and sufferings Angelou describes. Its bestselling status – it remains a chart-topper today in the wake of Angelou's death in 2014 – marks out women's autobiography as both radical and liberatory yet also echoes the point made by Gwendolyn Mae Henderson in 1989 that black women's writing *in general* is special since it must, of necessity, address several audiences simultaneously:

> As gendered and racial subjects, black women speak/write in multiple voices – not all simultaneously or with equal weight, but with various and changing degrees of intensity, privileging one *parole* and then another. As such, black women writers enter into testimonial discourse with black men as blacks, with white women as women, and with black women as black women. At the same time, they enter into a competitive discourse with black men as women, with white women as blacks, and with white men as black women. (Henderson in Wall 1989: 36–7)

Henderson's brilliant insight into the complex author/text/reader dynamics that fashion black women's writing helps explain its appeal to a white female readership (i.e. readers are relating to those elements in the texts that are common to all women), even while acknowledging that they may, on occasion, also be challenged and/or alienated.

The figuring of life-writing as a tool for feminist empowerment is doubtless why the genre featured so prominently in the lists of books published by the UK feminist presses throughout the 1980s and into the 1990s. Autobiographical and biographical texts formed a considerable chunk of the lists of books published by Virago (and still do), The Women's Press, Sheba and Pandora, for example, with The Women's Press publishing autobiographies and memoirs by Janet Frame (1990) and May Sarton (1986), Sheba releasing Audre Lorde's auto-biography (1985), and Pandora outputting autobiographical writing by Agnes Smedley (1989) and Sue Johnston (1989). At both Pandora and Virago, the UK's largest feminist publisher, life-writing constituted a tenth of total output. As former Virago publisher Carmen Callil herself reflected in interview: '[P]olitics through memoirs, politics through stories of [. . .] life stories. Which is very much actually the way people today absorb things' (10 November 2004).

Post-1990, as Judith Butler's ideas around gender performativity began to take hold in the academy following the publication of *Gender Trouble* (1990), the autobiographical genre began to be examined from a new, 'queerer' perspec-tive. Nancy Miller took on the Butlerian destabilising of not just gender (i.e. masculinity/femininity) but also sex (male/female) (see Chapter 2) to argue that earlier examinations of autobiography (including hers) had been oversimplistic, since they rested on a unified (and unifying) notion of 'woman'. She concluded that such a simplified subject does not exist, but that telling autobiographical stories provides a space in which the complexity of identity can be explored – by the reader, as well as the author, since it is in reading others' stories that we come to consider our own (Miller 1991).

Other feminist scholars, meanwhile, explored the ways that autobiography 'queers' the meaning of 'real life' stories. Liz Stanley, for example, argued that memory is always selective and limited, so that 'each reader of written lives is a biographer, producing their own authorised version of that life' (Stanley 1992: 124). Laura Marcus similarly explores the ways that women's autobiographical texts 'expose the double-edged nature of the psychic construction of feminin-ity', where, on the one hand, there is autobiography as expression of the female self, while, on the other, there is revelation of the ways in which one 'becomes a woman' (Marcus 1994: 221). Women's autobiographies were therefore increas-ingly seen to reveal the instability of gender as a cultural construction, while simultaneously offering the 'deconstructed' female reader reassurance that she is not alone.

These 1990s/post-millennial interrogations of the significance and function of gender in autobiography are firmly situated within feminism's third wave, influenced as it was by the ideas of queer theory and Butlerian restagings of *all* identities – male, female or other – within an overarching paradigm of con-sumerist culture. Indeed, the foregrounding of consumption within both queer theory and third-wave feminism – both of which drew attention to the literal and psychic (re)construction of the self through the acquisition of consumer goods (a new appearance, new accoutrements or even a new body) – also had an effect on the telling and selling of autobiographical stories. The pervasive cult of celebrity, in which the singular/reified self was celebrated (ironically coinciding with the total deconstruction of the self in literary theory, of course) came to be tied into an increasingly commodified and consumer-driven culture. In terms of literary fiction and, of course, life-writing, this meant that authors' 'personalities' – as well as the books they wrote – were consumable commodities to be promoted and pushed. It was the era that marked the arrival of what Joe Moran calls the 'star author' (Moran 2000).

During the third wave, then, consumer culture's focus on the telling of 'real' stories, and the selling of the personalities behind them, as well as its reification of fame, created a new appetite for celebrity memoirs – an appetite that has not been sated in the years since. Annual book sales lists are now routinely dominated by celebrity autobiographies, with even the less well-known 'famous faces' (the so-called 'minor celebrities') finding their way onto bookshelves and bestseller lists. Although many of these books are published by popular presses, the trend has also had a significant effect on the publishing industry as a whole, with distinctly 'literary' imprints unable to avoid the trend. The lasting impact of feminism (and particularly feminist publishing) has meant that women writers are well represented among these autobiographical voices, since there is deemed to be a market for the life-stories of eminent writers and reformers alongside other social groups. Virago, which helped establish the market for feminist life-writing in the 1970s and 1980s and is now the only second-wave feminist publisher still in business, has recently added the memoirs of Janis Joplin, Gloria Steinem, Dolly Wilde, Mae West and Mary Wollstonecraft to its lists. Virago's sales figures provide striking evidence of the overall rise in the amount of life-writing being published year on year; autobiography and memoir now accounts for around one-fifth of its total output, more than double the proportion of earlier decades.

Although this trend will be read by some as rather depressing evidence of the relentless rise of consumerism/individualism in the Western world, the feminists working at Virago are more pragmatic and see themselves as exploiting the trend for the best of political purposes. Indeed, the head of publishing at Virago, Lennie Goodings, was not ashamed to admit in interview that the shift towards publishing more autobiographies is both deliberate and politically effective: 'subversion is the way forward. I don't think you can change people by banging them over the head. That's why I think the memoirs are really working now, actually' (8 May 2008). In publishing autobiographical writing from a range of women who continue to challenge the constraints of their gender in different ways, notwithstanding their celebrity or 'star' status, Virago continues to communicate its 'pro-woman' messages. Second- and third-wave feminist analysis of autobiography, and the many and various reinventions of the genre by women writers, are now being harnessed to capture the interest of the mainstream and – at very least – women's life-writing continues to be heard.

Bibliography

Andermahr, Sonya. 2009. *Jeanette Winterson*. Basingstoke: Palgrave Macmillan.

Angelou, Maya. 1984. *I Know Why The Caged Bird Sings*. London: Virago.

Benstock, Shari (ed.). 1988. *The Private Self: Theory and Practice of Women's Auto-biographical Writings*. London: Routledge.

Bostridge, Mark. 2004. 'Introduction'. In *Testament of Youth*. Vera Brittain. London: Virago.

Brittain, Vera. 1931. In *Nation and Athenaeum*, 24 January.

Brittain, Vera. 1933. *Testament of Youth*. London: Virago (2004).

Broughton, Trev Lynn (ed.). 2007. *Autobiography: Critical Concepts in Literary and Cultural Studies* (4 vols). New York: Routledge.

Callil, Carmen. 1980. 'Virago Reprints: Redressing the Balance'. In *The Times Literary Supplement*, 12 September.

Day, Elizabeth. 2013. '*Testament of Youth*: Vera Brittain's Classic, 80 Years On'. In *The Observer*, 24 March.

Ellis, Carolyn. 2004. *The Ethnographic I: A Methodological Novel About Auto-ethnography*. Walnut Creek: AltaMira Press.

Felman, Shoshana. 1993. *What Does a Woman Want? Reading and Sexual Difference*. Baltimore: Johns Hopkins University Press.

Frame, Janet. 1983. *To the Island*. London: The Women's Press.

Frame, Janet. 1985. *The Envoy from Mirror City*. London: The Women's Press.

Frame, Janet. 1990. *The Complete Autobiography*. London: The Women's Press

Gilman, Charlotte Perkins. 1892. *The Yellow Wallpaper*. London: Virago (1981).

Jacobus, Mary. 1986. *Reading Woman: Essays in Feminist Criticism*. London: Methuen.

Jelinek, Estelle (ed.). 1980. *Women's Autobiography: Essays in Criticism*. Blooming-ton: Indiana University Press.

Jelinek, Estelle C. 1986. *The Tradition of Women's Autobiography: From Antiquity to the Present*. Boston: Twayne Publishers.

Johnston, Sue. 1989. *Hold on to the Messy Times*. London: Pandora.

Kaufman, Sue. 1967. *Diary of a Mad Housewife*. London: Michael Joseph.

Lorde, Audre. 1984. *Zami: A New Spelling of My Name*. London: Sheba.

Lorde, Audre. 1985. *The Cancer Journals*. London: Sheba.

Marcus, Laura. 1994. *Auto/biographical Discourses. Theory, Criticism, Practice*. Manchester: Manchester University Press.

Martineau, Harriet. 1877. *Harriet Martineau's Autobiography*. London: Virago (1983).

Miller, Nancy K. 1991. *Getting Personal: Feminist Occasions and Other Autobio-graphical Acts*. London: Routledge.

Mills, Sara and Lynne Pearce. 1996. *Feminist Readings/Feminists Readings*. Hemel Hempstead: Harvester-Wheatsheaf.

Moran, Joe. 2000. *Star Authors: Literary Celebrity in America*. London: Pluto.

Mullan, John. 2007. 'True Stories'. In *The Guardian*, 27 October.

Nussbaum, Felicity A. 1989. *The Autobiographical Subject: Gender and Ideology in Eighteenth Century England*. Baltimore: Johns Hopkins University Press.

Owen, Ursula. 2009. 'True Tales From a Revolution: The Non-fiction Classics Now Hidden From Feminist History'. In *The Independent*, 7 May.

Roberts, Michele. 2014. '*Testament of Youth* by Vera Brittain, Book Review: Repub-lished Memoir of Great War Remains an Evocative Account'. In *The Independent*, 27 March.

Sarton, May. 1985. *Journal of a Solitude*. London: The Women's Press.

Sarton, May. 1986. *May Sarton: A Self Portrait*. London: The Women's Press.

Smedley, Agnes. 1989. *China Correspondent*. London: Pandora.

Smith, Sidonie. 1987. *A Poetics of Women's Autobiography: Marginality and the Fictions of Self-representation*. Bloomington: Indiana University Press.

Smith, Sidonie, and Julia Watson. 2010. *Reading Autobiography: A Guide for Interpreting Life Narratives*. Second Edition. Minneapolis: University of Minnesota Press.

Spacks, Patricia Meyer. 1976. *The Female Imagination: A Literary and Psychological Investigation of Women's Writing*. London: George Allen and Unwin.

Stacey, Jackie and Janet Wolff (eds). 2013. *Writing Otherwise: Experiments in Cultural Criticism*. Manchester: Manchester University Press.

Stanley, Liz. 1992. *The Auto/Biographical I: The Theory and Practice of Feminist Auto/Biography*. Manchester: Manchester University Press.

Stanton, Domna C. 1984. *The Female Autograph*. New York: New York Literary Forum.

Steedman, Carolyne 1983. 'Introduction'. In *Jipping Street*. Kathleen Woodward. London: Virago.

Steedman, Carolyne 1986. *Landscape For a Good Woman*. London: Virago.

Wall, Cheryl (ed.). 1989. *Changing Our Words: Essays and Criticism, Theory and Writing by Black Women*. New Brunswick: Rutgers University Press.

Winterson, Jeanette. 1985. *Oranges Are Not The Only Fruit*. London: Pandora.

Winterson, Jeanette. 1987. *The Passion*. London: Penguin.

Winterson, Jeanette. 1995. *Art and Lies: A Piece for Three Voices and a Bawd*. London: Vintage.

Winterson, Jeanette. 2007. 'First Fruit'. In *The Guardian*, 3 November.

Winterson, Jeanette. 2011. *Why Be Happy When You Could Be Normal?* London: Jonathan Cape.

Woodward, Kathleen. 1928. *Jipping Street: Childhood in a London Slum*. London: Virago (1983).

10 Historical fiction

This chapter explores the literary category 'historical fiction', which is distinct from other kinds of writing set in the past. A clear definition is required here, as writing about the past or setting a novel in the past does not necessarily constitute the writing of a historical novel. Although some critics and commentators have treated works like Sarah Waters' Victorian trilogy *Tipping the Velvet* (1998), *Affinity* (1999) and *Fingersmith* (2002) as historical fiction, for the purposes of this chapter I have chosen to work with Suzanne Keen's definition:

> historical fiction includes a wide range of works with a basis in biographical details and historical events, set in periods other than the writer's and contemporary readers' times, and representing characters in interaction with settings, cultures, events, and people of the past. (Keen in English 2006: 167)

According to Elodie Rousselot, a work of historical fiction uses real events and people from the past to weave a fictional story with meaning for the present. It makes the political personal:

> the focus on personal details at the expense of a broader sense of history may indeed sometimes seem to artificially bridge the gap between the 'then' and the 'now', and to create a deceitful proximity with fictional historical characters. (Rousselot 2014: 87)

The chapter will set out a feminist chronology of historical fiction that highlights women's many contributions to the genre. Feminist critics have traced this back to the sixteenth century, and I identify in particular the writing of early-twentieth-century female novelists in establishing women's voices in historical fiction writing as the genre itself came to be theorised by and within the academy. The chapter then moves on to look at the contemporary reformulation of the historical novel to incorporate a more postmodern perspective, interweaving aspects of the past with the present, real with imagined, fact with fiction.

It uses as case studies three of the most successful and respected female writers of the British contemporary literary scene: Jeanette Winterson, Pat Barker and Hilary Mantel. Their experiments with the historical novel have resulted in radical re-imaginings not only of past periods, people and events, but also the historical fiction genre itself. Winterson takes on the Napoleonic wars in her novel *The Passion* (1987), undercutting the military power and authority of the French general by portraying him from the viewpoint of his army chef – among others. Barker's Regeneration trilogy takes on the landscape of the First World War to problematise the received, often nostalgic, view of this conflict alongside interrogations of gender constructedness and sexual fluidity. Mantel's *Wolf Hall* (2009) and *Bring Up The Bodies* (2012), meanwhile, follow the often historically overlooked character of Thomas Cromwell to explore Tudor attitudes to morality and mortality, and thus allow the author to illustrate both continuity and change between the past and the present. These exemplary texts show the development of the historical fiction novel into the contemporary, blending the real with the imagined and using the lessons of the past to illuminate realities in the present. Mantel has been venerated for the first two novels in her planned trilogy on Cromwell, with both texts being awarded the Booker Prize for Fiction. As novelist Margaret Atwood – whose own meticulous research for her 'speculative fiction' novels (see Chapter 8) can be compared to Mantel's – said on publication of *Bring Up The Bodies*: 'historical fiction has many pitfalls, multiple characters and plausible underwear being only two of them [. . .] Mantel sometimes overshares, but literary invention does not fail her: she's as deft and verbally adroit as ever' (Atwood 2012). Mantel is now firmly established as one of the most important contributors to the historical novel genre.

A feminist history of historical fiction

In Mary Spongberg et al.'s useful anthology of women's historical writing, the roots of the historical novel genre are traced back to the sixteenth century, when religious writers and pedagogues sought to enforce a hierarchical distinction between history and storytelling (Spongberg et al. 2005: 240). In Spongberg et al.'s text, it is argued that it was a woman, Madeleine de Scudéry, who wrote the first historical romances (published under her brother's name) in the 1640s, 1650 and 1660s, interweaving her elaborate stories of love and intrigue – and multiple abductions – with portrayals of real-life society figures who would have been recognisable to her contemporary readership. Making the political personal is fundamental to the historical fiction genre, which allows the writer (and consequently the reader) to imagine the emotional and psychological motivations behind historical events:

> this emphasis on the private life behind the public stage became critically important to the practice and theory of historical fiction for women authors, who enunciate their prerogative both for fiction and for history through the rich interpenetration of public and private history which became their speciality. (Spongberg et al. 2005: 240)

There followed, in the early nineteenth century, a proliferation of historical novels published after the conclusion of the French Revolution, as writers explored the dramas of preceding years by imagining the ways that individual motives had consequences for the general populace. György Lukács, in his influential text *The Historical Novel* (1937), argued that one of these works of historical fiction, Walter Scott's *Waverley* (1814), was the originator of the genre. In *Waverley*, Scott takes on the Jacobite rising of 1745 to explore the personalities behind the politics, and his novel was a hugely popular success in its time. There is now a literary award named after him, with the Sir Walter Scott Prize for Historical Fiction, established in 2009, offering one of the largest monetary rewards on the literary prize-giving circuit.

Lukács set out a working definition of historical fiction that includes several key points: the transformation or reshaping of lives through historical events; the featuring of historical figures, albeit as oblique or marginal characters; the foregrounding of undistinguished or historically obsolete characters in order to tell the story; the contestation of declining and ascending political powers; and the affirmation of human progress in and through the conflicts that are described. Lukács' theory largely defined the historical fiction genre during the latter half of the twentieth century but, as with so much other literary theory, it fails to acknowledge the contributions of women writers. Alongside Scott, working in the historical fiction genre there were also many 'women writers [. . .] at the forefront at experimentation in these forms and in consolidating the genre of the modern historical novel', including Jane Porter, Maria Edgeworth and, later, George Eliot (Spongberg et al. 2005: 241). For these women writers,

> historical fiction provided (and still provides) a means by which women could ap-
> propriate a past that had largely been denied them. The realist form these women
> writers chose was peculiarly suitable for their chronicles of the newly learned, or
> imagined details, of distant family lives and successions. (Shaw in Monteith 1986)

The historical fiction genre is especially empowering for women writers, then, as it allows them to manipulate and participate in history through storytelling – a process from which women have traditionally been excluded because of the patriarchal structuring of the monarchy, the church and the state.

Diana Wallace's 2008 overview of the female tradition in historical novel writing opens with a bold statement of the power of the genre for women: 'the historical novel has been one of the most important forms of women's reading and writing during the twentieth century' (Wallace 2008: ix). Her landmark study traces the development of women's historical fiction throughout the twentieth century, but identifies Sophie Lee's *The Recess* (1783) as the first historical fiction, in opposition to Lukács' assertion that Scott had originated the genre and Spongberg et al.'s identification of Madeleine de Scudéry as a historical fiction writer. Wallace's study provides further analysis of the definition of the 'historical novel' and contributes to the task of recovering lost work by female writers spanning the 100 years from 1900 to 2000, citing the abundance of such texts as validation for the genre's importance in the literary field: 'the sheer number of historical novels published by women writers over the twenti-eth century is a testament to the importance of the form' (Wallace 2008: 4).

Throughout the twentieth century, the impact of feminism meant that there were changes in the way the historical novel was written – and received – by women. Modernist authors such as Virginia Woolf, for example, used the genre to radically reimagine the figure of the hero and to insert a female perspective into their portrayals of historical events. In *Orlando* (1928), Woolf's protagonist travels through the courts of Elizabeth I and Charles II, meeting famous poets, including Alexander Pope, along the way. The full title of the text is *Orlando: A Biography*, which conspires with the illusion that it is a historical document rather than a work of fiction. Throughout the text, Woolf uses her protagonist to illustrate the changing, and often arbitrary, nature of gender rules in the dif-ferent historical periods she depicts, thereby using the past to speak to the issues that were of concern to first-wave feminists (for more on the interrogations of gender made in this text see Chapter 2). Her novel thus exemplifies that 'histori-cal fiction is not simply fiction set in the past. It is marked too by an engagement with the present and the future' (Spongberg et al. 2005: 245).

Following Woolf, there were other significant British historical novelists, including Georgette Heyer, Naomi Mitchison and Mary Renault, all writing in the immediate aftermath of both the first wave of feminism and the First World War. Wallace argues that this war was one of the catalysts 'which made women aware of their own existence as subjects within history' (Wallace 2008: 220). It is therefore unsurprising that it prompted an outpouring of female writing which aimed to make women newly visible at different moments in history. Heyer is now celebrated for helping to establish the (popular) historical romance genre, taking Jane Austen's writing as inspiration for her 'realistic' depictions of the Regency period, replete with historical details and portrayals of significant individuals from the time. Naomi Mitchison wrote prolifically across a wide range of genres but especially historical fiction, taking in periods and places that ranged from Ancient Greece to eighteenth-century Britain, and garnering a reputation as one of the great writers of the genre. Mary Renault, mean-while, set her historical novels in Ancient Greece, painstakingly researching her settings in order to authentically evoke the scenes and characters of that time: 'modernism's rediscovery of Classical culture marked much historical fiction by women writers in the first half of the twentieth century, as in the work of Mary Renault, celebrated for its meticulous historical research in the depiction of ancient Greece' (Spongberg et al. 2005: 246). Renault, herself a gay writer, used these historical settings to explore homosexual lifestyles (among men) in a time and place when such relationships were culturally sanctioned. Her historical novels were a way, then, of legitimising such relationships, by presenting them as part of a narrative stretching back into the ancient past: 'fiction and history are not engaged in finding the truth but in meaningful ways of remembering the past' (Spongberg et al. 2005: 248).

Following the Second World War, more high-brow British historical fiction became somewhat moribund. On this point, literary critic Suzanne Keen distinguishes different kinds of historical fiction, separating the popular writing of Georgette Heyer, Patrick O'Brian and Catherine Cookson from the more 'literary' texts that had preceded them (Cookson's historical romance texts, for example, were hugely popular in the post-war period, with her near 100 books selling 123 million copies worldwide). Keen then marks the 1980s as the decade when there was a 'turn' to the historical once again in literary fiction, crediting the influence of Latin American 'magic realism' in helping to create the postmodern historical novel:

> that recent British and Anglophone fiction has taken a historical turn has become an axiom of critical commentary on the contemporary British literary scene. The historical novel, a subgenre of the English novel with a continuous presence since the eighteenth century, has in the past two decades flourished, enjoying popular success with a devoted readership, undergoing significant feminist and postcolonial adaptations, and commanding significant critical attention. (Keen in English 2006: 167)

Wallace, meanwhile, notes a striking difference between male and female writers' engagement with the genre during this period:

> Male-authored historical novels frequently elided the female, either erasing women altogether or presenting them as the enigmatic 'Other', [while] women's historical novels were politically driven, refashioning history through fiction as part of the need to tell 'her story'. Women's history had to be recovered and reconstructed before it could be deconstructed. (Wallace 2008: 176).

Keen also argues that historical fiction is able to transcend some (if not all) of the criticisms made of genre fiction, and is thus deemed worthy of 'literary' status because it can allude to eminent figures, significant episodes or other legitimate historical artefacts as 'facts'. She notes, too, that in spite of women's long association with the genre, the post-1980s reframing of historical fiction has once again engendered it as a 'male' form of writing (Keen in English 2006: 167). Novelists such as John Fowles, Peter Ackroyd and D. M. Thomas all made their names by writing what was seen to be 'serious' historical fiction (much of it overtly postmodern or metafictional) and the 'value' ascribed to it lives on today in literary prizes like the Booker, which always includes a number of texts dealing with what are often the darker episodes in British and/or colonial history.

Significantly, Keen also observes that the contemporary trend for 'literary' historical fiction coincides with a modern preoccupation with the past, and with a problematisation of an idealised version of especially military history: 'the prominence of historical fiction has also accompanied, and arguably stimulated, a booming heritage industry's focus on a positive, marketable past capable of inspiring patriotism and attracting tourists' (Keen in English

2006: 169). The contemporary historical novel, then, is distinct from both the low-brow and middle-brow historical novels, and historical romance writing, which had during the post-war period of the latter part of the twentieth century combined to make up most literary production in the genre. Instead, 'the new postmodern historical fiction represents an emergent form, one that has attracted a great deal of critical approbation, but which has not yet displaced its precursors' (Keen in English 2006: 173).

Fellow literary critic Perry Anderson similarly describes the emergence of this new form of historical novel:

> now, virtually every rule of the classical canon, as spelled out by Lukács, is flouted or reversed. Among other traits, the historical novel reinvented for postmoderns may freely mix times, combining or interweaving past and present; parade the author within the narrative; take leading historical figures as central rather than marginal characters; propose counterfactuals; strew anachronisms; multiply alternative endings; traffic with apocalyptics. (Anderson 2011)

Historical fiction in the contemporary era, then, may be seen to be marked by a tension between traditional and postmodern formulations of the genre. The case studies that follow– discussing works by Jeanette Winterson, Pat Barker and Hilary Mantel – evidence this postmodern 'turn' even as they demonstrate that, on this occasion, the revaluation and rebranding of a genre have not been at the expense of women authors. As Rousselot observes in gender-inclusive listing: '[O]ver the last few decades, historical fiction has experienced a remarkable recrudescence, with a growing number of critically acclaimed authors (such as Hilary Mantel, Ian McEwan and Sarah Waters) exploiting the creative possibilities the genre affords' (Rousselot 2014: 1). It is for this reason that the historical fiction genre represents a particularly fitting, and broadly optimistic, final chapter for this book.

Working in the wake of post-structuralist and postmodernist theory, authors of the contemporary historical novel have been very focused on the inherent 'unknowability' of the past and the elusiveness of what would once have been spoken of as 'authentic'. As critic Fredric Jameson points out: '[the] historical novel can no longer set out to represent the historical past; it can only "represent" our ideas and stereotypes about that past (which thereby at once becomes "pop history")' (Jameson 1991: 18). So, for example, Pat Barker's Regeneration trilogy retells the story of the First World War by interweaving real-life poets and historical figures with the author's fictional creations, especially women, in order to overtly challenge our assumptions about what we think to be 'true' about this period – one which is in so many ways familiar because of the wealth of material on it produced in popular and literary culture (see Case study 10.2, 'The 1990s – Pat Barker's Regeneration trilogy'). Barker's intention is to expose the gaps and silences in our received knowledge of this recent past in order to proffer an alternative version of history and, indeed, to make us question what we think we already know. Such self-conscious – and consciousness-raising – practices are now a common feature of the contemporary historical novel, as Keen observes: 'looking back to expose the crimes of the past, to engage in revisionist story-telling, or to bring up-to-date historical insights to readers of fiction have proven strong motivations for contemporary historical fiction' (Keen in English 2006: 179).

Contemporary historical novels also feature many stories of the dispossessed, as historical novelist A. S. Byatt describes:

> one very powerful impulse towards the writing of historical novels has been the political desire to write the histories of the marginalised, the forgotten, the unrecorded. In Britain this has included the histories of blacks and women, and the whole flourishing and brilliant culture of postcolonial novels. (Byatt 2001: 12)

This new, 'neo-historical' fiction (spearheaded by the extraordinary boom in neo-*Victorian* fiction, in particular, since the late 1990s) creatively and critically engages with mainstream history and is also defined by its situatedness in contemporary culture's fascination with the past (see Heilmann and Llewellyn 2014). If we look at the work of one of its best-known proponents, Sarah Waters, we can see the way that such fiction has the capacity to speak to both the future and the past, inserting alternative lives into historical settings with the purpose of envisaging a better future. In *The Night Watch* (2006), for example, Waters evocatively recreates the everyday life of wartime London during the Blitz and the years immediately after – including its cultural values such as the British 'fighting spirit' and 'stiff upper lip' – to depict, in parallel, a period of intense social upheaval in which gender roles were being loosened and alternative sexualities brought into the open. Although, as noted, her writing would not be considered 'true' historical fiction in terms of the definition offered at the head of this chapter (in that it does not contain any biographically identifiable characters from the period or retell recorded history), it is certainly worthy of mention for its success in capturing and revisioning the cultural life of the period, a good deal of it previously hidden from history.

Indeed, as Rousselot has observed, Waters' writing 'hinges on the trick of rewriting history from the point of view of lesbians and gay men' while also warning about the dangers of 'history tourism' and the contemporary preoccupation with romanticising the past (Rousselot 2014: 97). Her inclusion of gay culture in past timeframes, featured not just in *The Night Watch* but also in her neo-Victorian novels, is both deliberate and feminist, as Rina Kim and Claire Westall observe: '[h]er work is noted for its historical engagement with working-class lesbian life and, one might argue, can be read as an attempt to validate an existence that has consistently been written out of the pages of history' (Kim and Westall 2012: 204). While Mary Renault wrote about gay men in Ancient Greece as a covert means of validating gay existence in her contemporary setting, Waters is more explicit, inserting lesbian characters into her historical retellings of the more recent past. Her work may thus be

seen as part of feminist women writers' ongoing project, dating back to the
seventeenth century, of using the historical fiction genre to stake their claim to
a place in history.

Case study 10.1 Jeanette Winterson's *The Passion*

Jeanette Winterson's novel *The Passion* was published in 1987, and marked
a turning point in the author's career, after which Winterson could claim
to make a living from her craft. The plot centres on two characters – Henri,
who serves as a foot soldier in Napoleon Bonaparte's army, and Villanelle
(a *vivandière* or sex worker in the camps), who 'loses her heart' to the wife
of a rich and powerful man. In the course of the action, the two meet and,
in true 'magic-realist' fashion, set off on a quest to recover Villanelle's 'lost
organ'. The story, set at the turn of the nineteenth century, thus ostensibly
follows Lukács' 'rules' of historical fiction as set out above: it shows the
reshaping of lives through the historical event of the Napoleonic wars; it
features as a peripheral figure the hugely significant French military and
political leader Napoleon Bonaparte; it foregrounds the undistinguished
ranks of foot soldiers and sex workers in Bonaparte's army; it shows the
decline of Bonaparte's powers; and it ends with an affirmation of human
progress in the form of Henri and Villanelle's child. But that is not the
whole story.

As Winterson weaves her story through the changing terrain of France,
Russia and Venice, the narrative mixes not only history with fiction, but
also with fable and magic. This is a deliberate 'untelling' of history as we
know it, a destabilising of fact and fiction to reveal the constructedness
of what we receive as 'official' histories. It is a conscious manipulation
on Winterson's part: 'I wanted to use the past as an invented country. So
I knew I was going to land on some moment of history and rediscover
it' (quoted in Reynolds and Noakes 2003: 19). As with other postmodern
stagings of historical fiction, Winterson's novel both presents aspects
of accepted history and contradicts them, using the generic conventions of historical fiction to reveal the arbitrariness of what we come to
know as 'real'. The novel's central quest – to regain Villanelle's captured
heart, imprisoned by the beautiful 'Queen of Spades' – runs alongside
Bonaparte's quest for power. This mixing of magic and 'reality' sets an
allegorical quest to free a captured heart alongside one of Europe's most
dramatic and important military quests, fancifully pitting a web-footed
woman in drag (Villanelle has supposedly been born with webbed-feet)
against a megalomaniac man on a horse for the reader's sympathy. The
novel culminates in a staged retreat not only from history but also from
'reality' itself, as its other protagonist, Henri (who has lost his own heart

to Villanelle), descends into madness and the story ends by questioning the existential boundaries between what is real and imagined.

Like Mary Renault and Sarah Waters, then, Winterson uses her novel to record and reinstate the histories of the marginalised and the dispossessed: this is evident in her writing of the lesbian affair between Villanelle and the Queen of Spades, as well as her depiction of the lives and experiences of the disreputable characters she portrays in the casinos and brothels that are a feature of the novel's historical backdrop. The final chapter, too, records the fate of Henri as he is cast into that most marginalised of groups, the insane. The narrative thus captures and records all these notionally insignificant lives and presents them to the reader within the more familiar landscape of a military battle.

One of the central motifs of *The Passion* is the idea of chance. Gambling features throughout the story, and is the device on which many of its most important plotlines are centred: 'gambling is not a vice, it is an expression of our humanness. We gamble. Some do it at the gaming table, some do not. You play, you win. You play, you lose. You play' (Winterson 1987: 73). Villanelle's affair with the Queen of Spades begins in the casino where she works:

> The roulette table. The gaming table. The fortune tellers. The fabulous three-breasted women. The singing ape. The double-speed dominoes and the tarot. She was not there. She was nowhere. My time was up and I went back to the booth of chance full of champagne and an empty heart. 'There was a woman looking for you,' said my friend. (Winterson 1987: 60)

Winterson's story shows love as a gamble, a risky venture without which nothing can be gained.

When Villanelle falls in love with the married Queen of Spades, she realises the odds are stacked against their happiness, and attempts to leave the 'game' that is their affair by marrying a man she despises: 'there is no sense in loving someone you can never wake up to except by chance' (Winterson 1987: 95). This relationship, in turn, is ended on a bet that Villanelle loses, resulting in her being sold as a prostitute for Bonaparte's men, which is where she meets Henri, turning a losing bet on its head. This emphasis on gambling suggests that history itself is no more than a series of random events predicated on chance; in constructing her novel as a historical fiction, Winterson thus invites the reader to interrogate not only the arbitrariness of how 'history' comes to be, but also the unpredictability with which only some of those events are passed down through time.

It is not only love that is gambled on during the course of the story. Bonaparte gambles with *lives*, the highest of stakes, risking hundreds of thousands of others in pursuit of his own desire for power:

He believed he was the centre of the world and for a long time there was nothing to change him from this belief [. . .] He is repulsive and fascinating by turns. What would you do if you were an Emperor? Would soldiers become numbers? Would battles become diagrams? Would intellectuals become a threat? Would you end your days on an island where the food is salty and the company bland? He was the most powerful man in the world and he couldn't beat Joséphine at billiards. I'm telling you stories. Trust me.
(Winterson 1987: 13)

Winterson's depiction of Bonaparte is intended to undermine and contradict the historical construct of him as a great Emperor – she is using the conventions of the historical fiction genre deliberately, recasting history itself. Through Henri's experiences in Bonaparte's army, we see at first hand the 'real' (i.e. psychologically flawed and dangerous) man rather than the legend, and share in Henri's disappointed realisation that 'greatness' itself is merely a construct.

The Passion, then, is a work of historical fiction that pushes the boundaries of the genre within which it sits. Winterson engages, as well as abandons, the conventional aspects of the historical novel, and in so doing interrogates the concepts of love, truth, reality and history. She undermines the reliability of everything we accept as 'known', from the history of Bonaparte's reign to the mythology of the web-footed woman or the idea of true romance. Winterson's novel may thus be seen to take up Jameson's ideas about the inherent unknowability of the past and to put that to the test in fiction. It remains one of the most imaginative and exciting examples of the contemporary reformulation of the historical fiction novel.

Case study 10.2 The 1990s – Pat Barker's Regeneration trilogy

The first book in what would become Pat Barker's trilogy of works focused on the First World War is her 1991 novel *Regeneration*. The story begins at Craiglockhart, a hospital in Scotland where casualties of the war are sent for treatment. Barker amasses a cast of both real and imagined characters here, including the war poets Wilfred Owen and Siegfried Sassoon and the psychologist W. H. R. Rivers, using many of their actual words, gathered from published works, in the course of telling her story. As the trilogy continues with *The Eye in the Door* (1993) and *The Ghost Road* (1995), Barker's focus moves more to the fictional character Billy Prior, although real historical figures remain present throughout the narrative, which concludes poignantly in the days before the Armistice is announced.

As with Winterson's *The Passion*, the Regeneration trilogy defies easy categorisation as historical fiction. As Claudia Pierpont observed following the publication of the final volume in the series:

> while Ms. Barker is meticulously true to both the military and personal aspects of her history, she is never constrained by her sources. *Regeneration* (published in 1991), *The Eye in the Door* (1993) and now *The Ghost Road* are too imaginatively free-ranging and immediate to seem quite 'historical novels', too concerned with moral and sexual battles to seem quite 'war novels', too striking as hybrids of fact and possibility, easy humor and passionate social argument to be classified as anything but the masterwork to date of a singular and ever-evolving novelist who has consistently made up her own rules. (Pierpont 1995)

Barker's trilogy, then – which has netted her two Booker Prize awards – has helped define the historical fiction genre for a new millennium, introducing to it a sensibility and a sensitivity that extends across class and gender identities as well as feminist ideology: 'this war trilogy is as feminist and as class-embattled a work as Pat Barker has ever written' (Pierpont 1995). Indeed, critics have drawn a line of inheritance from her trilogy back to Rebecca West's *The Return of the Soldier* (1918) and Virginia Woolf's *Mrs Dalloway* (1925). Both these novels, like Barker's, use the setting of the First World War to express ideas about contemporary formulations of masculinity and femininity.

Regeneration focuses on the real-life Captain John Rivers' work treating British army officers suffering from 'shell shock', or what we would now call post-traumatic stress disorder (PTSD). Barker shows through Rivers' treatment of the soldiers – treatment she had meticulously researched through case notes and other archival material – a kind of gentle masculinity that was in many ways at odds with the construction of manhood typical of the Edwardian era, especially in the context of war. As she explained to Rob Nixon in an interview: 'I think the whole tenor of his way of dealing with therapy, which was to express the emotion and not run away from it, is, of course, implicitly a questioning of Victorian ideals of manhood' (Nixon 2004). Barker thus makes clear that her presentation of Rivers is a deliberate disruption of accepted notions of gendered behaviour in this historical period.

However, the text goes further than this, also evoking a connection between the Victorian construct of female 'hysteria' and the passivity of the trenches that broke so many of the soldiers of the First World War. In this she follows the work of feminist critic Elaine Showalter, in *The Female Malady* (1985), which Barker acknowledges in her author's note at the end of *Regeneration*. The work of clinicians such as Rivers was built on the developing ideas of psychoanalysis first put forward by Sigmund Freud and those of neurology set out by Jean-Martin Charcot, and positioned the high incidence of hysterical symptoms in shell-shocked soldiers within new discursive formulations of mental illness. In Rivers' hospital the masculine is feminised and the feminine is masculinised, and men are shown being compassionate towards one another – even in the horrifying context of history's bloodiest war. Barker thus subverts dominant discourses of trauma and portrays an alternative version of 'manhood', in contrast to the sombre and stoical heroism that is so embedded in our cultural narratives of the First World War.

Male sexuality is also a central concern of the Regeneration trilogy. Sexual ambiguity runs throughout the novels, and homosexuality is both evoked and suppressed within the narrative: 'Willard hesitated. "It's not just that." He bent towards Rivers. He's one of those." Rivers looked and felt stunned' (Barker 1991: 137). Here Barker employs one of the central tropes of historical fiction – inserting marginalised groups into past settings from which, in traditional narratives, they have been erased – to install the experiences of gay men into war stories. The presentation of Wilfred Owen and Siegfried Sassoon's relationship, for example, constitutes one of the trilogy's most important subtexts, giving voice to the silenced and sidelined, and presenting alternative versions of what the 'war story' constitutes. Barker draws a comparison here between the military's attempt to suppress Sassoon's protest and the silencing of gay lives – showing, through Rivers' efforts to reinstate the health of his mute patient, the importance of emotional honesty in order to be mentally as well as physically well.

The Eye in the Door, the second of the Regeneration novels, continues to challenge the silencing of dissenting voices in history: 'by highlighting the war's persecuted sexual and political dissenters, *The Eye in the Door*, like all of Barker's work, shows her commitment to the process of reclaiming silenced voices' (Coe 1993). In this instalment of the trilogy, Prior is discharged from Craiglockhart after 'successful' treatment and sent to London to work in an intelligence unit, investigating the activities of pacifist groups. This work returns him to his roots in working-class inner-city London, forcing him to address his allegiances – whether they lie with the people he grew up with or with his country. Barker shows through this internal conflict, as well as through the fates meted out to the working-class pacifists she portrays – not to mention the terror of being discovered to be a homosexual as experienced by married man Charles Manning – the lack of humanity of the 'war machine'. But she is sympathetic, too, to the law enforcers, and shows all sides of the story: 'Barker shows a remarkable empathy for the clipped, business-like tones of her upper- and middle-class officers, whose studied neutrality is mirrored in the dispassionate narrative voice' (Coe 1993). *The Eye in the Door* shows how those who resist as well as those who enforce orders are policed and coerced into conformity, thus providing a radically different, and subversive, version of the First World War.

The final novel in the trilogy, *The Ghost Road*, continues this interrogation of the dangers of imperialist nostalgia. The story here intersperses Prior's experiences in the present with Rivers' recollections of time spent in Melanesia in the past, allowing Barker to contrast not only timeframes but also cultures in order to show the arbitrariness of what comes to be culturally sanctioned. Barker contrasts, for example, Western and 'oriental' approaches to the body in order to highlight the lack of integration of body and mind that underpins Western medicine, to its detriment. The 'savage' medicine of the Melanesian people is kinder, and more effective, because it foregrounds the giving of care rather than drugs. Through Rivers' experiences in Melanesia, Barker not only reflects on Britain's colonial past but also proffers an alternative view of culture that is focused on the human, not the military or medicinal. She uses one of the tricks of the historical novel – the distance and difference created in the portrayal of past settings – to reflect on the experience of living with and accepting difference, making the political personal in order to deliver her ideas.

In *The Ghost Road* Barker also explores in more detail the personal motivations of her female characters, alongside the friendships and romances that motivate Prior. She shows that, while the women in her novel are required by the conventions of the time to present an air of 're-spectability', they harbour all the same lusts and longings that Prior acts out (those with whom he is sexually intimate include his lover in London, fellow war veteran Charles Manning, a prostitute in Scarborough, his fiancée Sarah Lumb, and a French boy in a town the British have taken from the Germans). Barker allows us to glimpse these women's hidden desires as they keep the home fires burning and their houses in order, with Sarah, for example, longing for her dead fiancé rather than the living one. Barker thus inserts the mundanity, as well as the melodrama, of women's experiences of the First World War into our narratives of this historical period, contrasting the domestic with the apocalyptic in ways that evoke critic Perry Anderson's definition of the postmodern historical novel. Barker's Regeneration trilogy thus explores the construction of gender and sexuality through time by showing the reader the irresistible influences of cultural rules, national attitudes and historical events on personal motivations. It rewrites our understanding of the First World War at the same time as it redrafts the parameters of historical fiction itself.

Case study 10.3 **The 2000s – Hilary Mantel's *Wolf Hall* and**
Bring Up The Bodies

Before Hilary Mantel undertook the task of writing her trilogy of works
chronicling the life of the sixteenth-century statesman Thomas Cromwell,
she had already written two historical novels – *A Place of Greater Safety*
(2006), about the French Revolution, and *The Giant, O'Brien* (1998), about
an eighteenth-century Irishman who becomes a scientific curiosity. But it
is without doubt it is her work on the Tudors that has had the greatest
impact not only on the English literary canon but also on contemporary
understanding of this critical period of English history. The finale of her
Tudor storytelling is yet to be published (*The Mirror and The Light* was
perhaps one of the most hotly anticipated books at the time of writing)
so the focus of this section falls on the first two instalments: *Wolf Hall*
(2009) and *Bring Up The Bodies* (2012).

Mantel's novels show her awareness of the requirement of the
historical novelist to retell the past in new ways: as she puts it in the first
book of her trilogy, 'beneath every history, another history' (Mantel 2009:
66). The protagonist of her story, Thomas Cromwell, is recast from the
villain of earlier portrayals (such as that put forward by his biographer,
Robert Hutchinson; or in the novels of Ford Madox Ford and Philippa
Gregory; or in Robert Bolt's script for *A Man For All Seasons*) to figure
as a rational, logical and thoroughly 'modern' man. Mantel's Cromwell
is shown to be capable of love and loyalty as well as calculating precision,
at ease mastering the elements, just as he masters the law and the courts:
'at home in courtroom or waterfront, bishop's palace or inn yard. He can
draft a contract, train a falcon, draw a map, stop a street fight, furnish a
house and fix a jury' (Mantel 2009: 31). Mantel employs the historical
novel's trick of elevating 'lower-status' characters from history to a central
role, putting the blacksmith's son Thomas Cromwell at the heart of the
royal court's power plays during the tumultuous years of the Reformation.

Mantel is adept at making the political personal, and creates in her
character Cromwell a likeable as well as relatable figure through whom
we can understand the personalities as well as pettinesses that led to
England's momentous break from Rome in 1534. Importantly, she makes
him human: from *Wolf Hall*'s opening scene of the young Cromwell
being beaten by his alcoholic father, through to the moving descriptions
of his wife and children's illness and death. Mantel thus builds a picture
of her protagonist which helps us better understand the psychological
motivations behind Cromwell's work at court – she moves him from a
two-dimensional player in Henry VIII's retinue to an almost heroic character for whom readers find themselves rooting.

The author makes the political personal through her construction of her historical figures' private lives and includes in her depiction of Tudor history, perhaps for the first time, a range of female characters and experiences as well as details of the private, domestic realm. It is not only Anne Boleyn's story that is (re)told in Mantel's novels: we see a cast of other women who have been absent from descriptions of this period of history. Mantel fleshes out Cromwell's wife and their extended family of daughters, sisters and nieces, and captures in the early years of the Cromwell household a happy, functioning family life. This is contrasted with the ugly misogyny of Sir Thomas More, who treats both wife and daughter with cruelty and disdain:

> 'Eat, eat,' says More. 'All except Alice, who will burst out of her corset.'
>
> At her name she turns her head. 'That expression of painful surprise is not native to her,' More says. 'It is produced by scraping back her hair and driving in great ivory pins, to the peril of her skull. She believes her forehead is too low. It is, of course. Alice, Alice,' he says, 'remind me why I married you.'
>
> 'To keep house, Father,' Meg says in a low voice.
>
> 'Yes, yes,' More says. 'A glance at Alice frees me from the stain of concupiscence'.
> (Mantel 2009: 230)

This reframing of the character of Thomas More as vain, misogynist and cruel is a radical revision of the martyr who looks out from history books: the great humanitarian visionary (he was the author of *Utopia*, first published in 1516) and deeply religious man. As critic Christopher Tyler points out in his review of *Wolf Hall*:

> [More is] made repulsive even more by the self-adoring theatricality behind his modest exterior than by his interest in torturing heretics and contemptuous treatment of his wife. He ends up stage-managing his own destruction out of narcissism and fanaticism, or at best a cold idealism that's contrasted unfavourably with Cromwell's reforming worldliness. (Tyler 2009)

By portraying More in this way, Mantel highlights the fallibility of the received wisdom handed down in our history books – another trick of the historical novel – while also reminding the reader that the lot of women in these times was very often one of servitude and disempowered endurance.

Mantel also expertly crafts her depictions of Henry's first wife, Catherine, his second wife, Anne, and his intended third wife, Jane Seymour. These three very different women are shown, unusually, as more than mere cyphers, the familiar progression of names whose fate the reader knows too well. Critic Bettany Hughes writes:

It is a welcome thing to have the wives of Henry here in sharp focus. In the Tudor age popular theology described women as an affront to the very nature of God himself. The sin of our sex led many, like Anne, to be damned as whores and eradicated. This book brings back many bodies. (Hughes 2015)

In depicting the impact of these Tudor attitudes to the 'sin of women's sex', Mantel shows the ways that women both suffered and benefited from the construction of their gender and sexuality in sixteenth-century culture. Catherine's failure to produce a male heir leads to her being ejected from the royal court, ultimately to a lonely death, while Mantel's Anne Boleyn is cunning and clever, using her sexuality to commit Henry to a forbidden second marriage – leading, indeed, to the dissolution of the Church in England.

Boleyn's astuteness is, in turn, in stark contrast to the guilelessness of Jane Seymour, who seems to somnambulate into the predatory Henry's arms at the end of Mantel's first novel in the trilogy. But all three women share, ultimately, a powerlessness that leaves them entirely at the mercy of Henry's whims. The King is ruthless and determined in his desires, and although it is not only women who are sacrificed in his quest for an heir, it is they who are shown to be most often vulnerable:

Wolf Hall, the Seymour family seat, is a site of scandal in the novel, a place where men prey on women and the old on the young. It's also where Jane Seymour first caught Henry's eye – an event that falls just outside the book's time scheme, but which serves as a reminder that, whatever their status in 1535, most of the major characters will end up with their heads on the block. (Tyler 2009)

Throughout the two novels, Mantel hints at the contemporary reader's knowledge of the historical events she portrays – she drops in mention of Thomas Wyatt's renowned love poems for Anne Boleyn, for example, and of Holbein painting his famous masterpiece *The Ambassadors* – but succeeds in creating so compelling a version of these events that the reader forgets the inevitable outcomes of the story. Jerome De Groot identifies a 'double effect' in Mantel's work:

this self-conscious conjuncture of 'history' and the novelization of history, the rendering of the work of historicizing obvious to the reader, is key to the novel's 'double effect'. It presents us with a familiar history, a set of characters and stories and events that are almost excessively well known. Simultaneously, Mantel allows the unseen, the unheard, the unclaimed to permeate. (De Groot 2016: 27)

In this way, Mantel effects a blurring of fact and fiction, crafting a historical novel that forces readers to interrogate the veracity of what they understand to be 'real'. However, in texts which are ostensibly realist in form, this is a very different strategy – one that very much depends upon what the reader brings to the interpretation – from Winterson's fantastical storytelling or Barker's painstaking creation of fictional characters that are as 'real' as the biographical ones. For Mantel, this 'double effect' is something she has to work hard at to sustain. As she observes in *Bring Up The Bodies*:

> what is the nature of the border between truth and lies? It is permeable and blurred because it is planted thick with rumour, confabulation, misunderstandings and twisted tales. Truth can break the gates down, truth can howl in the street; unless truth is pleasing, personable and easy to like, she is condemned to stay whimpering at the back door. (Mantel 2012)

Although Mantel is not typically regarded as a feminist writer in the way that Winterson and Barker both are, in writing *Wolf Hall* and *Bring Up The Bodies* she has retold Tudor history in such a way that it creates a much broader understanding of female experience during the period, as well as contesting stereotyped constructions of its key characters. She has created works of fiction that have, ultimately, altered our understanding of history itself, linking her project to that of early-twentieth-century female historical novelists such as Mitchison and Heyer, who also wrote as a means of inserting women into history. Therefore, whether self-consciously feminist or not, Mantel's use of the historical fiction novel effects a feminist objective: as Diana Wallace reflects, the historical novel 'has allowed women writers and readers the considerable pleasures of cross-writing and cross-reading – of trespassing in time to masquerade as a highwayman, a pirate, a Jacobite rebel or Merlin himself' (Wallace 2008: 227). It is a genre with great liberatory potential for women, both as writers and as readers.

Bibliography

Anderson, Perry. 2011. 'From Progress to Catastrophe'. In *London Review of Books*, 33:15, 28 July.
Atwood, Margaret. 2012. '*Bring Up The Bodies* by Hilary Mantel – Review'. In *The Guardian*, 4 May.
Barker, Pat. 1991. *Regeneration*. London: Penguin (1992).
Barker, Pat. 1993. *The Eye in the Door*. London: Penguin (2008).

Barker, Pat. 1995. *The Ghost Road*. London: Penguin (2008).

Byatt, A. S. 2001. *On Histories and Stories*. Cambridge, MA: Harvard University Press.

Coe, Jonathan. 1993. 'A Window on the World'. In *The Guardian*, 21 September.

De Groot, Jerome. 2016. *Remaking History: The Past in Contemporary Historical Fictions*. London: Routledge.

Eagleton, Mary and Emma Parker. 2015. *The History of British Women's Writing, 1970–Present, Volume 10*. Basingstoke: Palgrave Macmillan.

English, James F. (ed). 2006. *A Concise Companion to Contemporary British Fiction*. Oxford: Blackwell.

Heilmann, Ann and Mark Llewellyn. 2014. *Neo-Victorianism: The Victorians in the Twenty-First Century, 1999–2009*. London: Routledge.

Hughes, Bettany. 2015. '*Bring Up The Bodies* by Hilary Mantel – Review'. In *The Telegraph*, 22 January.

Jameson, Fredric. 1991. *Postmodernism*. London: Verso.

Kim, Rina and Claire Westall (eds). 2012. *Cross-Gendered Literary Voices: Appropriating, Resisting, Embracing*. Basingstoke: Palgrave Macmillan.

Lukács, György. 1937. *The Historical Novel*. Translated by Hannah Mitchell and Stanley Mitchell. Harmonsworth: Penguin (1981).

Mantel, Hilary. 2009. *Wolf Hall*. London: Fourth Estate.

Mantel, Hilary. 2012. *Bring Up The Bodies*. London: Fourth Estate.

Monteith, Moira (ed.). 1986. *Women's Writing: A Challenge to Theory*. Brighton: Harvester Press.

Mullan, John. 2012. 'Regeneration by Pat Barker'. In *The Guardian*, 24 August.

Nixon, Rob. 2004. 'An Interview With Pat Barker'. In *Contemporary Literature*, 45:1, pp. 1–21.

Pierpont, Claudia Roth. 1995. 'Shell Shock'. In *The New York Times*, 31 December.

Reynolds, Margaret and Jonathan Noakes. 2003. *Jeanette Winterson: The Essential Guide*. London: Vintage.

Rousselot, Elodie (ed.). 2014. *Exoticising the Past in Contemporary Neo-historical Fiction*. Basingstoke: Palgrave Macmillan.

Showalter, Elaine. 1985. *The Female Malady*. London: Virago.

Spongberg, Mary, Ann Curthoys and Barbara Caine (eds). 2005. *Companion to Women's Historical Writing*. Basingstoke: Palgrave Macmillan.

Tyler, Christopher. 2009. 'Wolf Hall by Hilary Mantel – Review'. In *The Guardian*, 2 May.

Wallace, Diana. 2008. *The Woman's Historical Novel: British Women Writers 1900–2000*. Basingstoke: Palgrave Macmillan.

Waters, Sarah. 2006. *The Night Watch*. London: Virago.

Winterson, Jeanette. 1987. *The Passion*. London: Bloomsbury.

Woolf, Virginia. 1928. *Orlando: A Biography*. London: Hogarth Press.

Index